DUCK BILLED PLATITUDES

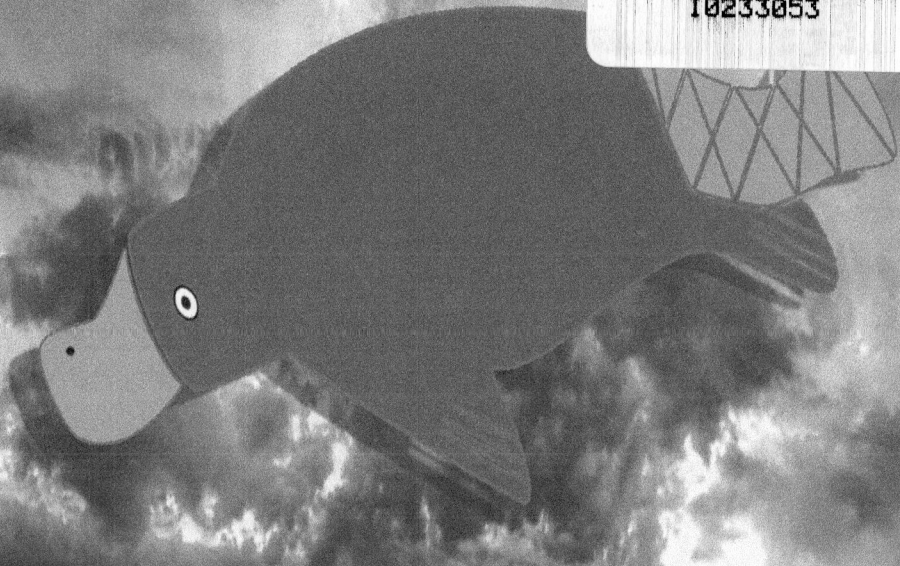

writingas about various things and stuff
Jonathan Downes

Typeset by Jonathan Downes,
Cover and Layout by SPiderKaT for CFZ Communications
Using Microsoft Word 2000, Microsoft Publisher 2000, Adobe Photoshop CS.

First published in Great Britain by CFZ Press

CFZ Press
Myrtle Cottage
Woolsery
Bideford
North Devon
EX39 5QR

ISBN: 978-1-909488-54-0

For Richard Dawe

(I always promised that I would dedicate a book to you,
I am just sorry it wasn't while you were alive, but who's fault was
that?)

AUTHOR'S NOTE

Dear friends,

The other day I was reading a similar anthology to this, which – for the sake of all concerned – shall remain nameless. I've found that I was very much enjoying reading the assorted literary footprints of a journalist for whom I have always had a fair amount of regard. It was (like I hope this is) one of those books that you can leave quite happily on the bathroom windowsill, to read during those moments when one is communing with nature. It is a book that you can dip into at random, and it is a book that can – occasionally – lead one onto new journeys of one's own.

I was sitting reading that book, when I thought 'I can do this!' and so I did!

However, there a couple of differences between that book and this.

That book has every entry carefully dated, with annotations, and mini-essays putting each essay into a cultural and historical perspective! This one doesn't. Why?

Although the author of that unnamed book only did what I tried to do with the series of Fortean anthologies that we started through CFZ publishing some years ago, reading such things in the context of a collection of breezy anecdotes, and relatively light hearted editorial content seemed to me to be self-aggrandizement of a level which mildly irritated me.

The stuff in this book is not dated.

It is not annotated – and there has been no attempt to put it into any historical or socio-political context.

Why?

Precisely because the vast majority of this stuff is lightweight, hopefully easy to read, and hopefully entertaining. It is a mixture of editorials, some book reviews, and a few feature articles, which have been taken almost at random from stuff that I wrote between 2013 – 2016 in a magazine called *Gonzo Weekly*, of which I am the founding editor.

If I may quote, somewhat out of context, Mark Twain:

"Persons attempting to find a motive in this narrative will be prosecuted;
persons attempting to find a moral in it will be banished;
persons attempting to find a plot in it will be shot.

BY ORDER OF THE AUTHOR per G.G., CHIEF OF ORDNANCE".

To which I shall only add that I hope that it affords you some little amusement.

Hail Eris.
Love and peace.
Jon Downes.

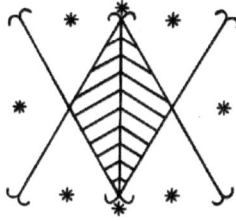

HOW PLEASANT TO KNOW MR BLAKE

I have been a music journalist, man and boy, for well over thirty years, and I have met a wide range of people. I have met some gibbering idiots and some complete nonentities who happened to get lucky. In between them all I have met some genuine artists, and a few extraordinary characters.

There is a slowly dwindling list of people whose music has touched me and that I have always wanted to meet. I say 'dwindling' because each year some of them doe, or disappear into a limbo from which I am never likely to encounter them. But occasionally I meet someone that I have always wanted to meet, and manage to cross a name off my mental checklist.

The most recent of these characters, that I have always wanted to meet, and finally managed to, is Tim Blake. What? You've never heard of him? Well wash your mind out with soap child, whilst I pass you over to those jolly useful people at Wikipedia:

Timothy 'Tim' Blake (born 6 February 1952, at Queen Charlotte's Hospital, Shepherd's Bush, west London), is a keyboardist, synthesist, vocalist, and composer with both Gong, and Hawkwind. Blake is best known for his Synthesizer and Light performances as Crystal Machine, with the French Light Artist Patrice Warrener.

They were sometimes joined on keyboards by the young prodigy Jean-Philippe Rykiel.

Blake first worked as the engineer at Marquee Studios, where Daevid Allen was recording his first solo album *Bananamoon* in 1971. At the end of the sessions Allen had invited Blake to come back to France to be Gong's sound mixer, but he refused. He eventually joined Gong full-time in September 1972 as the band's keyboard/ synthesizer player, being among the first to bring the synthesizer out of the studio and on to the stage. He appears on all 3 albums of the *Radio Gnome Invisible* trilogy; *Flying Teapot, Angel's Egg*, and *You*. He left Gong in early 1975, prompting the

7

eventual departures of almost all of the other members of the 'classic era' (with the exception of Pierre Moerlen, who continued the band under the name of Pierre Moerlen's Gong).

Blake began a solo career under the name of Crystal Machine, which is noted for being the first live act to introduce the use of Laser lighting in the entertainment world. After two solo albums 1977's *Crystal Machine* and 1978's *Blake's New Jerusalem*, Blake joined another noted "space rock" outfit, Hawkwind, for a short stint between 1979 and 1980, and has sporadically rejoined them on several occasions, and since December 2007, is still with Hawkwind, with whom he performs on Theremin and what he chooses to call "Virtual Lead Guitar".

I first heard Blake, operating under the soubriquet of 'Hi T Moonweed' making gloriously peculiar whooshing noises on the first album of *Gong's* Radio Gnome Invisible trilogy (now expanded at least to a quadrilogy, but this is a complete diversion). I was a spotty fourteen year old who had discovered the glorious noises of rock and or roll some years before but had grown tired of the sounds emanating from Top of the Pops each Thursday night. It was the autumn of 1973 when I spent a weekend at my friend Tim's house. His elder brother who had a moped, sideburns and a blonde girlfriend called Christine who looked a bit like a goldfish, played us this weird record called *The Dark Side of the Moon* and neither me or Tim had ever heard anything like it before. But it blew me away, and I realised for the first time that there was life outside the top 20.

Then the next spring one of the older boys on the school bus gave me a copy of something called *The New Musical Express* and I read it avidly from cover to cover. The next week I bought my own copy, and soon I was reading all of the music papers each week. Then one day in the summer term I read in the pages of the *NME* that a band called *Gong* were selling an album for 49p. Gosh I thought, and I went and bought it.

I had no idea what it was going to sound like. I vaguely thought that it might sound a bit like a *Deep Purple* album that someone had taped for me, and was totally confused by it when it didn't. But it was the only LP I owned and I had spent several weeks pocket money on it, so I persevered and grew to love it. And so, my life was changed for good. Soon afterwards I heard *Flying Teapot* for the first time and totally adored it—it wasn't until many years after that I found out that it was a substantially different band from that which had recorded *Camembert Electrique*, but what I did know was that although I shall always have a soft spot in my heart for my first LP, *Flying Teapot* was (and is) an immensely more satisfying piece of work, And the main musical difference was the advent of Tim Blake.

I always thought that his extraordinary sonic landscapes with *Gong* came from the same sort of place as *Tibetan Bells* by Henry Wolff & Nancy Hennings which was one of the peculiar records that dominated my listening for a while in the mid 1970s, even after I found that T Lobsang Rampa was actually an enterprising plumber from onew of the suburbs of Plymouth. Then in the late 1970s and early 1980s when I tried unsuccessfully to find nirvana through substance abuse and talking metaphysical bollocks, my soundtrack of choice was often *Blake's New Jerusalem* on which Tim Blake channelled the spirit of his famous semi-namesake (who as far as I am aware was actually no relation, but probably should have been), and to this day it is one of my favourite records.

So when I met him, I was very pleased to be able to sit down and interview him.

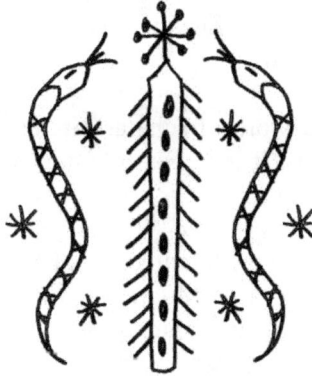

REVIEW

NEMO: ROSES OF BERLIN:
by Alan Moore and Kevin O'Neill

I have been a fan of Alan Moore for many years, since—back in 1982— I read the story of Sir James Jaspers, a renegade and completely insane British Prime Minister who did all sorts of extraordinarily horrible things to the British people. I was a student at the time, and even Mrs Thatcher hadn't reached the zenith of her awfulness. Thank Goodness that it couldn't happen here, I thought secure in the smugness of being a student. Twenty something years later as this country lived through the post Iraq horribleness of Tony Blair, I thought back at those times with a grimace. How little did I know. And once again I had to agree with *Pop Will Eat Itself* who once upon a time intoned that "Alan Moore knows the Score". He certainly fucking does.

It is not just that he tells good stories, with an elegantly brutal and stylishly macabre turn of phrase but he has this unique way of making what he doesn't tell; the spaces in between the plot and the characters, if you like, just as important as the storyline. In one of the early issues of the *League of Extraordinary Gentlemen* for example, the two street urchins working for an elderly Artful Dodger, are young versions of two characters from *Eastenders*; something which has no effect on the plot itself, but gives a warm glow of satisfaction to those who—like me—rather enjoy spotting carefully hidden pop culture references, and have sprinkled around not a few of my own.

But his attention to detail is not confined to pop culture. *From Hell* his massively erudite retelling of the Jack the Ripper mythos, has more voluminous endnotes, and references than one could ever possibly have imagined in a comic book. In fact, not for the first time in his career he redefines what comic books are all about, and their relationship to mainstream literature.

From Hell is, in many ways, a work of scholarship, and although I am afraid that I don't agree with his conclusions, it is impossible not to be ridiculously impressed at the sheer scale of his achievement.

The film, however, is a completely different kettle of fish. It is terrible, as are most of the films that have been attempted of Moore's books. The exception is *Watchmen* which I personally love, although there are a heck of a lot of people who don't, including Moore himself.

Although I am a fan of the film, I dislike the way that the ending was completely rewritten to provide a scenario more in tune with the cultural mores of the post 9-11 generation of American consumers.

Hollywood has not been good to Moore, although I have to admit that *V for Vendetta* had its moments. Probably the worst example is the movie of *The League of Extraordinary Gentlemen* which is a complete travesty and pisses all over Moore's original grand design, adding new characters (again to appeal to the American market) and featuring an appalling performance by Sean Connery as Allan Quatermain, (the literary hero who inspired my Mother to bully my Father into working in Africa in the late 1940s.

The series of books, however, of which this present volume is part, are magnificent. This is the second part of a trilogy featuring the descendants of Captain Nemo, aka Prince Dakkar, who is not only the hero of two books by Jules Verne, but the most impressive character in the early volumes of the comic book series.

This volume features his daughter Janni who first appeared in Volume One of another trilogy in the series. In *Century:1910*, Janni is a fifteen year old who rebels against the wishes of her dying and despotic father and runs (ok swims) away, ending up in Edwardian London where she changes her name to 'Jenny' in a deft and stylish retelling of Brecht and Weill's *Threepenny Opera*.

Working as a skivvy in a particularly shitty dockside hotel where she is abused and finally raped she assumes the mantle of the titular heroine of *Seeräuberjenny* and eventually masterminds a satisfyingly violent end for those who would have oppressed her. *The Black Freighter* is of course *The Nautilus* (this is the second appearance of this song in the canon of Moore's work, because the ship also appears in the pirate subplot of *Watchmen*). Janni takes command of her father's ship and sails off into the abyss.

Wikipedia describes the plot of this current volume:

"This story takes place in 1941. After Janni Dakkar and Broad Arrow Jack's daughter Hira and her husband Armand Robur are captured by Adenoid HynkelsNazi-forces, Nemo and Jack go to Berlin on a rescue mission only to find out they have been lured into a trap. They are soon pursued by the remains of the Twilight Heroes, Maria and Dr. Caligari. Dr. Mabuse later helps the pair evade capture and reveals to the them the plot had been orchestrated by Ayesha, who has become an ally of Hynkel, to get her vengeance after the events of "Hearth of Ice." Dr. Mabuse tells Nemo and Jack that Hira was pronounced lost at sea and Armand Robur is currently being held by Hynkel. Nemo and Jack raid Gestapo H.Q. and free Armand but has to Jack sacrifices himself so that Nemo and Armand can escape. Nemo kills Dr. Caligari which causes his soldiers to destroy Maria. Nemo kills Ayesha in a brutal sword fight. The Robur-aircraft arrives and picks up Armand and Janni. Hira, revealed to have survived the downing of The Terror, uses Robur's aircraft to level Berlin. "

But again it is the attention to detail from both authors which make this such an impressive book, Adenoid Hynkel is the character Charlie Chaplin played in *The Great Dictator*, for example.

Moore's characterisation is completely spot on. The fifteen year old Janni of 1910, would have grown into the 46 year old Janni of 1941, and in an alternate 1966, somewhere on a quantum level of reality, the 70 year old Janni, interviewed in the pages of a gossip magazine, and used for the appendix of this volume is a completely logical progression.

Roll on part 3 next year. I can hardly wait.

DIPPING MY TOES INTO THE IDEASPACE OCEAN

I remember back in the Easter holidays of 1977, when I was home from school for the last time (I was expelled a couple of months later, but that is another story) I went into Bideford and bought the three weekly music papers, *The NME, Sounds* and *Melody Maker*. The first of these was always my favourite. I walked mildly shiftly past what was then the Stella Maris convent, and slipped in through the unlocked gate of Bideford football ground. I got out my cigarettes, a pork pie and a bottle of cider, and settled down to read the music press in peace.

I remember an article about how all the various punk bands were signing to different labels, which started off (and I paraphrase, because for heavens sake, it has been 37 years) "I was going to start this article with the sentence 'now that The Pistols have signed to A&M', but I have been overtaken by events…"

The front cover story was, indeed, that *The Sex Pistols* had signed to A&M records and been kicked off after about a week. I let out a cheer. This was the band which spoke to me! The fact that I was a pretentious public schoolboy with a taste for *Pink Floyd* and things psychedelic mattered not a jot. As I read the list of little bands who allegedly couldn't play, but had nevertheless signed to record companies and were about to achieve fame and fortune, I felt a warm glow of pride. I was part of something!

Now, 37 years later I feel much the same. The other night I was listening to the excellent new CD by *Bridget Wishart and Spirits Burning* when I heard something extraordinarily life affirming coming out of the speakers. "I thought I was the only person mixing acoustic music, rock and dance music in an attempt to make something truly transcendental". I shouted, but neither the dogs, cats or Lobby the Lobster in the tank in the corner made any comment.

But its true. Ever since I read John Higgs' monumentally Fortean book about chaos magick and the KLF, I have been working on a concept of fusing all the different things that I like into a 21st Century, English analogue of Gram Parsons' *Cosmic American Muzic.* Many years ago I had a psychedelically lucid conversation with the late Will Sinnot of *The Shamen* about this very idea. If he had lived, the band would have gone to some extraordinary places, and I am unworthily following in his footsteps, It is heartening to discover that Don and Bridget are fellow travellers along a very similar road. Watch this space!

MEETING MISTER COLQUHOUN

Andy Colquhoun is a guitarist with a peerless pedigree. He first came to the notice of the music press when in 1977 his band Warsaw Pakt recorded an album (Needle Time) that was in the shops 24 hours after the first note was recorded (viz the session ended at 10 p.m. on Saturday 26 November 1977 and the album was ready to be sold by 7a.m. on Sunday 27 November 1977.).

The band was trying to make a point about technology in doing this, and the album sleeve was a 12" square brown bag with stickers and rubber stamping to display the band name and album title. After Warsaw Pakt, he joined Brian James' Tanz Der Youth, (described as the world's first hippy punks) subsequently moved on to the band The Pink Fairies, and then a band with ex-MC5 guitarist Wayne Kramer.

For the best part of thirty years he was songwriting partner and collaborator with the legendary Mick Farren; a partnership which only ended with Mick's sad death in July 2013.

In 2001 he released his first ever solo album He writes: "There comes a time in the life of every guitar player when he or she gets the chance to make a solo album. This is my attempt, and I've put as much guitar on it as possible".

But now there is a brand new one. I spoke to him recently about it...

JON: So, tell me about the solo album.

ANDY: Well, yeah, with the solo album; very, very pleased with the artwork and the way it's coming together. I've already seen the CD in advance and I'm very happy about the way that's going. It's got twelve original tunes on it that I wrote, and I originally recorded those in 2010. And then there's been an addition of another seven tracks that are all covers of songs that I like, and like playing. This is an instrumental album. The album I did before this, *Pick Up The Phone, America!*, just had four instrumental tracks on it. I think because I was working such a lot in the States with Mick Farren I didn't get around to writing a lot of lyrics, so the lyrics that really meant something to me went on that album. Then after talking over what I was going to do next with some of my friends, I decided to do a solo of just instrumentals, and then just sat down and wrote them. Got the recording process quite together so that by the end of it I could just start on a song and finish it by the end of the week but it took a lot more time than that to get started. I think the first tune I really approached on it is one of the bonus tracks; that was 'River Deep, Mountain High' – everyone knows that tune and I've always loved it; and that was the one I got my friend Philthy from *Motorhead* to do the drums on. And following that, I think I did 'Black Hole Sun', which was a song I'd heard on the radio and I was so knocked out by it, I had to pull over and listen to it properly. You know how sometimes a song gets you like that?

JON: Oh, yes.

ANDY: And so then I just did a straightforward translation of the merseyline [?] on to lead guitar and reconstructed the backing, and did it that way. So that's how it kind of started, and that took quite a long time, by which time I'd figured out the rest of the rest of the numbers I was going to do. I did carry on doing the standards but the challenging part was to come up with original tunes. So it starts off with this one title, 'Back in the Day', which is basically a Blues number – a slightly different sequence to a normal Blues tune – I was very pleased with that when I finally finished it and it went on from there.

The sequence on the album is pretty much the order in which the numbers were recorded, 'cause I'll do one, and then that will be the start and then I'll say, "Well, what it needs now is something a bit more up-tempo," so I'd write another one. And at the same time I was concurrently doing videos of the tunes.

So yes, it was like, the second track would be 'Blue Lagoon', which has kind of got a different feel; it's a bit more up-tempo. One of the notes I make on the CD is that when you're writing an instrumental you're not actually putting word-shaped thoughts in people's heads s when they listen to it they're a little freer than they might be if the storyline is written out.

The other thing, which contributed to going instrumental, I was working with Mick Farren, who of course is a prolific wordsmith and there are his wonderful words so there wasn't actually a call for any lyrics at that point in time and so I was free to explore the melodic ideas that you get in an instrumental. And, of course, when you're writing songs you might get a guitar break in the front and one in the middle and perhaps one in the out-trap. But it's a whole different discipline to writing instrumentals.

JON: It's also a style of music, which people wouldn't immediately connect with you.

ANDY: Very possibly. Very possibly.

JON: You're associated in most people's minds with a certain sort of music. Are the instrumentals still in that style, in that sort of genre, or have you explored different genres doing it?

ANDY: Well, it definitely has given me the chance to go into other fields. I mean, when I started out I was writing punk-rock tunes. Well, even before that I was playing and writing, to some extent, British R&B-type tunes; sort of feel-good stuff, you know. So you do progress, you know, and you try different things. There's quite a lot of fields in this, on the CD that's going to be released. Where there's a strong similarity would be sort of track twelve, 'Exit Stage Left.' It's very much in the same mould as the *Fairies* or *Deviants* . You know, sort of hard and heavy. And there are other tracks that are on there that are like that. Like the third track, 'Hot Rod'; that was a deliberate attempt to write an instrumental such as you might have heard coming out of a group in the sixties or seventies, perhaps, even. The fourth track, 'Electroglide', was basically a rock song. It's a sort of like small bass-y song, you know. Modern rock and blues; that's the one I'm referring to. Then the sixth track; that's another punky thing that's been given a guitar, and that's followed by a ballad, and so on. So it's quite a cross-section, you know.

JON: Who else is playing on it?

ANDY: Well, David plays bass on five of the tracks, mostly on the covers; you know, the standards. And Philthy from *Motorhead* is playing on 'River Deep, Mountain High.' But otherwise, it's me and a load of machines and instruments.

JON: Do you like playing with machines rather than people? 'Casue it's a very different discipline, isn't it?

ANDY: Yes. I do like sitting down and just making up a tune, and not having [laughs] to then get other musicians to over-dub into it. It can't really be done. Once you've done that, you then have to start again with other musicians and build the whole thing up again. And if that's easy, that's great. If you've got a band going, and you've got the space and time to do those sort of things, then I probably prefer that. But it doesn't happen every day of the week so I find it very useful to use the modern technology that we have, and I guess I'm going into a sound that's based in the sixties and seventies, which is kind of where I'm coming from.

JON: Where did you record it?

ANDY: Well, at Cyber Music, which is what I call my home recordings, so that would be in various locations. It was all done in LA on Hollywood Boulevard.

JON: Golly. I keep on forgetting that it was only a few years ago that you came back.

ANDY: Yes, we came back in 2011 so we're into the third year that I'm back in Blighty and it's been great so far, apart from the tragedy last year, of course, with Mick dying.

JON: That was horrible.

ANDY: Yeah, it was.

JON: I was really, really touched by the level of love that everybody showed in the obituaries and tributes to him.

ANDY: Yeah, it was amazing, wasn't it?

JON: It was the day the sixties died in the end, wasn't it?

ANDY: I think by that time people recognized what a force he'd been. For me and the band members, you know, he'd always been that sort of – what would you say? – a force of nature that was – he wouldn't compromise about anything. And he was still stuck to exactly the same principles and so on that he'd had in the first place and nothing had changed his mind about anything. In fact, it only confirmed his worse suspicions [laughs] as events unfolded, you know.

JON: I think we need somebody like him now more than ever.

ANDY: Well, I don't know what's gonna replace him....

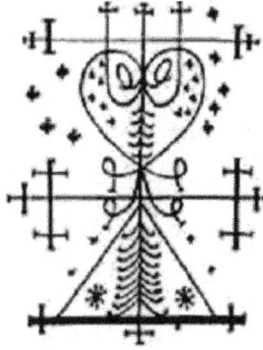

REVIEW

WAGING HEAVY PEACE
Neil Young

Blimey. This is a monumentally peculiar book. It is disjointed, repetitive, and meanders from subject to subject with a total lack of focus. I also like it a lot. Neil Young writes how he has given up alcohol and marijuana some months before commencing work on this long-awaited autobiography, and there are times within these 400+ pages that he reaches a new lucidity about events of his past, almost as if he is revisiting them with a new and sober vision.

The disjointed and episodic nature of the book is disconcerting in the first few chapters, but after a while one realises that it has its own internal structure and logic and that if he had written the book in a more conventional linear manner it just would not have worked anywhere near as well. He keeps revisiting his current obsessions; the LincVolt project, and his PureTone process which he hopes will replace mp3s as the industry's standard for digital streaming of music.

He is a strange, but oddly likeable fellow; and although he appears to have been brutally honest about his chequered past – the break ups of his relationships prior to meeting Pegi, for example – he still comes over as a nice man, and more importantly, a man of steadfast integrity. His accounts of his relationships with his two sons, Zeke and Ben, who were both born with cerebral palsy even though they had different mothers, are oddly touching, and I was very impressed by the way he always refers to them as Zeke Young and Ben Young in the text. Doing this, rather than just using their Christian names as nearly everybody else on the planet would have done, emphasises that he sees them as true individuals, and wants us to do likewise; not ignoring, but seeing past, their disabilities. This is a massively laudable thing, and I take my hat off to him. He also doesn't attempt to brush over his brief relationship with Charles Manson, although the song Revolution Blues which appears on his On The Beach album from the mid-70s does appear to be more admiring of the Family ethic than the account given in this book. However, unlike the retrospective accounts by Dennis Wilson, which are quoted in *Heroes and Villains* by Steven Gaines, Neil Young does not indulge in retroactive histrionics. He just states the facts, gives a wry smile, and moves on.

He is obsessed with cars, and motor vehicles in general. His LincVolt project, for example, seems to be particularly dear to him. It is an attempt to convert large luxury cars to sustainable eco-friendly methods of power. This is something that if I had the money, I would be involved in as well. I miss driving a Jaguar, but I'm only too aware that each time someone does so it is a another coffin nail into the casket of pollution which surrounds the 'green hills of Earth'.

I like the way he names each of his cars, and most of his instruments; his favourite guitar – the one he recorded so many classic albums with – is called Big Black. I was oddly sad to finish the biography late last night, and I am very pleased that Neil seems to have got the writing bug and intimates that there will be more books of autobiography on the way. This is good, because he has only scratched the surface of his remarkable life in this book. Long may he run.

REVIEW

AT THE APPLE'S CORE
Denis O'Dell

Once again I have a *Beatles*-related book for review this week. However, for once I will miss out the bit about having been a *Beatles* fan and collector for many years, because –let's face it—if you actually *read* my inky fingered scribblings each week, that has probably become self evident.

Rashōmon is a 1950 Japanese period drama film directed by Akira Kurosawa, working in close collaboration with cinematographer Kazuo Miyagawa. It stars Toshiro Mifune, Masayuki Mori, Machiko Kyō and Takashi Shimura. The film is based on two stories by Ryūnosuke Akutagawa: "Rashomon", which provides the setting, and "In a Grove", which provides the characters and plot. The film is known for a plot device which involves various characters providing alternative, self-serving and contradictory versions of the same incident.

More and more, when I read a book by someone who used to work with, or was somehow involved with *The Beatles* I am reminded of this seminal slice of Oriental drama. This book is particularly interesting because unlike the other memoirs that I have read recently O'Dell was a seasoned entertainment industry professional before and after he met *The Beatles*. In contrast, however, Chris O'Dell was a superfan, and rock chick who carved herself a niche in the industry, and Alaistair Taylor was an employee of Brian Epstein who got lucky, and then got very unlucky surprisingly quickly.

O'Dell sheds some interesting light on the plans to make a movie of *Lord of the Rings* featuring all four *Beatles* in different roles. This is something which has been alluded to in a number of different books, but I have not read the details until now.

O'Dell is also in a privileged position to have been able to write this book because he was one of the Directors of Apple, but coming from a more conventional background than many of the others he is a bit more objective about the creative chaos which surrounded it.

I have always been an admirer of the Apple Records ethos, and saddened by what happened to this quixotic and noble vision. With the benefit of hindsight (good old hindsight) it is easy to see what went wrong. There were too many hangers on and freeloaders, and - having attracted more than a few such people to my own enterprises over the years - I can sympathise with the feelings and motives of those who sought to get rid of these blots on the Apple Corps escutcheon.

This book gives a useful insight into the Apple years, and is a good compliment to some of the more rock and roll orientated books on the subject that have appeared over the years. Unfortunately, however, for my tastes, this is a bit too much of a showbiz memoir, and smacks of all the things that I dislike about the entertainment industry.

But I mustn't bring my own prejudices on the subject into the limelight. Being totally dispassionate about it, this is not a book that I particularly enjoyed. Nor did I warm particularly to the author; mainly because the conventional side of showbusiness and showbiz politics is not something that interests me, and - indeed - it is something which grates with me on a political level.

But it is an interesting read, and has enough hitherto unavailable information within its 220 pages to guarantee it a place on my ever expanding bookshelves of *Beatles* books for the foreseeable future. Also it only cost me £1.20 plus postage from Amazon so I really cannot complain.

AUSTERITY MY ARSE

We are living in strange and disturbing times. I know that this is primarily a music magazine, but as intelligent people it is very difficult to ignore the things which are going on around us.

It is very difficult to ignore the behaviour of those who have been set in authority over us; any pretence that those whose responsibility it is to look after the weakest and most vulnerable members of society is rapidly going out of the window. Successive governments have done their best to demonise the unemployed and to terrorize those people who are on sickness benefits of one sort or another.

The popular conception that people who are too idle to support themselves only have to go to a sympathetic doctor with some made up ailment or other in order to get a lifetime of living high on the hog at the expense of the poor hard working tax payer is completely false, but it is a fallacy which has been promoted to a ridiculous extent by the government and its lackeys in the media. This has got to such a ridiculous extent that I know personally one young man in his twenties who is so severely handicapped that he cannot speak coherently, that he is doubly incontinent, and cannot walk unaided, had his benefit cut off recently and was told he was fit for work. Luckily common sense and some sort of concept of fair play prevailed, but this is only one incident out of many that I could quote.

A friend of mine who is severely dyslexic, has the computer skills of a three-toed sloth, and can only afford a 15 year old laptop running Windows XP had his benefits stopped purely because he didn't understand how to log in to the government jobseekers website which – apparently – does not allow computers running Windows XP to access it.

There is something absolutely horrific about all this. In my writings I have often been accused of being unfair to American politicians, and some have even accused me of an anti-American bias.

This, as you can tell from my writings here is simply not the case. I am biased against any political system which victimizes and oppresses those people who do not have the skills or the power to protect themselves.

I am not going to write about the situation in the United States here in this column because I know nothing about the welfare situation there, but I suspect that it will be as bad, or worse, than it is in the UK. Something is going to have to change, and at the moment I admit I have no idea what it is going to be, but I have a horrible suspicion that something particularly nasty is around the corner.

Why am I dedicating my editorial in what is meant to be a music magazine over a holiday weekend to such a depressing and disturbing subject? It's simple kiddies. Easter is a time of rebirth and a time of redemption. No matter what religion you have, or indeed, whether you have a religion at all, you must be aware that for many people this is a season which has a much deeper meaning than just having chocolate eggs you can scoff.

One of the reasons that I put so much time and effort into this magazine is because I believe that music has been important to the human race since the earliest days and that if used correctly it is a unifying and uplifting medium that brings people together. In these increasingly dark times we need solidarity more than ever.

I am happy to say that there is a vibrant and mutually supportive community building up around this magazine and I think it really is starting to do the job I have wanted it to do ever since Rob Ayling and I first talked about it nearly a quarter of a century ago.

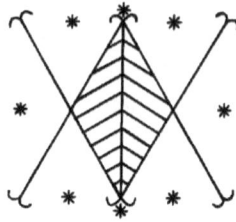

REVIEWS

DARK HORSE: THE LIFE AND ART OF GEORGE HARRISON
Geoffrey Giuliano

HERE COMES THE SUN: THE SPIRITUAL & MUSICAL JOURNEY OF GEORGE HARRISON
Joshua M Greene

This week's review continues my trawl through various Beatles related books that I have picked up for a song on Amazon.co.uk. Last week I got a little bit philosophical on you and equated the burgeoning library of books on 'The Fab Four' which continues to expand and show no real sign of abating despite the fact that the band fizzled out well over 40 years ago, with a Japanese film and play called *Rashōmon*.

The whole crux of this play is that everybody recounts events that have happened to them from a personal perspective, and I realised – some four decades after beginning my collection of Beatles books – that much the same could be said about my Beatles library especially when the books are written by people who for some reason or other had been involved with the band, or its individual members, back in the day. I found the contrast between memoirs written by someone who had risen from the ranks, as it were, as one of the aides to Brian Epstein with the account written by somebody who had been involved in the wider world of show business both before and after their tenure with the Beatles. The contrast was remarkable.

This week, however, my post bag included two biographies of George Harrison; both written by people who had known him, and furthermore known him for similar reasons. These were not music business cronies, or fellow musicians. These were people who had encountered 'the quiet Beatle' during his quest for spiritual enlightenment, and they tell two very different stories.

Here comes the sun: The Spiritual and Musical Journey of George Harrison is probably the better of the two books, and gives a much more rounded view of Harrison's life than the other book *Dark Horse: The life and art of George Harrison* by Jeoffrey Giuliano, if only for the simple reason that it was written after Harrison's death when the story was over and there was nothing left to tell.

Giuliano's book was written in 1997, just after George had pulled the plug in a rather unsatisfactory manner on any chance of the 3 remaining Beatles continuing their fragile association in the wake of the Anthology project. Giuliano, who had given a very interesting, sensitive and insightful look at Harrison's spiritual path obviously felt that George was drifting away from the faith which had sustained him for so many years. Furthermore, Guiliano makes it clear that this new pursuit of materialistic aims, as he saw it, was not something that was good for George, or the myriad of followers whom he had garnered over the years and who had – in many cases – adopted similar spiritual practices as a result of George's example.

However, as we all know, within a year of Giuliano's book, George had his first bout with cancer. Two years later he had the near fatal encounter with Michael Abram, and two years after that he was dead.

In those four years between Giuliano's book and George Harrison's departure from this material world he not only demonstrated his renewed faith in Krishna, but resolved his problems with the other two remaining Beatles, and generally put his emotional, financial, social, and – above all – spiritual affairs in order.

If you are looking for an analysis of the career of this enigmatic and massively talented musician who had the misfortune to be a very good songwriter in the same band as two classic ones, neither of these books will give you what you are looking for.

Here comes the sun is probably the best of the two and does give a fascinating insight onto Harrison's ill fated 1974 tour containing information I have never read anywhere else, but both books could be described as being woefully lacking in this respect. But that is a bit like complaining that Tesco is a very bad tropical fish shop, because neither of these books set out to cover George's professional career.

Joshua Greene, for example, was one of the musicians on the sessions for the Radhe Krishna Temple album, whereas Giuliani is also a fellow traveller in the

Krishna movement. Both of them come closer to explaining why a complex, shy, and often unhappy man who was born the son of a Liverpool bus driver ended up finding peace and fulfilment in an obscure branch of Hinduism. After reading these books I feel that I understand Harrison much more than I did a week ago.

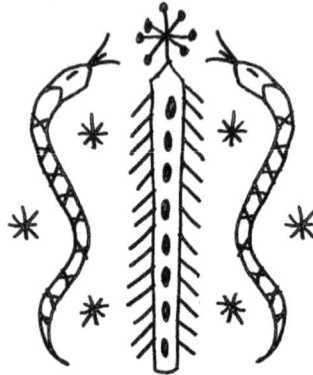

MEMORIES OF A FREE FESTIVAL

One of my favourite rock biographies is *Alias David Bowie* by Peter and Leni Gillman. It was first published in 1987 when I was working as a staff nurse at Western Hospital, Crediton. Apparently the man himself wasn't impressed by the amateur psychoanalysis in there which related a lot of his life and career, and in particular, his lyrics over the years to his relationship with and the subsequent death of his schizophrenic half brother, Terry. The motif of madness is certainly a recurrent one in his work, and one piece of circumstantial evidence that massively supports the Gillmans' hypothesis is that one of the proposed covers for Bowie's 1970 album *The Man Who Sold the World* features a painting of Cane Hill psychiatric hospital in Croydon, which is where Terry lived at the time, and continued to live for many years.

I think it is quite likely that another reason Bowie didn't appreciate this book, despite the fact that it was quite probably the first in depth and properly written biography of him was that – to be brutally honest – he didn't actually come out of it very well in many instances.

One such instance involves the Free Festival which was organized by the Beckenham Arts Lab, which was held at Croydon Road Recreation Ground in Beckenham on 16th July 1969. They describe how Bowie, despite being only twenty-two, behaved like a bad tempered old git for much of the time that day, alienating and snubbing many of his closest supporters, including his future wife, and the guy with whom – according to most people around at the time – they were both sleeping.

Bowie's memories of the day were somewhat different:

The Children of the summer's end
Gathered in the dampened grass
We played Our songs and felt the London sky
Resting on our hands it was God's land

It was ragged and naive it was Heaven
Touch, We touched the very soul
Of holding each and every life
We claimed the very source of joy ran through
It didn't, but it seemed that way
I kissed a lot of people that day

Whether or not it was that way it actually happened doesn't really matter. I don't know whether Bowie actually did "kiss a lot of people that day" or whether he strutted about the place like an insufferable prick, or whether – as I strongly suspect – it was somewhere in between.

What I do know, is that it was the social function of events like the Beckenham Free Festival to bring people together and to create a sense of community amongst the attendees, and if you believe in such things, amongst the wider population who would have been blessed by the healing vibes which emanated from the event, when around them the world was getting increasingly strange and unpleasant. Just think of it: only a month before men had stood on the surface of The Moon for the first time, only ten days before the Manson family had invaded Cielo Drive, there was carnage in South East Asia and political unrest across the Western World.

Arguably the socio-political situation facing us today is even worse. There is carnage of the vilest sort across the Middle East and political unrest of an unprecedented nature looming at home. I have a horrible idea that, unless we are very fortunate, life is going to get a whole lot nastier for many of us. I am not going to even try and pretend that I believe that an old fashioned dose of hippy good vibes is going to cure all this. It certainly won't, but all that any of us can do is to try to light our own small candle in the darkness and do what we can in our own little corner of humanity.

A few weeks ago, I presided over the fifteenth Weird Weekend. It may not have been a free festival, but the vast majority of people there got in for nothing, and the whole point of the event was, is, and always will be, to bring people together, and to spread good vibes amongst all and sundry. If reading that makes you suspect that I am an old hippy, and this surprises you, then I really think you should take a proper look of the photograph of me which is emblazoned across this editorial.

Work has already begun on next year's event, which will once again feature several Gonzo luminaries and I have a suspicion that you will be reading about it in these very pages sooner rather than later. I came very close to calling it a day this year. My health is declining, my energy levels likewise and after fifteen years nobody can really accuse me of not having given it my best shot. But it was a beautiful event; it made me and a lot of other people very happy, and so it will continue at The Small School in Hartland for the considerable future. It brought a lot of people of different backgrounds together and I believe that many long term friendships have been forged.

And yes, I did kiss a lot of people that day.

TALKING ABOUT CLEPSYDRA

I have written before how I am not a fan of Facebook. I dislike its facile approach and the way that it conveniently replaces so much of importance with a shallow analogue.

For example, people are convinced these days that they are doing their bit for social change, not by marching on a protest demonstration, manning the barricades or making Molotov cocktails, but by clicking 'I like this' on a Facebook petition.

There are also so many pictures of people's pet cats that one can possibly stand to look at in any given period, but I am the first to admit that I am becoming a curmudgeonly old sod.

However, as I have admitted on many occasions on these pages, Facebook is undeniably a very convenient way of keeping in touch with people, and the other day I sent an instant message to Andy Thommen and asked him if there was any news from the Clepsydra camp.

For those of you not aware, Clepsydra is a magnificently tuneful progressive rock band from Switzerland.

In 1991 Clepsydra released their first album *Hologram,* which was followed by the EP Fly Man in 1993.Clepsydra then signed to InsideOut, who released their second album More Grains of Sand in 1994.

This CD included the song *Moonshine on Heights*, which by many is regarded as neo-prog classic. 1994 also saw them performing two songs on national Swiss TV, a rare occurrence for a progressive rock band at that time.

Says Andy, "We had no idea that there was a progressive rock scene. In fact we never heard the expression progressive rock until about three months after the release of Hologram in 1991."

In 1998 Clepsydra released their third album Fears, the first album with Marco Cerulli on guitar.

In the wake of the album release Clepsydra had a 10-day-long European tour and was booked for a concert in Canada on the strength of this production. In 2001 the band released Alone with Nicola De Vita on bass. This album came with three different album covers: The Chicken, The Octopus and The Fish.

Following these four albums Clepsydra entered a state of hiatus. At this point they had established themselves as a popular entity among fans of neo-progressive rock, and they were often compared to the likes of Jadis, IQ and Fish-era Marillion.

In 2013 Clepsydra announced they were reuniting, with Andy Thommen back on bass guitar, and a reunion tour scheduled for 2014. Says Andy about the reunion, "On Sunday June 23 we met and decided to go for the reunion. The day after we did one single post on Facebook announcing the reunion, within 24 hours we had the first 3 concert offers!"

There have been whispers on the internet that the band's reunion has been so successful that they were planning to continue beyond this reunion tour. Andy began by saying:

"We're approaching the end of the reunion tour, with the last three concerts to come ..."

And confirmed that the band is working on a live DVD recorded on a multi-cam at the RoSfest earlier this year in Gettysburg, USA, when Clepsydra shared a stage with the legendary Caravan. RoSfest, or to give it its full name, the Rites of Spring Festival, is an annual progressive rock festival in Pennsylvania. This was its 11th year, and as they say:

"RoSfest has always been at the forefront of bringing new and upcoming progressive rock bands to an American audience, while also bringing in bands that were at their peak during the heyday of prog rock in the '70s."

John Lennon always said that were the Beatles ever to re-form he would want them to go into the studio and see what they could produce rather than just play a series of what are now known as heritage gigs. I have always taken this as a yardstick by which bands' re-unions work and are judged so I am very glad to hear that, as Andy told me:

"We have started talking about the recording of a new album."

Although these plans are at a very early stage. I asked him whether they had written any of the material for the new album yet. He replied:

"No writing, just ideas, concepts and the decision that we WILL DO IT!"

He told me that the release date for the DVD is planned for the end of this year, and that:

"The DVD will contain the full uncut concert, which is about 100 minutes, plus a bonus tour backstage footage."

I am sure that all Clepsydra fans will agree with me that this is really exciting news, and that we are all looking forward to finding out what the 'pearl of Switzerland' does next.

IN SEARCH OF THE ACID KING

At Christmas two years back my presents included a copy of the Philip Norman biography of Mick Jagger. I have always liked Philip Norman, ever since reading his biographies of The Beatles and The Rolling Stones thirty odd years ago.

In his biography of the latter band he discussed the infamous 1967 drug busts at some length. Undoubtedly the most enigmatic character involved in this unfortunate series of events was a Canadian known as "Acid King" David Schneidermann/Snyderman/Sniderman (take your pick) who disappeared soon after the bust never to be heard of again. Bizarrely Norman insinuated that he was basically a phantasm of the times, a tulpa-like character who sprung into existence for the duration of the Redlands drug busts and then disappeared again.

Despite my Fortean leanings, I always thought that this was somewhat unlikely, especially as in Albert Goldman's scurrilous *The Lives of John Lennon* published a few years later, Schneidermann turned up as a bit player in Goldman's description of the 1969 Toronto Rock and Roll Festival.

Imagine my surprise, when - on Boxing Day, after Olivia had gone home, and Corinna, Mother and I had settled down to our various activities, I discovered that not only had Schneidermann lived for several decades in Los Angeles under the nom de guerre of 'David Jove', but that both Jagger and Marianne Faithfull were aware of the fact. Norman also stated that Schneidermann/Snyderman/Sniderman/ Jove was an employee of the security services intent on discrediting The Rolling Stones.

Bloody Hell I thought and had a pootle about on line. I not only discovered that this was now fairly common knowledge, but that other books had been written claiming that he was no spy, but an employee of *The News of the World*. I began to get rather obsessed, and fair hammered my paypal account buying a whole slew of Rolling Stones books on eBay, until I discovered this - a biography of the man by the bloke who was probably his best friend. What's more it turned out that Schneidermann/ Snyderman/ Sniderman/Jove was also a singer songwriter, and - a quick go on YouTube showed me that he was a rather good one.

Intrigued, and with a head full of questions I wrote to Ed Ochs, the author...

I enjoyed the book very much, but a couple of things confused me. In all the Rolling Stones books written until Philip Norman's biography of Mick Jagger last year, it is either stated or implied that David disappeared, and no-one knew where he was. But he was in clear view all the time, and it appears that both Jagger and Marrianne Faithfull knew all about him. Have you any idea why it took so long for his whereabouts/identity to be made public?

Good point. If Jagger had really wanted to find David he could have found him in Toronto until 1970, nightly acting out a cross between James Bond and Robin Hood. By then he had changed his name to David Britton, which fogged his trail as he zig-zagged through Europe. After changing his name a few more times, he settled into Jove -- and "Schneiderman" disappeared until Marianne stumbled across him in LA in the '80s. He lived the life of an underground filmmaker off the grid, but the irony was he craved attention and stood out wherever he went, whatever he did. By the way, David performed Shakespeare in England and, most mysteriously when discussing disappearing acts, he had an older sister, Barbara, who lived in England and is/was married to a judge. I don't know her married name. She's probably still there... (I'm not precisely sure what time period you're referring to here -- immediately post-Redlands or years later. Let me know if I strayed from your intended question.)

Right from the beginning he appears to have been an elusive character. Even in the mid-1960s, false passports were not that easy to obtain. How did he get hold of them? And why did he live such a charmed life?

Good question. Actually, fake passports weren't all that hard too obtain in the mid '60s. You have to understand: That was the height of the Vietnam War draft in the US. Fear and paranoia ran rampant. There were books circulating with titles like "How to Create a New Identity and Disappear" and "The New Identity Tool

Kit." Millions were looking for any way out of the draft and death in a rice paddy; many jumped to Canada. David had a lot of money. (His father, Max, was a successful realtor and gave him whatever he wanted.) He could buy as many passports as he wished on either side of the border -- no problem. In 1970, having skipped bail in Toronto, all those passports came in very handy indeed.

He attributed his charmed life of escaping tight spot after tight spot to being "protected," by which he meant protected by his magical spiritual training as heir to Crowley, which meant he could talk his way in and out of just about every situation imaginable. Then again, how charmed a life was it really for a man on the run from the law for most of his life, drenched in drugs, booze and paranoia, who never got the recognition for being the enormously talented artist he was, and never went home again.

It is obvious from the book that you were very fond of him. But it is also obvous that he was not an easy character to work with. Could you have written the book while he was still alive?

Brilliant question. The answer is no. He would never have cooperated. He wouldn't talk about his past. He worked hard to conceal it and reveal nothing. The last thing he wanted was a book about him, and certainly the last book he wanted was an honest book that revealed his past and him as a human being with flaws. Whenever the past came up he quashed it, changed the subject. He was very disciplined like that. He lived completely in the moment, moments that could last for hours, days. While I was fond of him I was also profoundly disappointed in his sabotaging everything we did and after a while it became vital to my survival that I keep him at arm's length or risk losing everything in his whirlpool. If I lost my my job, my girlfriend and my home he would have been happy with that because he thought I could then hang with him full time. I knew if I didn't have a life of my own he would snatch it and take it over for his own use. I was endlessly conflicted. I was fond of him and also very burned by him at the same time. Not only was he not an easy character to work with, he was impossible. You worked for David, not with him, despite what you may have thought or hoped, because it was always and forever all about him.

Do you know whether there are any plans to reissue any of his music? Or indeed the record that you made with him? I have heard snippets on YouTube and they are much better than I was expecting.

I don't think the online snippets are of decent quality or representative. I could imagine, in the hands of a bold entrepreneur, his two LPs might make an interesting Stones novelty item in the UK. Someone would have to place an inquiry with his daughter, rock violinist Lili Haydn, in LA and make a basic licensing deal for his LPs. As for our EP, "The Bones of Hollywood," his former business manager holds the masters. Funny to think that one of Rod Stewart's former producers/writers ("Do Ya Think I'm Sexy") co-produced it; we wanted that rock-disco sound... Cold financial fact of the matter is that nobody here sees any money to be made in marketing this material at this time -- or has the creative vision to foresee what a great story, with David, the Stones, Redlands and the historic trial, it all is and what a great movie it would make... and buy the rights and grab the headlines that would come with it.

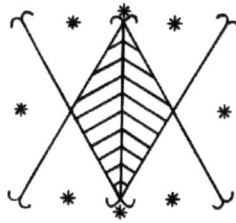

ANGRY? YOU TOO?

Something has been worrying me this week. I don't understand *why* so many people are angry with the recent iTunes promotion of U2's new album. Now, don't get me wrong. I am not saying this because I am a fan of the band, or because I think it is a remarkable record. It's not, and I'm not. The band have made much better records in the past, and they have made considerably worse ones. That isn't the issue. There have been times in my life when I have been quite impressed with the band's output, although I would never have called myself a true blue fan. But that isn't the issue either.

The issue is why are so many people incensed by the fact that iTunes paid the band an undisclosed sum (said to be in the multiple millions) to send a copy of the record to everybody who had an iTunes account on the day in question? Those beneficiaries included me, by the way – twice.

The album can be removed from your playlists with a couple of clicks of a mouse, and although I believe it is slightly more complicated if you have an iPhone, I truly don't think it is going to be that much of an issue.

Why, therefore, are people treating this event as if the Jimmy Savile Fanclub had taken it upon themselves to flood millions of people's iPhones, iPads, computers, etc., with a series of unfortunate images? It doesn't make sense to me.

However, on a smaller scale, I have managed to engender this level of outrage in some people; in 2009 when I started the CFZ Daily Blog network, and again a few years ago when I took over the Gonzo Blog and made it daily; I decided that it would be quite a nice thing to do to post daily notifications on to some of the relevant news groups. This provoked a shit-storm of quite peculiar proportions.

The fact that these notifications were made by email, and therefore could be deleted with one click of the mouse, didn't stop some people from objecting so vehemently that you would have thought I was disseminating something quite offensive. I know that some people don't like prog rock, but .....

Something that makes the whole thing even more peculiar is that this is by no means the first time that people have used this sort of marketing. I didn't have any Apple machinery back in 2011, so I paid no attention to the promotion that happened when a unique Paul McCartney album was presented through the medium. And I don't remember anyone making a fuss about it.

Then again, staying with Paul McCartney, his album 'Memory Almost Full' was given away for free with one of the Sunday newspapers, as was a Prince album a few years ago. I don't remember similar howls of indignation from *Mail on Sunday* readers complaining of the level of 'Liverpudlian filth which had been foisted on them by their local newsagent.'

No, this appears to be a purely internet-based phenomenon, and I would hazard a guess that like so many other internet-based phenomena that we now take for granted, it has its roots in the fact that although intellectually we know that our computer is in contact with other electronic devices across the globe, because said electronic communications device is situated in the privacy of our own homes, or – if we are talking about a telephone – in the privacy of our own pockets, somehow an unwanted email seems like a dastardly invasion of privacy. In reverse, this is how, in my opinion at least, (and I am neither a sociologist or psychologist by trade) the 21st Century phenomenon of internet sexuality has become both such a widely indulged-in practice and a potentially worrying sociological happening. Think about it this way:

Most people wouldn't dream of inviting a total stranger that they had known only an hour or so (sometimes less) into their homes, let alone their bedrooms. But if your laptop is by your bed, or your tablet is in your pyjama pocket, it could well seem that you have already attained a certain level of emotional intimacy with the person with whom you are chatting online, and therefore cybersex or whatever does not seem such an illogical next step.

So, following this paradigm, when the *Mail on Sunday* gave away a Prince or a Paul McCartney album then, to the minds of the hapless consumer, it was no different to any other of the other crap that you get with your Sunday newspapers: you either enjoy it or you don't. If you enjoy it you keep it, if you don't it goes in the recycle bin.

However, when iTunes gave away 500 million digital copies of Songs of Innocence, many people perceived it as being as if Bono at his most annoyingly unctuous had turned up with his pals, uninvited in one's sitting room and started playing a load of music interspersed with his pontifications on the state of the world.

This, I think, has been PR mistake for both U2 and iTunes, although I am sure the biggest band in the world, and one of the biggest corporations, will recover from it sooner rather than later. However, it has been a fascinating exercise in cyber-sociology, and one which PR people across the entire gamut of human enterprise would do well to take on board.

REVIEW

TRAVELLING DAZE
Alan Dearling

I want to introduce you to the jolly nice people at Enabler Publications who are doing a sterling job issuing books (amongst other things) on the free festival and 'traveller' culture of Britain, which has largely disappeared in the past twenty years. Alan Dearling sent me a copy of their new book, Travelling Daze which tells the story of the Free Festival and Traveller movement from then until now. First of all, let's get the review bit out of the way. This book is a magnificent achievement from a socio-cultural point of view; it documents a period of British social history that would otherwise have been forgotten, and it is essential reading for anyone who has ever turned their wild staring eyes towards the open road, or even put Hawkwind or Gong onto the CD player. That means approximately 98% of the people who read the Gonzo Daily. So go out and buy it.

But it also opened a whole slew of emotional cans of worms which I had thought were buried deep in my psyche, never to be opened again. Because, for many years, I was almost a traveller. I say 'almost', because I always had a house of bricks and mortar to come back to. And in a body blow to my anarchist credibility, I owned said house (or rather - at the time - Abbey National PLC owned it). But for great stretches of time for about twelve years from the late 1980s, I spent a lot of my time (and what is more important, my happiest times) on the road between various events at which I sold my wares and danced like an idiot. There are people and places in this book that I had nearly forgotten. The descriptions of the Treworgey Tree Fayre, for example, were spot on, and brought back all the glorious insanity of those days with an immense rush of joy and pain.

Because of the very nature of the book, it celebrates what was good, creative and positive about the scene, which is exactly what it should do. It doesn't attempt to gloss over the negative aspects, but it doesn't dwell on them. I stopped being part of the culture because of people such as 'The Brew Crew', a bunch of filthy dirty brigands off their heads on Carlsberg Special Brew, the dole fraud, the widespread use of heroin, the sexual promiscuity and violence amongst some traveller children, and the low-life scum (including grave robbers, amateur pornographers, and car thieves) who ended up part of the scene once it was no longer able to police itself effectively.

The book has done something very important for me, and something for which I can never thank Alan Dearling enough. It has reminded me why I first got involved in the Traveller Culture, and what I had first found attractive, nay irresistible, about it. It encapsulates a beautiful part of our shared history; a time when people of integrity preferred a shared communal existence in the open air, and turned their back on the increasingly unpleasant face of Thatcher's Britain. The fact it all went wrong wasn't their fault. In fact, it could be argued that the scum who ended up forcing so many people, including me, to turn away, were actually just as much children of Thatcher's policies as the yuppies, the outsider dealers, and those annoying women with ponytails who used to say "OK, Ya" a lot. They were selfish, unbridled capitalists, with no thoughts or care for the society in which they had planted themselves. Pure Thatcherites, in other words. This is a fantastic book, and I cannot recommend it highly enough. Go to the Enabler Publications website. Knock three times and say Jon Downes sent ya!

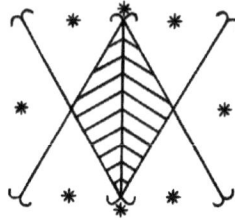

SOME DAY MY PRINCE WILL COME

I am surprised by the negative vibes being directed towards the two new Prince albums (OK, if you want to be pedantic, the Prince album and the Prince with 3RDEYEGIRL album). Personally I think they are both smashing and grow on me with each subsequent playing.

Prince is a weird little bugger, but I have been a big fan for the last twenty years, and although he has his off periods, like Neil Young and the late Frank Zappa, he is so prolific (when he wants to be) and covers so many bases that he is never gonna be able to please all the people all of the time. I think I prefer the solo album to the 3RDEYEGIRL one, but that may just be because I heard it first.

There is no doubt that Prince is a consummate musician, and his guitar playing is excellent. In fact, he first came to my notice in the late 1980s when none other than Keith Richards was extolling his virtues, following which – a few months later – various Rolling Stones shared a stage with the Purple One at an after show gig.

But the 3RDEYEGIRL album provides a chance for Minneapolis's favourite diminutive guitar god to unleash his inner stadium rocker and produce riffs which would not have been out of place 40 years ago played by Paul Kossoff. This isn't a criticism, I like Paul Kossoff, particularly his work with Free, but the most successful bits of the *Plectrum Electrum* album are the bits when the heavy guitar stylings are fused with (and sometimes give way to) Prince's trademark bedroom funk.

However, on both of these albums there is scientific proof that there is, indeed, a male menopause because, for the first time in my experience, Prince's lyrics are no longer entirely written by his cock. One of the things that mildly irritated me about him has been the fact that an enormous majority of his lyrics have been about his sex life. Sexual reproduction, is, of course, the primary concern of every multi-cellular life-form because – it may well be argued – that the prime duty of any multi-cellular life-form is to pass on its DNA to the next generation. I am a firm believer in Darwinism, which is where this theorem originates, but even the originator, Chuck Dee himself, would probably have balked at 'sexy motherfucker'.

But I am not going to be over-critical here. These two records are amongst the best I have heard all year, and – unusually for someone who is generally considered to be a heritage act – this new album is quite possibly as good as most of the things he has recorded in the last 35 years. It is not quite *Sign O the Times* or *Lovesexy*, but then again, what is?

The new Leonard Cohen album is particularly impressive. I enjoyed the previous one which was basically him reciting poetry over a musical backing, but on this one he is singing again and often sounding like Frank Zappa. The tone is much darker, and more to my taste. It is gloriously bluesy, and I have to wonder whether the reviewers who have described it as a folk album have actually listened to the bloody thing!

This is the nastiest he has been in decades and the music is all the more improved for it. Leonard Cohen has always been at his best when he has assumed the role of a sexualised auteur, and - to my mind at least - he never fitted into the role of the Zen elder statesman half as well.

To me at least, Cohen's voice has always been like a mixture of dark chocolate and some unspecified opiate, and it is wonderful to hear him singing again.

Cohen was eighty a few days ago, and - just according to the laws of nature - he must be nearing the end of his career, However, on the evidence of this magnificent record, one thinks that as long as his ageing body holds up, he will be able to produce several more astounding records to top off what has - by anyone's standards - been an astounding musical career.

The new Marianne Faithfull album is a little odd. *Give my Love to London* opens with the title track which is ragged as hell and comes over like a stoned bunch of folkies playing 'Waiting for the Man'.

On first listen, such a rag tag opener does not set the scene well for the rest of the album, but it soon tightens up and tracks like *Late Victorian Holocaust* which was written by Nick Cave, are magnificent. The whole album has a peculiarly unfinished feel to it with count ins left in and fragments of studio noise. However, when you go back to the beginning and start again the title track now does not sound out of place at all. In context with the rest of the album it makes perfect sense.

Against a peculiar amalgam of Waterboys and Velvet Underground she sings:

"The river's running bloody, the Tower is coming down
I'm singing Pirate Jenny, while the black ship's bearing down"

and one wonders whether she has read the Alan Moore novella of a few years ago when characters from the League of Extraordinary Gentlemen universe live out their own drama to the interactive soundtrack of *Seeräuberjenny.*

This zeitgeist of fantasy and impending horror is a recurrent theme throughout the album, and even the love songs are a portent of some unspecified horror lurking just around the corner for the hapless protagonists of the song.

We are living in strange and disturbing times, and this paranoid and unsettling album provides rather a good soundtrack to them.

A SERMON

My father was a Church of England lay preacher, my brother is a high-ranking army chaplain, and my aunt was a deaconess, although I have to admit I don't actually know what that entails, so I have preachers aplenty in my family, which is why – probably – it could be argued that I have a tendency to treat my weekly editorial for this column as a sermon.

It's my nature, innit?

And so, having basically realised that preaching sermons is indeed in my nature innit, I have decided that there is very little I can actually do about it, so today, brothers and sisters, my chosen text is that yes, sometimes miracles do happen! I have several (well two, actually) examples to cite in defence of this aphorism.

First of all is the remarkable case of Wilko Johnson. At the beginning of last year the poor bastard was told that he had pancreatic cancer and only a few short months to live. His bravery under these circumstances was extraordinary, and he behaved in the way that I hope that I would under the same circumstances. He went on the road to do a farewell tour and made a record with Roger Daltrey. As far as the latter is concerned, I think that they missed a trick because the record so should have been called 'Roger Wilko and Out', but not everyone has the same affinity for peculiar (some say painful) puns as I do.

However, times came and times went, and Wilko, though growing weaker, continued to play often unannounced dates. He even played in Bideford last year as special guest of Norman Watt-Roy; a gig which I have been kicking myself ever since for not having attended. But still he didn't die.

About six months ago doctors, amazed at this, re-examined him, found that he had a particularly rare form of cancer and carried out experimental surgery which to everyone's surprise (including one would imagine, Wilko's) actually worked, and this week Wilko announced that he was finally cancer-free. Although Johnson was incredibly brave and described that after being told he only had months to live "he never felt more alive", the last few years must have been an emotional rollercoaster for the poor bugger, and one imagines how he is going to cope with finding out that he now has his allotted life-span ahead of him once again. I can only think in terms of the various prisoner of war camp novels that I have read in which recalcitrant prisoners are made to kneel next to an open grave, whilst their tormenter holds a gun to their foreheads as if to execute them, only for the prisoner to find that when the trigger is pulled nothing more dramatic happens than a click. I have often thought that that must be one of the worst experiences that one can undergo, and wonder whether – behind his implacable visage – Wilko must be going through all sorts of psychological and emotional turmoil. Or maybe he is just taking it in his stride? I very much doubt whether we shall ever find out, and if I ever get round to interviewing him, I am buggered if I am going to ask. This is the man who wrote *Roxette* after all.

Whilst on this subject, which some people might consider morbid, but which I think is such an important part of the human condition that it really deserves to be discussed more, I was told this week that one of my friends, colleagues and clients is facing the final curtain. He, too, is being massively brave about it, and although I shall not name him, I believe that he reads this magazine each week and I just want him to know that all our good wishes are speeding across the aether to him and his family. People who have read my burblings in this column can hardly fail to have realised that my favourite author is the late, great Robert Anson Heinlein, and that my greatest influence is the equally late, and equally great, Gerald Durrell. Before I move on to the second part of my musings on miracles, I would just like to give you a quote from each of these writers, which say basically the same thing.

HEINLEIN

"There is no conclusive evidence of life after death. But there is no evidence of any sort against it. Soon enough you will know. So why fret about it?"

DURRELL

"Nothing except possibly love and death are of importance, & even the importance of death is somewhat ephemeral, as no one has yet faxed back a reliable report."

So what is my second miracle of the week?

Scott Walker has made an album which isn't wilfully unlistenable to!

For well over 20 years, Scott Walker has been my favourite singer. Like (I suspect) most of his fans, I have gone out and bought each of his records as they came out, and admired their artistic integrity, whilst secretly wishing that the man with a voice like molten chocolate mixed with opium, would stop making impossibly complex, high-concept music bristling with stupid noises and arcane sound effects, and get back to making records like he did in the late-1960s. We all know that that is never going to happen. But over the past 20 years his records have become more and more difficult to like. One can appreciate them on an artistic level, but – for me at least – they have become pretty well impossible to listen to.

In 1995 he released an album called *Tilt* – his first for eleven years – which, though it continued in the European avant garde vein, which he had been working within ever since the final 'Walker Brothers' album *Nite Flights* back in 1980, was a cornucopia of great tunes, peculiar orchestration, and amusingly obtuse lyrics. At the time his biographers claimed that this would probably be his final record, but eleven years later along came *The Drift*, which was spikier, more cerebral, and almost entirely bereft of tunes. A year later, he released an instrumental work called *And Who Shall Go to the Ball And What Shall Go to the Ball?* performed by the London Sinfonietta with solo cellist, Philip Shepard, which was music written for a performance by a London–based avant garde dance company. I actually liked it, in the same way as I like some music by 'Faust' but it was never going to make many friends, as it was 24 minutes long and took the listener into the darkest soundscapes of a diseased mind. Five years later came a record called *Bish Bosch* which was received with wide critical acclaim, and which I thought was merely annoying in its wilfulness. For the first time I got the impression that Scott was merely making stupid noises for the sake of it. This realisation was a massive disappointment for me.

Four years ago, the experimental drone metal band, 'Sunn O)))', approached Scott with the idea of a collaboration. However, although having collaborated with Natasha Khan on a glorious song for the 'Bat for Lashes' album *Two Suns* in 2009, and a monumentally peculiar contribution to an avant garde retelling of the Book of Exodus a few years before, Walker refused. However, a couple of years later, he apparently relented and a collaborative album called *Soused* was released this week. The collaboration with Sunn O))) is the first listenable album he has made in twenty years, and whilst firmly in avant garde territory is possibly his best record since *Nite Flights* in 1980. Corinna's and my adopted nephew, Max Blake writes: "I found myself nodding my head with the rhythm at one point. I felt disgusted with myself, and listened to the second movement of 'And *who shall go to the ball?* ...'"

There are tunes. The words make some sort of arcane sense. And then *Sunn O)))* provide a degree of melody and structure which underpin the whole thing in a way that is wholly satisfying. If he never does another record, the 71-year-old Scott Walker has finally produced something lasting that could provide a fitting epitaph for a self-indulgently brilliant career.

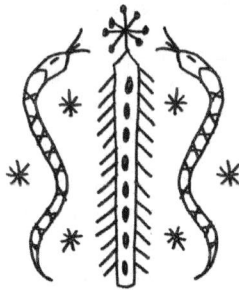

WALKER ON RED SHOES

I always try to be honest in these pages and, although I am not just about to eat my words, I might be just about to have them in preparation of being a tasty little *bon bouche*.

In my editorial this week I was very scathing about Scott Walker's *Bish Bosch* album from a few years ago. Then, in the aftermath of yet another listen to *Soused* I listened to the former album again and realised that it was nowhere near as bad as I thought it was. Although listening to it is not really an enjoyable experience, and it will never replace *Scott IV* in my affections, it is by no means as pointless and wilfully unpleasant as I had originally thought.

This brings me back to what we were talking about in my editorial a few weeks ago, when I mentioned that I was halfway listening through Kate Bush's albums in sequence.

When I listened to *The Red Shoes* for the first time since it came out I was very pleasantly surprised. I liked it a lot, and I am really not sure why I have spent the last 20 years thinking that it was woefully substandard. Even more peculiarly, although I loved *Aerial* when it first came out, this time around it was far too mellow for my taste. It only goes to show that music is wasted on reviewers.

But I had better not say that too loud, because I want you all to carry on reading this magazine.

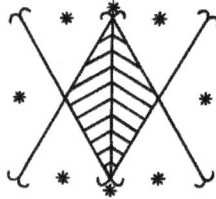

ASTRONOMUSIC

The tradition of 'Artists who do Science' and, indeed, 'Scientists who do Art' is a long and honourable one; it is well known, for example, that *Queen* guitarist Brian May has a Phd in Astrophysics after submitting his thesis in August 2007 (one year earlier than he estimated it would take to complete). As well as writing up the previous work he had done, May had to review the work on zodiacal dust undertaken during the intervening 33 years, which included the discovery of the zodiacal dust bands by the IRAS infrared astronomical satellite.

After a *viva voce*, the revised thesis (entitled *A Survey of Radial Velocities in the Zodiacal Dust Cloud*) was approved in September 2007, some 37 years after it had been commenced. It also works the other way. A science fiction author of whom I am rather fond is the late Leó Szilárd who was a Hungarian-American physicist and inventor. He conceived the nuclear chain reaction in 1933, patented the idea of a nuclear reactor with Enrico Fermi, and in late 1939 wrote the letter for Albert Einstein's signature that resulted in the Manhattan Project that built the atomic bomb.

The Friday before last I did something that I really should have done for a long time. As regular readers will know, we stream several weekly radio shows on Gonzo Web Radio, and write about them here on *The Gonzo Weekly*. For weeks, nay months, I had been intending to sit in on the chat room and listen to the awesome weekly show Friday Night Progressive hosted by my friend M.Destiny. So, finding that the registration process was far easier than I thought, I turned up unannounced in the FNP chat room and was made most welcome. I always find a range of exciting new music through this programme, and that night was no exception.

Astronomusic are a Brazilian duo who have been making music together for the last twenty three years. Larry Kolota wrote this in June 2007:

"Zózimo Rech and Adrianne Simioni have combined their efforts under the name Astronomusic. The cover artwork may suggest new age, but both musicians play guitar as well as keyboards and both combine synth music and instrumental progressive rock unlike anyone else. Unlike some electronic musicians who have little formal training or experience in bands, Rech and Simioni have both, and they certainly can play. In addition to time spent in rock and fusion bands, they were both in Orquestra Profana in the early 1990's, an ensemble dedicated to the interpretation of classical music with electric and electronic instruments. The Life of a Star is by and large a loud, bombastic progressive rock album that uses a lot of synths, but electric guitar prevails.

It was recorded back in 1997 but not released until 2006. Pictures of a Solar System (2006)is considered the sequel. This one has some electric guitar and some rock but is more of a symphonic/melodic/rhythmic synth album along the lines of Synergy, though with higher energy, and sometimes touching upon the style of Fonya.

It is compositionally the more mature album. Simioni plays electric and acoustic guitar and electric violin. Rech has arranging, co-arranging, and/or co-writing credits on all the songs on her 2006 album The Intelligible Sky, produced the album, and took care of the keyboards and sequencers. It is an album that is more progressive rock than synth music. It has more than enough energy and complexity for progressive rock fans, yet is full of sophisticated synth textures, both symphonic and spacey. The drums on all these albums are programmed, but they are well done; a human drummer would not have added much. The booklet for Pictures of a Solar System is particularly beautiful, 24 full-color panels featuring astronomy images created by Frank Hettick. Progressive rock fans should probably start with The Intelligible Sky, synth music fans with Pictures of a Solar System, but those open to both prog rock and synth music will find great music on any of these."

Seldom have I heard music so organic made with largely electronic instruments. They were kind enough to send me copies of their albums, and I have to say that these records have been jostling for space with the new *Rocket Scientists* album and *Steve Ignorant's Slice of Life* for my listening time over the last couple of weeks.

The band describes their work in more detail:

"It may be said that the seeds of Astronomusic were planted when, in 1991, Adrianne Simioni (violin and electric guitar) and Zozimo Rech (electric and acoustic guitar) were introduced to each other. The occasion was the creation of Orquestra Profana, a group dedicated to the interpretation of classical music with "profane" instruments, i.e., electric guitars and synthesizers. In their talkings, the subjects of science (mainly astronomy) and arts (mostly music) would come again and again.

It's not unusual to hear that the scientific point of view "sterilizes" or "unromanticizes" what it focuses. No matter how, it works and gives us access to wonderful advances in countless aspects of our welfare. Regarding this, suffice to acknowledge the evolution of an observation of a mere shining point at the sky by the naked eye (which also has a very special appeal in its own simple nature) into a hi-resolution digital image of a planet only possible through the joint effort of generations dedicated to techno-scientific understanding.

Aeons past, when primitive men sat around the fire, looked at the night sky and imagined the stars as others celestial fires, they certainly created art related to that. Nowadays, we contemplate the sky with knowledge of the life of the stars, that their light may be the support for civilizations in planetary systems and their collapse may affect catastrophically an entire region of the galaxy. It shouldn't be considered nonsense the fact that this new manner of seeing the skies might also generate a subjective manifestation. Thus, the "coldness" inherent to science does not create necessarily an obstacle to the artistic interpretation of its fruits and a creative mind will always discover new ways with dramatic potential yet to be explored. The study of the universe, its development, its beginning, its end will always have a strong call and the arts inspired by this theme will find people that appreciate them as much by the merit of the subject as, perhaps, through some instinctive association with art inspired by myths of creation and end of times .

So, our aim with Astronomusic is to make music to every person that has already contemplated the skies... been delighted... and eventually asked him/ herself.."

I have to agree with Larry Kolota. The first impression that one would normally get from instrumental albums based around the science of astronomy would be the most vapid of new age music.

But this extraordinary collection of recording is nothing like that; managing to be both cerebral and surprisingly visceral. Indeed some of it I can even dance to, insomuch as I can dance to anything these days (my type of dancing is now standing, propped up by my walking stick, and vaguely moving my head and one arm up and down).

One of the things I like most about my position is being able to bring you, the readers, new music and experiences that one might never have heard otherwise. *Astronomusic* are one such experience, and I cannot recommend them highly enough.

REVIEW

CHARLOTTE SOMETIMES
Penelope Farmer

As anybody who knows me will attest, one of my hobbies which surprise people who think of me as a sex, drugs and rock and roll fella, is collecting books from the classic era of children's literature. Surprisingly quite a few of my other friends and relations do the same thing and we tend to do our best to turn each other on to new titles as and when we find them.

For my 55th birthday in August this year my mate Richard Freeman, who is often described as 'the world's only gothic cryptozoologist' and who has risked life and limb on a series of intrepid expedition to far flung places around the globe, bought me this book.

The clue, I think, is both in the title and in Richard's appellation for – quite possibly – The Cure can be described as the *uber*-goth band and *Charlotte Sometimes* is one of their best known songs.

Knowing Richard as well as I do, and having known him for the last two decades, I was not at all surprised to find out that he discovered this book whilst pootling about on the internet trying to find out who the chick was in the video for The Cure's song. Goth chicks have sometimes, like brandy has for me, been his downfall. But I am digressing.

Whilst on this apparently fruitless exercise he discovered that the song was based upon a classic children's book by Penelope Farmer, and being that sort of fellow, he went onto Amazon and bought a copy. He was so impressed that he bought a copy for me.

But, enough of the back story.

This deftly written novel tells the story of how the protagonist (unsurprisingly called Charlotte) at a boarding school sometime in the late 1950s or early 1960s mysteriously travels back in time to inhabit the body of another schoolgirl – Clare – who attended the same boarding school in the closing months of the First World War. Over the next few weeks they mysteriously changed places during the night alternating between 1918 and Charlotte's time. Then, due to one of those banal but totally unforeseeable events in life that my oppo Graham calls 'curveballs', the two girls get stuck in each other's times, possibly permanently.

The difference between reviewing a novel and a non-fiction book is that when reviewing a novel you don't want to give away too much of the plot in fear of spoiling it for new readers. So I won't tell any more of the story. But what I will say, however, is that it is a beautifully written and sensitive novel which gently explores the emotions of each of the main characters, and leaves you identifying even with the nasty ones. Many books – especially in this centenary year – explore the horror of the trenches during World War One. But this book gives a poignant twist to that, and ends up revealing an utterly extraordinary punchline.

The book was first published in 1969, and I really do not know why I have not heard of it before. It also turns out that this is a third of a trilogy featuring the same characters. I know what is on my Christmas present list. Penelope Farmer is still alive and has written at least twenty five books. Apparently she is living in the Canary Islands, and her Wikipedia entry suggests that she is in straitened circumstances. If anybody could get me an email address for her I would be most grateful.

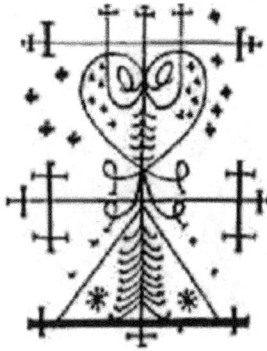

BLACK FRIDAY

Today is what the media have dubbed 'Black Friday'; something which I have never heard of in the UK before. Apparently there were queues of over-financed idiots queuing up from dawn outside our local Asda, and there were fisticuffs aplenty in the queue. I will accept that money is a necessary evil in our modern life, and that although I would love to live in a completely non-capitalist society, we don't and there is very little that I can do about it.

However, as far as I am concerned, financial transactions should be like going to the lavatory. Something concluded behind closed doors, and not mentioned in polite society.

The disgusting displays of self-indulgence and sheer greed which have played out across the western world today are proof, as if any proof were needed, that capitalism is both vulgar and socially divisive. I am very proud to say that to the best of my knowledge neither I nor any of my friends, family or extended household have had anything to do with this disgusting display of fiscal feeding frenzy, and this is a state of affairs which I strongly hope will continue. If you must talk about money, do it in private, and wash your hands afterwards.

I was going to post a picture here taken one of my adopted nieces of a slavering queue of human maggots desperately waiting in line outside Asda hoping to feed on the decaying corpse of the economy of the western world. But then I looked on line using Google picture search and found so many images of greed, avarice, selfishness, and sheer lust that – not for the first time – I really am embarrassed by some of the fellow members of my species. In a month's time it's all going to happen again as the western world celebrates the birth of a god that most of them don't believe in. Roll on January.

Bah humbug!

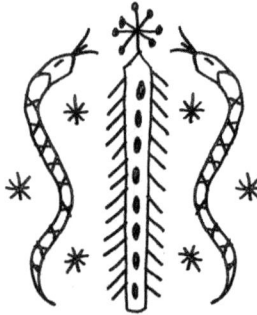

SEXIST PIG GENIUS

The best laid plans of mice, men and editors sometimes go pear-shaped. For months I have been planning a Frank Zappa special for Gonzo Weekly, to coincide with today - the 21st anniversary of his untimely death. But although it *will* happen, it won't be this weekend for a whole string of reasons with which I will not bore you.

But I *would* like to remember his passing both here in the magazine and on the Gonzo Daily blog. Because Frank Zappa was one of the most important, and certainly one of the most talented musicians and composers ever to come out of rock and roll music.

There is a panel in *Watchmen* that always makes me think of Zappa. It is the front cover of a nasty right wing newspaper which is emblazoned with the headline "Honor is like the Hawk - sometimes it must go hooded". Whenever I see that page I think how it should be changed to something like: "Art is like real life - sometimes it is stupid, sexist and utterly brilliant". And no-one did any of those things better than Frank Zappa. I was seventeen and just about to be kicked out of the rather unpleasant public school at which I was an unwilling pupil for a couple of terms, when I first discovered Frank Zappa through a fairly obscure compilation put out through Verve records sometime in the second half of the '70s. I bought it for the quite substantial sum of £2.50 and took it back to school where I played it to my peers who uniformly hated all of it except *What's the Ugliest Part of your Body* which made them snigger. Not for the first time, and by no means for the last, I realised that my tastes and those of the people around me were often going to be radically different, because I loved the record.

It gave me permission to be silly, and pointed out that the awful grey trench coated homogeneity of the circles in which I moved did not have the monopoly on ideas. Indeed silliness in music was as much of a thought crime as much of Zappa's perceived sexism is now. But I didn't care. I felt gloriously liberated, and from that day on my life was never the same.

Fifteen years later I knew that my hero was dying. But a world without Frank Zappa seemed unbelievable, and I was convinced that Frank would have a last minute reprieve like the one which only this year happened to Wilko Johnson. But miracles don't happen very often, *mors certa, hora incerta,* and 21 years ago today Frank Zappa died, and my life - but more importantly the world as a whole - was never the same again either.

REVIEW

WHITE LINE FEVER
Lemmy

There are three types of music biography/autobiography; the ones which are meticulously written and composed as a piece of literature. Morrissey's autobiography which was published to such acclaim last year is a fine example of that. The second type includes all the books which are deliberately written as works of reference, with scholarly references, footnotes etc. And the third type - in many ways the most common - happens after the musician in question sits down with a ghost writer and either dictates a stream of consciousness, or just tells rambling stories about his or her exploits which the ghost writer records, and then draws liberally upon in order to produce the finished product.

Guess which one this is?

Reading Lemmy's autobiography I was surprised to find that he is a vegetarian who practises tai chi and donates a large proportion of his royalties to a trust fund set up by an Indian guru whose name I have forgotten. No, of course he isn't. This book is a mildly entertaining romp thru drugs taken, vodka drunk, and groupies fucked in various positions over a career that has lasted for the best part of half a century.

He does lay out his stall as regard his philosophy of life:

"That's the great British legacy to the world, humour like *The Young Ones*, *The Goon Show* and *Monty Python*. Some people don't get it which is too bad for them. You are supposed to laugh in life. Laughing exercises all of the facial muscles and keeps you from getting old. Looking stern gives you terrible wrinkles. I also advise drinking heavily - it helps the sense of humour! Smoking pot helps the sense of humour no end, but after a while you lose it altogether, and all you can do is talk about the cosmos and shit, which is really boring".

I am pretty sure that this autobiography was basically put together in a series of pubs, where Lemmy necked back large amounts of vodka, and told anecdotes as the ghost writer Janiss Garza made notes and asked the occasional pertinent question. A woman ghost writer? It confirms much of what comes over in this book. Lemmy likes women, and not just in a carnal rock and roll animal sort of way. He likes them as people, and all the way through this book are descriptions of women he admires, women he has collaborated with, and women who are just simply his friends. There are plenty of groupies and more than his fair share of casual sex, but one is left with the impression that Lemmy has a fair bit more respect for these women than do some of his contemporaries.

The story is a rocky and pretty damn entertaining one. We follow Lemmy from his boyhood on Anglesey to his first faltering footsteps as a professional musician with The Rocking Vicars and Sam Gopal. Bizarrely, for many years I had always believed that the band was called Sam Gopal and the Rocking Vicars and had not realised that one was an Indian psychedelic musician playing a tabla, and the other was a very meaty rock and roll band. According to Wikipedia and other sources online, the latter band renamed themselves The Rocking *Vickers* because someone at their record company thought the name was blasphemous. Lemmy claims that the band continued until the early 1990s, with the band having morphed into somewhat of a comedy outfit, but I can find no confirmation of this on any of the various websites dealing with such things, including those with contributions from the ex-members themselves.

It is here where we encounter somewhat of a paradox. Whilst Lemmy's stories are undoubtedly entertaining, and often either shocking, amusing or both, they are not necessarily true. For example, right at the beginning he describes how his mother worked on a TB ward, and goes into great detail about how TB effects the chromosomes, leading to the birth of a baby "covered in rudimentary feathers" and another covered in scales. This is a massively good story, but complete bollocks.

Later in the book he claims that because of all the drugs he had taken, his blood was not human anymore, and would be completely toxic if given to anyone else in a transfusion. He quite possibly had so many drugs in his system that the second claim might well be true, but his blood and other bits would have stayed unquestionable human. Evolution just doesn't work like that.

I wished that he had written more about Sam Gopal, and about his tenure in Hawkwind. It would have been nice to know more about his relationship with The Pink Fairies, The Deviants and especially with folk like Mick Farren and Steve Took, but unfortunately whilst there is quite a lot about his relationship with the members of bands such as Metallica and Twisted Sister, there is far less about the time when he was one of the pivotal members of the Ladbroke Grove community, which is a great pity, because this is the time that interests me and about which I wanted to know more. However, I suspect that I am in a minority.

Motorhead have been treading the boards for very nearly forty years, and are unquestionably one of the iconic bands of heavy metal. There is only one problem here; I don't like heavy metal. It is one of the few types of music which does absolutely nothing to me except for to mildly irritate me. Admittedly Motorhead are by a long way up in the top echelon of the genre as far as I am concerned, and I do quite like them. I am coming at them from the direction of being a fan of Hawkwind and the MC5, rather than a devotee of the mainstream HM music. So whereas I am sure that most people who read this book, and indeed the main audience to which this is targeted, are fascinated by tales of how Metallica did this, or Twisted Sister did that, but I truly don't give a toss!

The truth is that whereas this doesn't work particularly well as a printed book, it would work much better as an audio book read by the author, and even better as a one man show with Lemmy, fag in one hand and Jack Daniels in the other telling the stories. However, I can't imagine Lemmy actually doing that sort of spoken word gig, and it would probably never happen. The best of all, of course, would be if you could sit in a quiet little bar somewhere, while Lemmy told you these stories one to one, and you both got shitfaced.

I can only dream.

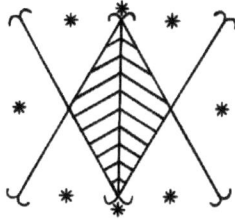

RAIDING THE ARCHIVES

Welcome to this, the second issue of Gonzo Weekly to be published in the brave new world of 2015. About ten years ago my favourite magazine was *The Word*, and I remember reading an editorial which said that in this aforementioned brave new world practically everything which had ever been recorded would eventually be available again. Well, this isn't entirely true, but I know what the author meant.

I am proud to say that a big part of this volte-face on the behalf of the recording industry is because of the machinations of the company for whom I now work, and its predecessor Voiceprint Records. They unearthed amazing pieces of rock and roll minutae thought lost forever, and continue to do so with releases such as the recent one by the late Peter Banks (the original guitarist with Yes) and his band Empire.

Of course some legendary recordings have still not seen the light of day, and probably never will. This is usually because they weren't terribly good, but also because some of them never existed in the first place.

A good example of the former is the legendary recording supposed to have been made on the night that The Beatles met Elvis.

Various pundits have built this up into a legendary masterpiece of colossal proportions, but it is almost certainly nothing of the sort. Most historians now agree that the event was never recorded, and if it was it consisted of Elvis playing a few bars of *I Feel Fine* on the bass guitar as the Fabs looked on sycophantically. Paul and John may also have sung a bit of one of Elvis' songs, but no-one can remember which, and the whole event seems to have been a damp squib.

Another legendary Beatles recording which has never seen the light of day is from January 1969 when Jim Morrison is meant to have turned up at the basement studios of Apple Records. What then transpired no-one seems sure, but I assume that it would be of no more significance than the film clip that I have somewhere on an old Betamax tape of Peter Cook and Dudley came visiting the sessions, which is just stoned drivel, but basically that is all that the vast majority of the Get Back sessions were, sad to say.

One legendary tape that finally surfaced a few years ago was recorded in 1974 and had been described in May Pang's book *Loving John*. Lennon was producing Harry Nilsson's latest album, Pussy Cats, when Paul and Linda McCartney dropped in after the first night of the sessions, aka "the Jim Keltner Fan Club Hour", at Burbank Studios on 28 March 1974. They were joined by Stevie Wonder, Harry Nilsson, Jesse Ed Davis, May Pang, Bobby Keys and producer Ed Freeman for an impromptu jam session.

Lennon was in his "lost weekend", separated from Yoko Ono and living in Los Angeles with Pang. Although he and McCartney hadn't seen each other in three years and had lashed out at each other in the press, according to Pang they resumed their friendship as if nothing had happened. The jam session proved not very productive musically. Lennon sounds to be on cocaine and is heard offering Wonder a snort on the first track, and on the fifth, asks someone to give him a snort. This is also the origin of the album name, where John Lennon clearly asks: "You wanna snort, Steve? A toot? It's goin' round". In addition, Lennon seems to be having trouble with his microphone and headphones.

Lennon is on lead vocal and guitar, and McCartney sings harmony and plays Ringo Starr's drums. (Starr, who was recording with Nilsson at the time but not present at the session, complained at the next day's recording session that "[McCartney] always messes up me drums!") Stevie Wonder sings and plays electric piano, Linda McCartney is on organ, Pang plays tambourine, Nilsson provides vocals, Davis is on guitar, Freeman (who was producing Don McLean in the neighbouring studio) fills in on bass, and Keys plays saxophone. Keys had been questioned on a number of times about the session, but he couldn't recall any of it.

I think that if I had been present I would do my best not to remember it either. It is living proof, if any proof were needed, that drugs are not good things at recording sessions. Paul is being over unctious, even more so than usual, and John descends into a self-opinionated bad temper, which is what happened to yours truly the only time that I ever took cocaine twenty-six plus years ago, which is why I never bothered to do it again. The recording is at best unremarkable, and at worst embarrassing, and one can see why it took so long to see the light of day. It actually might well have been just as well from the point of view of the musicians concerned if it had stayed in the vaults. There are things that we know perfectly well exist in the Beatles vault, such as *Carnival of Light* which George Harrison refused to allow onto the *Beatles Anthology* project on the grounds that it was an over-long avant garde mess. This makes one wonder what he would have thought of the recent reissue of his second solo album, the practically unlistenable *Electronic Sound.* Even at the time it was released in 1969 it seemed an unlikely move for a musician famed for his meticulous approach to studio craftsmanship. The cover of *Electronic* Sound was painted by Harrison himself. The inside sleeve included minimal notes on the album and a quotation attributed to Arthur Wax: "There are a lot of people around, making a lot of noise; here's some more."

I write elsewhere about what I have dubbed The Mythologisation Process, so I won't describe it again, but the current generation of musical archaeologists can thank their lucky stars that things are easier for them back when I first wrote my debut book back in 1988. It was a book about Beatles bootlegs, and sold about a thousand copies, although I have no intention of ever reprinting it. If you really want to read it there is a copy in the music section of Exeter Library's Reference section, which I did a modicum of Joe Ortonesque decoration to one rainy afternoon about fifteen years ago. But it was written over five years before EMI opened their vaults and the Beatles archaeologising began in earnest. it was reliant on rumours and half truths. For example, all the way thorough the 1970s various of the weekly music papers regularly mentioned two unreleased Beatles singles: *What's the New Mary Jane*" and *Futting around* c/w *Do the Fut.*

To deal with the second one of these first, it is a confusion between a Bee Gees spinoff record and the withdrawn Apple single by Brute Force. Brute Force may be best known for a song that barely saw a release. *The King of Fuh*, a song produced by The Tokens, prominently included at least two intentionally obscene double entendres, referring repeatedly to a "Fuh King" and telling everyone to "all hail" with a pronunciation that made it sound suspiciously like "aw, hell." The record was admired by Beatles George Harrison and John Lennon. Harrison used the already recorded demo track, but had strings arranged and overdubbed for the record. Apple Records knew that partner EMI would never distribute it, so the company pressed and distributed 2,000 copies themselves in 1969 (catalogue number Apple 8). There was also a copy of the record on the US version of Apple, without a catalogue number (said to have been created as personal copy for an American Apple employee). Brute Force also attempted to have Major Minor records in Britain release the record, but with no success. Finally, the artist issued the record on his own label Brute Force Records with an alternate B Side, *Tapeworm Of Love*, which received airplay on the Dr. Demento radio show. More recently (2005), the Revola label issued both *King of Fuh* and its original B side (*Nobody Knows*) as bonus tracks on the CD release of *Extemporaneous*. In 2010, *The King of Fuh* was released by Apple Records on their first "best of" compilation album, *Come and Get It: The Best of Apple Records*. And the other song seems to be a made up title for *What's the New Mary Jane*, written by John Lennon (but credited to Lennon–McCartney) and performed by the Beatles. It was recorded in 1968 for the album *The Beatles* ("The White Album"), but was not used. I remember how disappointed I was when, back in the mid-'90s I got hold of a bootleg copy of one of the four versions recorded by John, George and Yoko during the sessions for *The White Album*, and how I marvelled at the knowledge that my hero John Lennon had actually planned to release the bloody thing as a single.

And this is only scratching the surface of the mythology surrounding just one band, albeit arguably the most important rock and roll band of all time. We are now, sadly, entering the time when more and more of that generation of musicians are beginning to succumb to old age, senility and death. One wonders whether we are now at the high point of our knowledge; a kind of rock and roll Age of Enlightenment where those who can remember are still able to do so, and the commercial acumen of those placed in guardianship over the vaults are prepared to release practically anything if they can sell it.

In twenty years time those that are left of the sixties generation will be in their nineties. Will the world still care about the activities of a bunch of talented longhairs seventy years before? And if so, with no-one left to corroborate the research, what outlandish folk myths will arise?

REVIEW

ROBERT PLANT: THE VOICE THAT SAILED THE ZEPPELIN
Dave Thompson

A few weeks before Christmas I had a nice surprise when this rather nifty tome popped through my letterbox and onto my doormat. I often have quite an esoteric postbag, as my hydra-headed careers as naturalist, cryptozoologist, musician and rock and roll boulevardier trundles on much as it has any time this past thirty years. However as we approached what is euphemistically called 'the festive season' even the best intentioned rock and roll boulevardier has to be careful which parcels he opens, even if they are addressed to him, because opening one's Christmas presents early was one of the cardinal sins in the eyes of my late Mother, and even though she has been dead thirteen years, I would hate to make her roll in her grave.

So I passed the parcel to my dear friend and partner in crime for the past twenty years, Graham Inglis, and he had a quick gander at it and told me that it was a review book, so I sat down to read it with gusto.

Now, before we get any further, let me stress one thing. I like Led Zeppelin; possibly not as much as I did twenty years ago, and certainly not as much as I did when I was a schoolboy lusting after the girl who sat opposite me on the school bus and wanting to give her every inch of my love YEAH, but still a hell of a lot more than I do most bands, of this or any other era. I also have quite a few books on the subject of the band and their career, and when receiving a new volume on any subject about which I know quite a lot already, the first thought of trepidation that one has is that the book will not tell the reviewer anything new. With this book that is certainly not the case.

One of the things that I find interesting - stylistically at least - about this book is the way that it is laid out. There are two separate narratives here; one starting (logically enough) with his birth, and the other starting (equally logically) with his rebirth into a solo artist in the early 1980s after the untimely (though not particularly surprising) death of Led Zeppelin drummer John Bonham.

I met Dave Thompson many years ago when he was fairly early into his career as a rock and roll biographer, and had just had a biography of Chris de Burgh published by Omnibus Press. At the time my ex-wife and I were working with the *Lady in Red* balladeer (don't ask) and we trekked across suburban London to meet Dave Thompson. Even then I was impressed by the quiet and unassuming self-assurance of his writing, and the way he combined meticulous research with elegant but understated prose to produce a book that few others could have produced about someone who really wasn 't that interesting.

Over the years I have read quite a few of his books, but even I was shocked when I read on the flyleaf of this present volume that he has authored over a hundred titles! Led Zeppelin are one of those bands like The Beatles or the Stones, whom - it could be argued - have been done to death. So what new could even such a consummate professional as Dave Thompson bring to such an oft told story?

Well, quite a lot really.

If I had to sum up this book in one word it would be by stealing the title of an American TV show that I did some work for years ago: It is a mythbuster!

Early on in the book Thompson quotes the late Peter Grant, who was Led Zeppelin's manager throughout their career and beyond, who admitted that like Colonel Tom Parker did with Elvis, his main job with Led Zeppelin was to create a myth. 'Somebody killed something, that's clear at any rate" said Alice, when she first heard the poem *Jabberwocky*. One can say something similar about Led Zeppelin. Somebody sexually violated a tied and bound naked groupie with a dead or dying fish.... That much is true, because Frank Zappa said so. And Frank Zappa would never lie about anything would he? He warned us not to eat the yellow snow.

Yes, the primary source for this rather revolting story is a song by Frank Zappa on the *Fillmore East 1971* album, and the secondary source is a scurrilous and unreliable account by ex-roadie Richard Cole which appeared in a book called *Hammer of the Gods* and the tertiary source is another book by Cole, of whom Jimmy Page said: "There's a book written by our former road manager, Richard Cole that has made me completely ill. I'm so mad about it that I can't even bring myself to read the whole thing. The two bits that I have read are so ridiculously false, that I'm sure if I read the rest I'd be able to sue Cole and the publishers. But it would be so painful to read that it wouldn't be worth it.".

The main protagonists (apart from the fish and the unnamed young lady) are allegedly members of Led Zeppelin and Vanilla Fudge, all - as far as I am aware - of whom have categorically denied that it ever happened.

In my other life as Director of the centre for Fortean Zoology, I have written widely about the socio-psychological way in which real events become myths, and the story of the unnamed rock musicians, the groupie and the fish is a perfect example of this.

Grant even admitted that the band behaved no worse on tour than most other rock bands on the road. I have been a young man on tour with a rock band, albeit one with only a fraction of Zep's fame, influence or cash, but I can confirm (as if any confirmation were needed) that the opportunities for debauchery and bad behaviour are unlimited, but after having read this book, one starts to doubt whether Zep were, indeed, the magnificently debauched scumbags they have been portrayed as.

One also realises that their demigod status was something bestowed upon them by the press, with a little manipulation by Grant, and that most of what you know about the band is simply untrue.

For example, Jimmy Page was almost certainly not the dark philosopher of legend. He collected books by Aleister Crowley (well, so do I) and bought Crowley's old gaff on the shores of Loch Ness (well, so would I if I had his money which I haven't). But I know that I am not the dark lord of anything, and I somewhat suspect that Page wasn't and isn't either.

Peculiarly, once one cuts through the mythologised bullshit, the story of Led Zeppelin is even more impressive than one would normally have expected. But the meat and potatoes of this book isn't the story of the band, it is the story of Robert Plant the person, and here I found myself treading into - what was for me - completely unknown territory. Like many people of my generation, I was very disappointed by the first two thirds of the 1980s, especially as far as my favourite bands from the previous decade were concerned. They all seemed either to have split up, died, or - worse - got very dodgy haircuts and made some even dodgier music. Plant (to me at the time) made a series of dodgy solo records that I disliked purely because it wasn't *Led Zeppelin*, and it was nearly ten years after the band split up that I started to listen to his solo records.

In fact, it was another ten years before I got to see him live. *The Priory of Brion* played at Exeter Arts Centre in the autumn of 2000, and they were utterly awesome. Robert Plant autographed my CD of Led Zep 4, and added his autograph to my vinyl copy which had already been signed by John Paul Jones a few years before. Surprisingly the book suggests that *Priory of Brion* never played outside the West Midlands when I know full well they played in Devonshire, but this doesn't really matter.

The important thing about this book is that Thompson's prose enthused me enough to spend several evenings over the Yuletide break working my way through a whole slew of Plant's solo albums which I had missed at the time.

I knew his output since the late 1990s, but everything else had completely passed me by, mostly due to my own intransigence, and this remarkable, but oddly humble little book, gave me a gift of incalculable worth.

As well as making *Led Zeppelin* humans rather than mystic deities with a penchant for fish, it reacquainted me with some peerless sounds, which would otherwise have surely passed me by.

Thank you Dave.

ABSINTHE MAKES THE HEART GROW FOUNDER

I am feeling a little shaky today because last night my partner in crime with Wyrd Music came down to see me bearing a bottle of black absinthe—something that I have never had before, and always vaguely wanted to try.

One and a half tiny liqueur glasses and I was tripping off my bonce. The last time I took hallucinogenic drugs was Boxing Day 1981, but this stuff definitely came closer than I had any intention of going. According to current thinking, absinthe is no longer thought to have hallucinogenic properties, but on the basis of my experience last night (which I think shall be my *only* experience, by the way) I think that this current thinking is mistaken.

And it *doesn't* make the heart grow fonder.

2015 is shaping up to be a very exciting year here in the potatoshed from whence I mastermind this magazine. Just released are three books—the Gonzo annual 2015, Neil Nixon's extraordinary *500 Albums you won't believe until you hear Them* and an intriguing little book credited to Frank Zappa et al, and entitled *The Real Porn Wars.*

Coming very soon are autobiographies by Roy Weard and Gregg Kofi Brown and several other interesting projects that I cannot talk about just yet. There are also big things afoot from the CFZ and from Wyrd Music, so, I think you will see what I mean when I say that this looks as if it is going to be a very interesting year.

Now, all I have to do, is to shake off this bloody hangover.....

KEEP TAKING THE TABLET

Backalong (as they say in Devonshire) I used to enjoy travelling across the country, and - indeed - the world, doing my own inimitable thing, but in recent years I have done less and less of it. This is partly because My health is slowly, but surely, deteriorating, and it is far more comfortable (and a damn sight less effort) for me to spend my time pottering about my tumbledown cottage in North Devon, where I have my books, my computers, my tropical fish and my dogs, not to mention many of my nearest and dearest, but it is partly because as I get older I have more and more on my plate, and more and more to do.

Now, I will make a confession here. I have always looked at those people one sees on trains and in supermarket cafes pootling about on their iPads with mild disdain.

But now I am one of those people. last summer Corinna got a new mobile phone, and as part of the deal she got a free iPad.

I vaguely wanted one, mostly so I could check how magazines like this one, and the other online things that I do, looked on a mobile device. What I was not expecting was for this blasted tablet thingy to take over my life.

Then I discovered that I can type into Microsoft Word documents using it, and that despite not having a proper external keyboard, it was very comfortable and easy to use, and in fact far more easy and convenient than using my laptop.

I then discovered that being what is colloquially called a fat bastard that I could sit back in comfort in my favourite armchair, with Archie the neurotic Jack Russell on my lap, rest my iPad on my overlarge belly and type in extreme comfort, especially if I took my glasses off.

And then, earlier this afternoon (it is last Saturday from when you will be reading this, if that doesn't sound too Escherlike), I found that if I have my two cameras hung round my neck (as is my custom when on road trips) I can rest my iPad on them, and type perfectly comfortably from the passenger seat of the hire car as Corinna, (my beloved and terribly long-suffering wife, for those of you who don't know) drives across the arterial roads of the United Kingdom.

I have always liked the idea of field recordings. Of art which reflects the place where it was made. I have always liked the concept promulgated by John and Yoko over forty years ago, where art reflects one's life. But this week I am going to try and do it with a magazine.

I have only the vaguest idea of what will be in this issue; but what I do know is that if will be formed against the backdrop of what I am doing this week. because this is far from being a normal week in the life of Jon Downes, cryptoozoologist, itinerant wordsmith for hire, and part time musician.

We are not at home this week. We are travelling for mile across the southern half of the British Isles. First we go to Oakham, the county town of the smallest of Britain's counties. Then on to Norwich, and a couple of days pootling about in Norfolk, before back to, Oakham for a couple of days, and a journey to Staffordqshire, before returning home next Thursday.

Hopefully, by then, I shall have an entire magazine written and composited via email and Facebook, and be able to transfer the whole thing to my computer, and then put it together with what my other contributors have written and puta this issue together. Then I shall sleep for a couple of days before starting normal life again on Monday.

It is, I am sure that you will agree, a fine ideal. Let's see if it works.

By the way, any of you who read last week's magazine, and in particular the end bit that is on the inside back page. I don't know what you call that bit. It is, I suppose, a closing editorial, but I am sure there must be a proper term for it. At least better than 'End Bit'.

But I digress. In that final few paragraphs I wrote about a baby pigeon which had been caught by my *quondam* intern's Grandmother's cat. It was brought to us to see if we could save it. Sadly this didn't happen, and - just like we thought that it probably would - it died, despite our best efforts. But it was not hungry, it was not thirsty, and it died in a quiet and peaceful place rather than being ripped apart by a cat, so I think we did something good.

When the universe sends us an animal or a person needing help, we always do our best, even though our efforts are often in vain, and sometimes turn around and bite us on the bum.

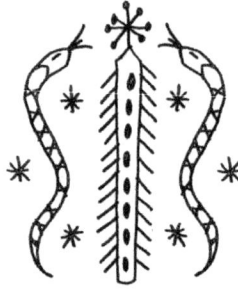

ON THE ROAD

CAPTAIN'S LOG: Dateline, Saturday afternoon, rural Gloucestershire

Our journey is well underway. We have driven over a hundred miles and have not only passed Bristol, but have reached the Michael Wood services on the M5. here we spent over fifteen quid on coffee and the sort of things that I only ever eat when we are on a motorway, because everyone knows that when you are on a motorway you enter a whole new realm of space-time where the laws of nature do not actually apply, and where Chocolatey bun things are not injurious to a person with diabetes. My main ambition for this journey, apart from seeing my grandsprogs is to try and buy the new Bob Dylan album on CD so that I can listen to it in the car.

So I go into the little shop and make a beeline for the record section. Yes, indeed there is a rack of shelves emblazoned with the sign 'New and Classic Albums by Classic Artists' so I actually had high hopes that the new Dylan album might be luring there. But, of course, it wasn't. There were several records by Daniel O' Jesus H, bald headed club footed freaking Donnell, the soundtrack to Grease, and greatest hits that I already own by The Beach Boys and The Who. The rest were horrid three CD bargain packs of Techno Classics, Reggae Classics, and 'Songs every Grandfather wants to hear'. As I am a Grandfather, and the songs I would want to hear on this particular journey would be by Nico, Throbbing Gristle, Crass, The Mahavishnu Orchestra and possibly Sun Ra, And certainly the new album on which Bob Dylan re-interprets the songs of Frank Sinatra, I had high hopes of this package. But it consisted of songs by Doris Day and various people that I had either never heard of, or wished that I hadn't and I made loud protestations of disgust which unfortunately attracted the attention of a sales assistant. She asked me what was wrong in an overly combative manner, and I explained to her that as a Grandfather I had every intention of taking The people responsible for this unpleasant artefact to court under the Trades Descriptions Act on the basis of fact that this package should have been entitled 'Songs that a Grandfather wouldn't be seen dead in a ditch wIth' . I then made my excuses and left...

SPURIOUS TRANSIENTS: Portraits of a landscape

"Recorded during 2012-2014 in Pembrokeshire and Ceredigion, "Portraits Of A Landscape" is a collection of musical pieces inspired by the Welsh countryside where the ancient landscape is juxtaposed against contemporary industry. The album is split into two distinct halves with tracks 1-5 reflecting the industrial landscape, while tracks 6-9 celebrate living alongside nature within the Welsh countryside. credits"

Gavin Lloyd Wilson is an old mate of mine, and although I knew that he was a musician (he is one of the on/off bass players for Welsh psych-wizards Sendelica) until now I have never actually heard his music. SO what does one do, when an old mate sends you a copy of his new musical project, with a covering letter admitting that it is well within the avant garde area of the musical spectrum? Well, to be brutally honest, one approaches with extreme caution. i hate reviewing my friend's records, because it puts one in a totally impossible situation. If it is good, then one always feels worried that people will think that you are only giving it a good review because of your friendship with the artist, and if it is bad...let's not even go there.

As most people know, I am massively overstretched for most of the time, and although I have music on in my office all the time, there is always a teetering pile of CDs waiting for me to play them, and so I make no apologies for the fact that this record has been hanging around on my office desk for some time waiting for me to play it. But as anyone who has even slightly read this week's issue will be aware, we are spending the week on the road visiting my stepdaughters and granddaughter, and are in a hire car with a rather nifty sound system, so I have brought along a whole slew of records that I have been waiting to play. ANd this is one of them.

I really shouldn't have worried, because this is an excellent, though massively peculiar record. For years I have been trying to make truly organic music mixing field recordings, acoustic instruments and electronica. To date the best I have managed are the opening and closing tracks of my last album (check it out on Spotify if you feel the need) but Gavin and his band have gone even further. This album, which has moments of very real beauty, is an unholy mixture of folk, psychedelic, electronic and avant garde music. Imagine Can, Throbbing Gristle, *Ummagumma* era Pink Floyd, and Fairport Convention having a tea party at which Roger McGuinn (in his raga rock phase) was given a birthday present of a whole slew of digital delays, and you might come close. But you wouldn't really. Because this music is indecribable, and crosses so many genres that it is totally impossible to classify.

But parts of it are very beautiful, others very scary. But it is almost impossible to turn off.

There is a new zeitgeist in the air, and various musicians and composers across the universe are tapping into it. And when, in however many years it takes, the music historians are writing the history of this gloriously insane time, this record will be seen as one of the major landmarks.

CAPTAIN'S LOG: Dateline, Sunday lunchtime, urban Rutland

Memo to self. Neither Corinna or Mother like me referring to the proprietors of an Oakham supermarket which I think should probably not be named as Neo Fascists because their cafe didn't serve breakfast, or have anything diabetic friendly that I actually wanted to eat, and didn't even have free wifi. And I should probably also note that the local council are not half witted dwarves who would benefit from a zombie apocalypse just because there weren't any· comfortable chairs left in the cafe and I was forced to perch on an uncomfortable wooden chair that was several sizes too small for me, eating something that will probably hasten my demise from diabetic complications. And no, they didn't have the new Bob Dylan album.

THE RELATIONSHIPS: Phase

"The Relationships are legendary purveyors of tweedy psychedelia and sparkling powerpop from Oxford, England. Their music mixes twelve-string guitar, postpunk urgency, and touches of prog with classic English songwriting in the vein of the Kinks, Robyn Hitchcock, and XTC.

Songwriter Richard Ramage and guitarist Angus Stevenson first crossed jangly guitars in mythic 80s ensemble Here Comes Everybody, which also featured Peter Momtchiloff â€" soon to become a founder member of John Peel favourites Talulah Gosh â€" and inspired Andy (Ride/Oasis) Bell to buy his first guitar. Diversifying via Razorcuts (Angus) and The Anyways (Richard), our two heroes regrouped in a desolate 90s landscape of grungy indie and Britpop-by-numbers to create the Relationships, who soon caught the eye of Californian label Twee Kitten. The bandâ€™s EP Country Catalogue (1998) and first album Trend (2000) followed. Andy Bell stepped in to contribute some wig-out guitar to the album, and Amelia

Fletcher (Talulah Gosh, Heavenly) put down some lovely backing vocals too.

With rhythm section Andy Smith (formerly of The Bigger The God) on bass and top sound engineer Tim Turan on drums the Relationships released their second album Scene on Trailer Star records of Nottingham (2005) and third album Space on Big Red Sky (2009). In 2014 they release fourth album Phase on Big Red Sky."

Not for the first time in my life I wonder why the-record that I have just listened to, and the exquisitely crafted press blurb that I have just read seem to have little or no relationship to each other. Don't get me wrong. I like this record very much indeed but I would have described it as sounding like a glorious piece of miscegenation between Barclay James Harvest and the Divine Comedy. I would have gone on to explain my theory that as musicians, and the folk who listen to them, are no longer spring chickens, that rock and roll is n longer a young man's game, and so the lyrical concerns of songwriters in general are changing, and how refreshing it was to hear a band like this writes songs about stuff that the listeners of my generation are more likely to be listening to.

I would have bitched slightly about the heavily processed drum breaks on one of the records, but would have then tempered that by explaining that unless you are Keith Moon, Ringo Starr on side two of *Abbey Road*, or possibly Ginger Baker at various times in his career it is impossible for you to produce a drum break let alone a drum solo that doesn't make me want-to projectile vomit. I would then probably have gone off on a totally irrelevant rant about the electronically treated drums on *Bonzo's Montreaux* on Led Zeppelin's *Coda*, and have lost 95% of my readership in trying.

I really like this record, and am going to investigate other material by the band as soon as I Can get back to my particular brand of reality back in Woolsery. In the meantime I am going to let this particular brand of neopsychedelic whimsy lull me through the long and interminable journeys across the arterial network of motorways which criss cross this sceptre'd isle.

CAPTAIN'S LOG: Dateline, Monday night, rural Norfolk

For years I used to refuse to eat at Macdonald's because if their heinous record of environmental crimes, but recently they have not only cleaned up their act, but opened restaurants that are open all night long, so even though it is 2am somewhere west of King's Lynn, we can get a cup of coffee and something to eat. I think we must look a rum crew. Corinna goes first, looking like a galleon in full sail. As she gets older she becomes more and more like a cross between the hippy analogue of an aristocratic County lady and the mad cat woman on *The Simpsons*. Following her are me, dressed in black with Crass T shirt and leather jacket looking like an ageing Groupie for the Anti Nowhere League, and - holding my hand - Mother who seems to get smaller, and more delicate looking, every day - like an anthropomorphised dunlin tiptoeing across a salt marsh.

The three of us bluster into the restaurant where - apart from a couple of surly looking youths in hoodies, and two very gay truck drivers - we are the only customers. I am leaning heavily on my walking stick, which makes clacking noises like Blind Pew's crutch (if you don't know what I mean you either have a dirty mind, or have never read *Treasure Island*) on the polished polycarbonate floor. There is music playing and I immediately start to laugh.

The trouble is that I have a particularly loud and piercing laugh, and it has been said that when I find something amusing, people know all about it a quarter of mile away. Some years ago we were in ASDA, coincidentally at the same time as my adopted niece Jessica and her family. We were at opposite ends of the hangar-like building and unaware of each others presence. However, I found something amusing and started to laugh and Jessica was so mortified at the possibility that she would become tainted by association with someone with such an embarrassing laugh that she refused to go across and greet us, despite me being her favourite uncle. For similar reasons I was always forbidden to go and collect her from school.

Corinna glared at me and jabbed me in the ribs with her elbow as I chortled away. "What on earth are you making such a spectacle of yourself for?" She hissed sotto voce. Between gasps I tried to explain.

The song was being performed by a bint with a sultry tremolo, and featured the refrain *Our Day will Come* which is and has been, the motto of various terrorist organisations across the globe including the Provisional IRA, and I had been giggling at the image which came into my mind's eye of Gerry Adams, Martin McGuinness et all on backing vocals dancing like the horridly effeminate blokes in The Floaters back in the day. "Hi, I'm Martin and I am Sagittarius" he would lisp scowling at the camera.

I thought (and still do think) that this was a massively amusing concept. However, Mother, Corinna, and the slightly vacant looking chap behind the counter looked horrified, and obviously don't find terrorism amusing. So I kept my own council for the rest of our sojourn in the restaurant and was not at all surprised to find that the new Bob Dylan album was not one of those selected to be on the playlist of Ronald FM or whatever the in house radio station was called.

ROCKET SCIENTISTS: Looking Back

"Rocket Scientists was formed in the late 1980s by keyboardist Erik Norlander and vocalist / guitarist Mark McCrite. The two released their first CD, "Earthbound", in 1993 joined by then - session bassist Don Schiff. Schiff quickly became a part of the band for their second release in 1995, "Brutal Architecture", and the three toured in the US and Europe in 1997 culminating in the live CD, "Earth Below and Sky Above: Live in Europe and America". In 1999, Rocket Scientists released "Oblivion Days", raising the bar on already high expectations.

At the turn of the century, Norlander, Schiff and McCrite all worked on solo projects in addition to backing symphonic rock vocal icon Lana Lane on several tours around the world. After an eight year hiatus, Rocket Scientists released its fourth studio album "Revolution Road" in 2006 to high accolades from the press and fans worldwide. In January 2008, Rocket Scientists released their first box set entitled "Looking Backward", a 5-disc collection containing remastered versions of their first three studio albums, "Earthbound", "Brutal Architecture" and "Oblivion Days", along with a 4th audio CD of new recordings of classic Rocket Scientists songs reinterpreted by the band in 2007. The 5th disc is a DVD-9 containing video of the 2007 sessions along with extensive interviews and historical archive footage from sessions going back to 1993."

Erik is a mate of mine and was kind enough to send me a care package of Rocket Scientists and other material of his about a year ago. I had only ever listened to it in the comfort of my own home, either in my office or in the sitting room. Now was the chance to see if my suspicions were correct. And they were. This melodic, and surprisingly complex music, cerebral and visceral at the same time, is the perfect soundtrack to long, psychedelic journeys across the English heartland. I cannot recommend them enough.

CAPTAIN'S LOG: Dateline Wednesday evening, Biddulph, Staffordshire

Watching the Brits (why the blinking flip did they have to stop calling them the British Rock and Pop Awards?) en famille with Mother, Corinna, Shoshannah and her husband Gavin. Who the fuck are all these people? I don't mean Mother, Corinna, Shoshannah and her husband Gavin, but the procession of thematically almost identical walking shop dummies who are paraded before the audience of overdressed marching morons, for them to cheer maniacally like the crowd at the Coliseum every time another gladiator was disembowelled. However on this occasion they were howling their support every time another nonentity got an award.

I used to think that I was reasonably hip, but I have honestly no idea who most of these people are, and truly don't care. Taylor Swift? What the hell is that all about? Its bland, it is unchallenging and it has the artistic relevance of a Wimpy bar advert. And she is one of the good ones.

Shoshannah, who is, by the way, my eldest stepdaughter, admitted that Taylor Swift is completely vanilla, and does nothing to offend or challenge people. AND she is a fan!!!! Is this what Sid Vicious died for? Now my younger stepdaughter has joined in the fray vis email and it turns out that she is a fan of this anodyne bollocks as well.

Christ on a bike. But if you think my reaction is extreme, I will just try and give a pen portrait of what my delightful wife is doing. She is almost foaming at the mouth with rage every time One Direction are mentioned. I love her to bits, but she is in danger of becoming a seething mass of bile, as the programme continues with a parade of women with big shoes, and young men who all look like they were part timers at a DIY warehouse.

On comes Jimmy Page, who looks and sounds like he is auditioning for the job of Ant and Dec's comedy foil. I doubt whether Uncle Aleister would have approved.

On comes Kanye West, (introduced by his wife) whose performance contains so many swear words that half of it has been muted and there are some very long and intriguing silences. Then comes Take That. Corinna sniffs peevishly and says one word..."pathos".

Then comes on a skinny blonde boy called George Ezra. My stepdaughter says that this is the weirdest example of a voice/face mismatch. I have to agree with her, but for the first time in the evening I see someone with genuine talent, and true star quality. He probably won't replace Wild Man Fisher or Tom Waits in my affections, but he is obviously someone to watch.

Paloma Faith was excellent, and although I had vaguely heard of her, I had never heard her music before. I can, however, see why Shosh likes her so much, and like George Ezra, I shall be checking out her back catalogue once I am back in the office. Her acceptance speech for her award was also the best of the evening - funny, humble and engaging.

Then One Direction won the award for best video, and I was startled by a Satanic sounding hissing from the other end of the sofa. Corinna was hunched over, her face purple with apoplectic fury as she hissed and mouthed swearwords at the screen like a woman possessed. The rest of us stared at her with barely disguised horror and I think all of us thought that she was going to transform herself into some winged daemon from the pit, and materialise on stage ready to rip out Ant and Dec's throats.

Then at the end Madonna is pulled to the ground and nearly garrotted. Within minutes it was on YouTube and jokes a out it were proliferating across Twitter. All I would say to Madge is that she is a year older than me, and she really shouldn't be wearing shoes like that at her age.

MUCH LATER...

"Did you see that *Brothers in Arms* is back in the Top Ten?" asked my delightful older stepdaughter, who has a distressing taste for eighties stadium music. "God, we are all going to hell in a handcart", I replied and wished I had some brandy.

But I didn't.

We returned last night and while Mother and Corinna did their own inimitable things, I settled into the office and transferred all the stuff I had written this week into the magazine template, and am feeling rather pleased with myself that despite having been away all week, roughly the same amount of work as usual has been completed on the magazine. I would like to proffer big thanks to Graham who did a wonderful job while I was away. He is off on HIS travels tomorrow as it is his turn to pick up a hire car and travel across country.. to see his mother.

I always like this time of the year; the winter is just about over and as Spring begins, I usually get enthused with energy and positive vibes and produce a lot more than I would at other times of the year. This is probably a good thing, because there always seems to be a whole lot more to be done at this time of year than there is at other times, but whether this is a chicken and egg situation I am never too sure.

There are, however, all sorts of things in the pipeline both with Gonzo, The CFZ, Wyrd and every other thing that I use to fill my life up. I am planning to start a library and a Wildlife Rehabilitation Unit, for example (as if I didn't have enough to do).

But as far as I am concerned, the universe sets you challenges and if you rise to the occasion then your karma is immeasurably more positive than it would be if you didn't. But this week, probably because of the young ladies upon whom I lavished my affections this week (two Stepsprogs and two Grandsprogs) I am feeling remarkably chipper, and positive enough to meet whatever the multiverse decides to throw in my direction.

It probably won't last, but I cannot remember feeling as happy as I do now in a long time.

A KITTEN CALLED SQUEAKY

Everything was going as normal until Tuesday evening. Monday had been fairly productive and straightforward, and on Tuesday Jessica and I had spent a long, complicated day correcting proofs and were feeling really rather pleased with ourselves. Helen, Jessica's mum, who has been housekeeper here since my parent's day came in to see us in the office. She was being very affectionate, and obviously wanted something. "Would we be able to adopt another kitten?" She asked in a voice like honey and treacle mixed up into a potion by someone invented by Enid Blyton.

"Christ, not another cat", I began, and then noticed a smug look on Helen's face. She obviously knew something I didn't. Then the pin dropped. "Corinna has already said yes, hasn't she?" I said, realising that I would have to cooperate with the inevitable. Helen nodded, and she, Jessica and Corinna went to collect said kitten from one of Helen's many relatives in Hartland.

Not altogether to my surprise, when they returned several hours later Jessica was also clutching a kitten. I did my best to sound stern and resolute and insist that this little one (with whom I immediately fell in love would be our last. After all, I said, we now have four cats (Poppy McGregor, Lilith Tinkerbell, Captain "Peanut" Frunobulax the Magnificent, and the kitten), and that is enough for anybody. However, Helen's household now has ten cats, and much though I love her, I am not sure that she is that good an influence on my beloved wife.. The kitten has the temporary name of 'Squeaky' (more because of the noise she makes all day long than because of the Manson Family connotation).

But then things got weirder. Wednesday morning dawned bright and sunny, or at least I suspect it did, because after a late night up with Squeaky I overslept by a few hours. I hate oversleeping and coming down late, So I was not in the best of moods when I did eventually come downstairs. When I hobbled into the office, the kitten poking out of the front of my shirt as if I had somehow become a marsupial overnight (being a father figure rather than a mother figure, shouldn't that be a 'Pa-Supial'?) I found to my horror that the hard drive containing all the Gonzo, Wyrd and Music files had gone tits up. Some of it was backed up, but equally some of it wasn't.

There are some jolly useful people at a Data Recovery form in Barnstaple who have the drive now, and I am reliably informed that it looks probable that I shall get some if not all of my missing files back, but the whole process is taking longer than usual which is why I have not been operational for the last few days. However, I have always been proud of the fact that The Gonzo Weekly, like the Pony Express always gets through and like the Windmill Theatre we never close.

So there is a magazine this week, even though it is somewhat more truncated than usual.

And guess what?

Despite all the crap that has happened, I still haven't had a cigarette!

I have to admit that I am feeling rather proud of myself.

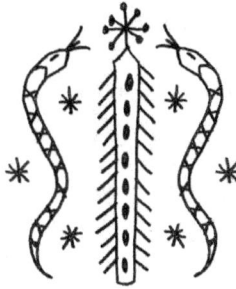

REVIEW

WAITING FOR THE BEATLES
Carole Bedford

I first read this peculiar little book soon after it came out in paperback for the first time in the late 1980s.

Although these days even a quick peek at what happens when you enter the term BEATLES into the Amazon.co.uk search engine, will reveal quite what an enormous business Beatlebooks have become, nearly thirty years ago it was a completely different kettle of fish, and I remember sitting down and making myself comfortable in the window seat of some café or other in Exeter High Street, and devouring most of the books in a single sitting.

It is the story of Carol Bedford, a teenage Beatles fan from Texas who travelled to London and became one of the main members of The Apple scruffs; a loosely-knit group of hardcore Beatles fans who were known for congregating outside the Apple Corps building and at the gates of Abbey Road Studios in London during the waning days of Beatlemania, in the hope of seeing or interacting with one of the band members.

It is a heartwarming story of devotion to an ideal even if that ideal was an unattainable one. Some commentators likened this devotion to more traditional spiritual pursuits as this quote from *Rolling Stone* in 1970 shows:

> *The Scruffs are sick of glib explanations. "One paper called us nuns," says Wendy. A nice idea that in principle; a group of girls "married" to four saints from Liverpool. It fits in with a piece in the Scruffs magazine which listed losing one's virginity as a reason for quitting the Scruffs. "Some of the original Scruffs have left, to get married, "explained Carol. "Tina, Lizzie, Joan..." She trails off. "Look we know that none of us is ever going to marry a Beatle, so forget that idea."*
>
> *"And don't," warns Chris, darkly "write any of that crap about 'mother instinct.'"*

Carol Bedford's book gives an entertaining overview of the story of the scruffs, and contains quite a few nice pieces of memorabilia to back up her assertion that she was particularly close to George Harrison. But although the letters from George to her do act as pretty good corroborating evidence of her story, recent claims have been made that cast doubt upon it.

This was taken from a Beatles forum:

> *This is Emma, and I am in the photos in Carol Bedford's book. I was actually appalled when I saw that book and photo's of me in the book as well! I have no idea how she got hold of those photo's. I do know that when she wrote about the girls going into Paul's house, she writes as though she*

was there. She wasn't, because I was and I can honestly say she wasn't there. So a few things in the book I took with a grain of salt! Anyway, my email address is xxxxxxxxx. I would love to hear from Lucy, Sue-John, Jill or Margo. I have often wondered what became of us all.

It also turns out that the pretty, shy teenager who was so in love with the quiet Beatle had a series of health problems as an adult, was in long term care, and recently died. In recent months I have sometimes written that "sometimes in life there are fairy tale happy endings". The story of Carol Bedford is a reminder that sometimes there aren't.

LOOK BACK IN ANGUISH

And so, boys and girls, we did it. Many apologies to the people who were left out this week, particularly Neil Nixon, but I hope you all realise that this proves the truth of what I have been saying for yonks - that computers are indeed the work of The Devil, and that they should be shunned by all right thinking people. But then again, as I have never pretended to be a right thinking person this is all fairly irrelevant.

I am particularly impressed that Corinna and I only made the decision to go ahead with this issue at just gone three this afternoon, and I am sitting here at two minutes to ten putting the last bits in. Not bad considering the whole thing was put together with none of my templates, without most of my graphics stuff, and mostly done on an iPad whilst I engaged in a wrestling match with a particularly voracious young lady who seems to be intent on either eating my braces or the iPad or both. Possibly giving the kitten the same name as one of the leading lights of the Manson Family was not as clever an idea as it seemed at first.

I have also been informed that we are in Mercury Retrograde, an expression that I had only ever heard of before in the books about John Lennon's final years when it seemed to be his excuse for all sorts of bad behaviour.

I am never sure about that sort of thing, so will not comment until I am in a position to find out more of my facts. But, like I wrote at the beginning of this magazine six hours ago, we pride ourselves on not giving in to the slings and arrows of outrageous fortune, and we always get each week's issue out. And once again, this we have done....

Slainte

YOUNG MAN BLUES

Once upon a time there was a popular beat combo from London, and they were called The Who. Mostly they sang songs written by their guitarist (who had a big nose) but sometimes they sang songs by other people, like this one by Mose Allison:

Well a young man
Ain't got nothin' in the world these days
I said a young man
Ain't got nothin' in the world these days

Well, you know in the old days
When a young man was a strong man
All the people stepped back
When a young man walked by

Now the two surviving members of The Who are over 70, and Mose Allison is nearly 90, and a young man still ain't got nothin' in the world these days, except his opinions, and an aptitude for change and taking new ideas onboard which his elders never have had.

Recently, Roger Waters has been shouting off in the press: "I feel enormously privileged to have been born in 1943 and not 1983. To have been around when there was a music business and the takeover by Silicon Valley hadn't happened, and in consequence, you could still make a living writing and recording songs and playing them to people. When this gallery of rogues and thieves had not yet injected themselves between the people who aspire to be creative and their potential audience and steal every fucking cent anybody ever made."

He does, of course, have a point. Quite a good point, in fact, but this is not what interests me about the affair. The thing that interests me is not what Roger Waters - an artist for whom I actually have quite a lot of respect - has to say, but the way he said it. The way that he blames the "rogues and thieves" of "Silicon Valley", for the changes in the music business is almost Luddite in its simplistic lashing out at advances in technology for changes in the music business. It reminded me irresistibly of my Father, many lifetimes ago, blaming the decline and fall of the British Empire on the popularity of The Beatles.

To both of them, the ex-Pink Floyd bass player, and the ex-Assistant Colonial Secretary of Hong Kong, I say the same thing: Bollocks. Luckily, Roger Waters is unlikely ever to read this article, and my Father has been dead for nearly a decade, so I can say this with impunity.

Bollocks!

The decline of the established record record business, like the decline of the British Empire is the result of a whole slew of socio-economic factors, and the "rogues and thieves" of "Silicon Valley", isn't actually one of them. The main reason is that music is not as valued as it was four decades ago. Yes, people expect to pay less for music, yes, people expect to get a lot of things, including music, for free, but the root cause of this is that music is just no longer as important to people as it was back in the day.

In the 1970s, the recorded music industry produced objects that one could and did fetishise. It is simplistic to say that this was something that disappeared once the recorded music industry no longer dealt with physical objects, because it was something that was disappearing long before that. When I was a boy I was fascinated by the paper sleeves which housed 45rpm singles, and I had quite a collection of them, and I was fascinated by their arcane symbolism. To an introverted fourteen year old the paper sleeves and the designs on the labels took on a far greater cultural significance than just the trappings that came with a three minute pop record. The noisome watercolour painting of a yacht in full sail on the RAK label always suggested that the content was breezy and ephemeral, for example, whereas the Mad Hatter on the Charisma label, the pervy Siamese twins on the Virgin label, the science fictiony Mooncrest label, and even the green wiggly thing on the Harvest label all signified various different head trips into their own brand of inner madness.

I don't think that it was just me.

What I do know is that my fetishisation of music declined with the advent of thermally heated record labels, and the end of heavy card gatefold sleeves for albums.

And I don't think that was just me either.

As the eighties became the nineties the packaging and presentation of records became more homogenised, and then sometime about two thirds of the way through the decade that taste forgot, came the compact disc, and - conditioned by the decline in the quality of vinyl presentation - lots of people, including - eventually - me, although I was a relatively late convert, fell for the nice shiny new concept. And so the rock and roll rebellion was finally harnessed and emasculated, and the mass transfer of MP3s and the streaming of music of which Waters so disapproves, became the logical end result.

One cannot blame the technology for what has happened. What has happened is almost entirely the fault of the conventional record companies who sold, and resold, the same material over again in one of the most egregious examples of unbridled capitalism that I can think of. I remember, for example, in the late 1980s I went out and bought Pink Floyd's *Momentary Lapse of Reason*' the day it came out from a little record shop in Crediton. About two months later I was in HMV in Exeter, and found exactly the same album bundled with a couple of concert posters for the same price. This is how the band (or at least EMI) rewarded those people who had been loyal enough to buy the bloody thing immediately, I started to shout, losing my temper. I was asked to leave HMV and never went back.

Sure the new technology has been the vector of some of the decline of the music industry, but it is also the way that all sorts of exciting new opportunities have taken place; this magazine for example could not have been conceived of more than four or five years ago. It also levels the playing field, allowing artists like me or quite a few of the other musicians who appear in the pages of this magazine to record complex music which would have been totally beyond our price range only a few years ago.

And, as far as packaging and presentation is concerned, things are also beginning to change, and - once again - it is down to the more level playing field presented and made possible by the new technology. Check out Reverb Worship for example at www.reverbworship.com. Their head honcho writes:

"Reverb Worship began in November 2007 with my first ever release which was *Keijo's* "About Around". It gained some excellent reviews and sold out quite quickly. Since then I have made many additions to the catalogue with various other releases by *Vapaa, Sand Snowman, Mountainhood, Wooden Spoon*, Mark Bradley, *Uton, LSD March, Kwannon, Directorsound, Phosphene*, Jeremy Kelly, *Sedayne, Timas 23, ST 37, The Hare And The Moon*, Sproatly Smith, *Wyrdstone, Dark Sun, Magic Carpathians*, Kawabata Makoto, *Motion Sickness Of Time Travel*, and many, many others. All of my Reverb Worship releases are limited edition. Each release is handmade and individually numbered. Each edition will range from 40 to 50 copies up to 100 copies maximum per release."

The records that his company releases are beautiful artefacts, and I would wave them snottily under the noses of people who say that the new technology has ruined the music industry. The new technology, as we wrote a few issues ago when we reviewed Gareth Murphy's *Cowboys and Indies* has - at worst - caused just the latest of the periodic blips, which like geozoological extinction events have rocked the recorded music industry at intervals over the last century and a half.

Like so much human endeavour on this beleaguered little planet, the music industry as it had become, was simply not sustainable. As a species we are living through strange and disturbing times, and when - as a species, but quite probably not as populous a one - we enter the next stage of our existence, we shall need music as much as ever, and I truly believe that it is companies like Gonzo, and Reverb Worship who are pointing the way towards the shape of things to come.

But before I get all apocalyptic, I shall go and play with the kitten,

Om Shanti

REVIEW

NO SIMPLE HIGHWAY: A CULTURAL HISTORY OF THE GRATEFUL DEAD
By Peter Richardson

Something that has struck me intermittently over the last four decades of collecting rock music biographies, is that whereas there are books on The Beatles, David Bowie,

The Rolling Stones and The Who for example, which perfectly complement my listening experience, whether or not the facts in them are 100% unvarnished (see last weekend's review of Carol Bedford's book about her life as an Apple Scruff, for a particularly good example of this), there are some bands and performers about whom I have never yet read a book with which I fully emotionally engaged. These include Bob Dylan, Neil Young, and yes... The Grateful Dead.

I first discovered The Grateful Dead by accident during the summer of 1976, when - flush with cash from my first job - I spent my newly earned money like a sailor on shore leave; mostly on books and records. One weekend I was in Bideford, at the end of Mill Street where there is now a Funeral Parlour. However, back in the day, the shop was Braddicks' record shop, one of two main record shops in the town, and as was my habit, I paid it a visit. There, displayed prominently in the racks was a double album containing both *Wake of the Flood* and *From the Mars Hotel*. The cover of the former of these resonated immediately with me, and although the double album cost nearly a fiver (a veritable fortune when you only earned twelve quid a week), I bought it.

Wake of the Flood was my favourite album that year, and launched me on a thirty nine year love affair with the music of this singular band. But I have never yet found a book about the band that even come close to complimenting the emotional response that I get from listening to the band's music. This book doesn't do so either, but it comes far closer than anything else that I have ever read about the band.

The story itself is reasonably straightforward: San Francisco freak take drugs, join a band, take more drugs, get famous, make a series of albums that are generally said to be not a patch on the sound of the band live, have health problems, reinvent themselves for the 1980s, become very famous, various members die, they split up. The history of the band has enough sex, drugs and rock and roll in it to be an interesting narrative, but it is true social history of the band, and even more importantly where they fit into the social history of the United States between 1965 and the present day, which is the really important and interesting thing. And this is without discussing and attempting some degree of meta-analysis of the music itself.

It has often been claimed that the nearest analogy that The Grateful Dead have in the UK are bands like Hawkwind or The Pink Fairies, but like most forced analogies, this one doesn't add up. One cannot imagine either of the two British bands, who - like the Grateful Dead have been dubbed "people's bands" - achieving the same position within the sociocultural infrastructure of the United Kingdom as has the American band across the pond, having whoever the UK equivalent of Tipper Gore (Samantha Cameron?) sit in with them on drums, no matter what the occasion. In fact it was discovering the position that the band actually holds within the American cultural map that was one of the two great epiphanies that I had whilst reading the book. The other was that The Grateful Dead are truly the best embodiment if Gram Parsons' "Cosmic American Music". The presenter of a radio show dedicated to the genre writes: "In the late 60's, in a time when country music and musicians were seen as the furthest thing from hip or cool, Gram Parsons and a few others began to embrace and incorporate country music into the rock and roll realm. Once, when asked if he was trying to play rock or country or soul or what, Gram responded that "it's all Cosmic American Music." Since then, the music world has never been the same. From Parson's vision, a whole new style of music was born and its popularity is still evident today. "Alt-Country,: "Americana," "New Weird American," "Anti-Folk," or whatever you want to call it, this music is linked by a sincere appreciation and acknowledgment of the music that came before it."

Until reading this book, which enthused me to listen to a whole lot more of The Grateful Dead's more obscure music in the past few weeks than I have done usually, I had not realised what a student of the different strains of sonic Americana, Jerry Garcia was, and also what a logical progression the band's trajectory actually was. Like so many people I always thought that their switch in stylistic direction between records like *Aoxomoxoa* and *Workingman's Dead* was a radical departure, and that the glossy production of their last albums was a rejection of everything that they had done before. But actually it was nothing of the sort, and after reading this book, I realise that it all makes a lot more sense than I thought that it did.

What a long strange trip, indeed.

REVIEW

BOB HARRIS: STILL WHISPERING AFTER ALL THESE YEARS
Bob Harris

It would be so easy to take the piss out of this book. But it wouldn't be fair, because Bob Harris is overall a decent, kind, and above all a nice bloke. He may have a distressing taste in ultra mellow vibes (as I suspect he would think of them), but he has stayed true to his ideals, and this book is testament to that.

It is a peculiar book, in that - like Viv Albertine whom we reviewed a couple of months back - it is almost painfully honest. Harris has had a most peculiar life, in which he has been buffeted and knocked about by the slings and arrows of outrageous fortune, but he has come through it remarkably unscathed. He is either a remarkable liar, or is truly not bitter about the way that he has been treated by various teams of management at the BBC who made him redundant on several occasions, and even by fellow DJ Bruno Brookes who made him bankrupt.

From the music buff's point of view, it is - of course - the earlier chapters of the book which are most interesting. His relationship with Marc Bolan in the late 1960s and the early 1970s is particularly interesting. He chronicles the break up of the relationship that Bolan had with John Peel in some detail, but the events that he describes have far more cogency than any of the other accounts that I have read, including Peel's. He also describes how Peel drew a line under his friendship with Harris himself, because he disapproved of the way that he was treating his first wife.

I had not realised that Bob Harris had been one of the original founders of *Time Out* - half the original editorial team, in fact.

With customary self-deprecation Harris describes the world of the 'underground' of the late 1960s in a way that suggests that he was far more of a mover and shaker at the time than I had ever guessed.

My interest in that particular movement was far more from the viewpoint of the revolutionary arm and in particular people like Mick Farren and his cohorts, but it was interesting to read about the other arm of the people who followed the good vibes of people like Harris.

One thing that comes over from the book, is that whilst he was only ever in line with what the mainstream media decided was public taste was for a few years in the early 1970s, when he won awards at the NME Poll-winners concert, for example, he has always had a sizeable public following. He seems bewildered at this, but also bewildered at the way the management at the BBC and other radio stations have ignored this groundswell of public opinion in favour of what they, or the focus groups, think that the public should like. His description of the night that he left the BBC for the second time is particularly poignant, and one truly feels for this straightforward but oddly naive man.

His health scares take up nearly as much of the book as do his marital problems, and they both add to the emotional rollercoaster which anyone with any empathy has to feel as they follow the ups and downs of this extraordinary life.

From a Gonzo point of view, (and I, of course, mean the record company which finances this magazine, rather than the genre of journalism spearheaded by Hunter Thompson and followed enthusiastically by yours truly at various times in my career) it is his description of working with the Yorkshire prog rock band Wally whose records can now be found proudly nestling amongst the Gonzo catalogue, that are particularly of interest.

I loved the anecdote about Rick Wakeman absconding from the hospital where he was recovering from a heart attack, to oversee one orchestral overdub.

This is also the only book that I have ever read that says anything positive or complimentary about Mohamed Al-Fayed, but he seems to be genuinely fond of the man who was both his wife's employer, and someone who has helped Harris out on at least one memorable occasion.

Something else which is notable is his friendship with his ex-wives. Most of the people that I know (including me) are on terrible terms with their ex-spouse(s), and I think it is testament to Harris' personality that he is friends enough with *his* exes that they all turned up to say nice things about him when he appeared on *This is Your Life*. I, on the other hand, am one of those people who are very glad that I will never appear on the show, if only because most of the people I have left in my past (including my ex-wife, and a couple of major ex-girlfriends) are firmly in my past, and both I hope stay there.

The thing that I wish that he had expanded upon, however, was the way that he has translated his very 1960s attitude to life into the Internet savvy world of the 21st Century.

Because it is here that Bob Harris has finally found his professional home. He has taken to online life like a duck to water, with a thriving community based around his website. He even gets his head around Twitter which is something that I truly do not understand at all. After finishing the book I spent a couple of hours pottering around his website, and was most impressed by the family vibe of it all.

This is an uplifting and heartwarming book, even though the catalogue of disasters at various places along the way, and the descriptions of some of the more over the top 1970s rock and roll music debauchery make uncomfortable reading. But this is par for the course for the book. Bob Harris does not sugar coat the difficult bits, any more than he exaggerates or becomes maudlin over the good bits. Like the book he has written, Bob Harris has integrity, and that is an increasingly valuable commodity in our increasingly unreliable and facile world.

Well done Bob. Whisper on, you funk soul brother.

THE GENERATION GAP

I have had Jessica - who is seventeen - here all week. She is just about to finish her college course that she truly never wanted to do in the first place, and that she only did because they wouldn't let her do the courses she actually wanted to do, at the local college - an institution for which I have very little patience or respect. I have had more dealings with them than I would have liked over the past couple of years, and I find it very hard to break my conviction that they are only there to massage the youth unemployment figures, and that they truly do not give a toss about those unfortunates who are placed in their care by a beneficent Government, *especially* if they are from a council estate, a broken home, or the foster system. I have had young people who come from various of these backgrounds working for me over the past few years, and truly, they have been amongst the finest youngsters that I have ever known, and certainly have shown themselves to be more impressive than many of the kids I have worked with who have come from far more privileged backgrounds, including those from my own *almer mater*.

But much though I dislike the educational establishment to which I refer, this is - believe it or not - actually not the subject about which I would like to hold forth this week. Jessica surprised me a lot this week; partly because of her aptitude with a computer programme that I have been using for fifteen years, and that she only picked up for the first time a couple of weeks back (Adobe Photoshop) and partly for another reason, which momentarily stunned me.

She didn't know who Bob Geldof was.

As regular readers of this magazine will know, Gonzo Multimedia, the company which finances this august publication, has recently announced the release of a DVD from 1978 featuring *The Boomtown Rats*, who both then and now have always been one of my favourite bands of the era. I came very close to seeing them, because they were playing at Glastonbury Festival in 1985 just as my first wife, our friend Alice and I were unpacking our tents, and they finished (playing the massively unseasonable *Do they know it's Christmas* just as we trudged over the brow of the hill. So I heard them, but never actually *saw* them, and am very much looking forward to the release of the DVD.

As regular readers of my inky fingered scribblings here and elsewhere will probably have realised, the insanely cramped converted potato shed which was once my father's study, and which is now the nerve centre of *Gonzo Weekly*, The Centre for Fortean Zoology, CFZ Press, CFZtv, and Wyrd Music, amongst other things, is also somewhat of a drop-in centre for the local arty crowd, and Jess and I were working hard on Luca Ferrari's excellent biography of doomed jazz muso Mike Taylor (out imminently from Gonzo), when there was a knock on the door and in walked electonica composer 4th Eden, aka Martin Eve, one of my collaborators and sometime contributor to this magazine.

He demanded tea, and the three of us sat chatting over a cuppa, when the subject of the aforementioned *Boomtown Rats* DVD came up. Martin teased me, suggesting that I should try to interview Sir Bob. I replied, truthfully, that the idea of interviewing Bob Geldof terrified me, and that I was far too much of a coward. Martin said something rude, and winked at Jessica, obviously hoping for and expecting, some form of corroboration.

She stared at him blankly. "Who is Bob Geldof?" She asked.

We were both shocked. Upon questioning it transpired that she had no idea who he was, had never heard of The Boomtown Rats or Live Aid. It was only then that we realised that Live Aid had taken place twelve years before she was born, that she had only been about seven when Live Eight took place, and would have been far more interested in The Tellytubbies than the miraculous reunion of Pink Floyd or the campaign to make poverty history. And this, I think is a valuable life lesson.

The people who are broadly my age, give or take fifteen years or so, are likely to know that the meaning of life is 42, that Peason is a wet and a weed as any fule kno, and that it has been twenty years ago today since Sergeant Pepper taught the band to play (even if it happened nearly half a century ago), but that things which are so well known as to be accepted by people of one generation, mean next to nothing to another one.

I am sure that I am not alone amongst readers of this magazine to have been raised by parents and teachers who thought that our interest in amplified nigger music (as one of my teachers described it) was tantamount to a taste for bestiality, and was symbolic of the fact that the nation, and life itself, was basically going down the drain fast.

I am also sure that I am not the only person reading these words who believed that *our* generation was going to be different, and that we would be the first generation to usher in The Age of Aquarius, with peace, love, tranquillity and free sex and drugs for all, blah blah blah. Well, of course it doesn't work like that, and lots of the people I know of around my age are at least as appalled by the sexual, chemical and musical mores of the current generation as our parents were about us, and - I suspect - that their parents were about them.

And that's about the only point that I want to make in my rant this week. Being old is not a virtue, being young is not a crime, The Boomtown Rats were a fantastic band whereas Skrillax are a fucking awful row no matter how hard I pretend to be him and try to like them. But that is right and proper, it is the way things are, and the way that I suspect things will always be. It is just about time that people of all generations got their heads around the fact, accepted it, stopped kicking against the pricks, and got on with their lives.

Now young whippersnapper, I want a cup of tea, and when you come back, I will tell you all abut something called *Woodstock......*

REVIEW

THAT'S ENTERTAINMENT: MY LIFE IN THE JAM
Rick Buckler & Ian Snowball

This is an interesting little book, and one which raises some useful points. First of all, let me say that apart from their output at the very end, I was never really a fan of The Jam, and that with very few exceptions I have never been overly impressed with Paul Weller's solo work either. It is OK if you like that sort of thing, but he has always been well into the second or even third division of rock stars as far as I am personally concerned.

However, I was 17 and unemployed in the year that the two sevens clashed, and I have always been interested in the history of British punk rock, so when I saw that those jolly nice folk at Omnibus Press had published the autobiography of the drummer of The Jam I decided to ask them for a copy.

First of all let's get the reviewing bit out of the way: It is a pretty entertaining read, and one comes away from the book rather linking the author, feeling completely ambivalent about Bruce Foxton, and feeling that Paul Weller is a bit of a prick. Or maybe that's just me. But let me put that into perspective. Earlier this year (or maybe it was the end of last year) I reviewed two Beatles related books that - tangentially - talked about Eric Clapton. And Christ on a bike, he was a complete and utter dickhead in the early seventies, if these two accounts are to be believed. And Paul Weller *at his worst* in this nifty little book comes over so much better he is almost Mahatma Gandhi in comparison.

Unlike some of the books I have read in recent weeks this book is remarkably unpolished. As an editor myself I know that most books turn up in my inbox in this condition and have to be pummelled into shape with the care of a fine lapidarist, and - indeed - most of the books that I read and review have been dealt with in just this manner. This book hasn't, which in some ways is refreshing, but sometimes just irritating.

One wonders the shedreasoning behind this lack of editorial involvement. Four possibilities come to mind here:

1. That the author was just so strong willed, not to say bloody minded, that all editorial suggestions were spurned. I have had authors just like that, and usually ended up telling them to go and commit a biologically impossible act of self-procreation. However, unless the author is a remarkably skilled liar, this would be totally out of character.

2. That the publishers didn't care. Again this is massively unlikely in my mind. Omnibus Press are one of the leading music book publishers in the world, and I have read many of their books. Seldom, however, one as unpolished as this one.

3. That this is a deliberate editorial ploy, to try and come over as a bit of

legitimate oral history. The true voice of the people if you like. Jah Wobble called his autobiography *Memoirs of a Geezer* but it was meticulously polished and edited. Other rock autobiographies I have read have attempted to be the voice of the people and come over ridiculously stylised. Dougal Whatsisname's book about his life on the road with Keith Moon is full of more deliberately stylised patois than *Confessions of a Windowcleaner* and has just about as many pretences to literary merit.

4. That the publishers used the wrong version. This is quite possible. I did it with my autobiography *Monster Hunter* back in 2004, and - mainly because I have never got around to it - the proper version has never seen the light of day. But Omnibus Press have far more publishing chops than did the CFZ back in the dark days before I met my lovely wife, and started to clean up my act.

But whatever the reason for this, it has actually worked out in Rick Buckler's favour, because it gives a human, and even slightly vulnerable edge, to what would otherwise have been a fairly dull list of gigs, tours and recording sessions. Because, and I truly do not mean to be unkind here, the history of *The Jam* is not a particularly interesting one.

They met at school, farted around doing cover versions and club gigs until they got a stable lineup, jumped on a bandwagon, got a record contract, started another bandwagon (or to be more exact, restarted an old one that most people had forgotten about) had some hits, and then split up when the main songwriter decided he could make more money doing something different.

But this is a bit like describing *Romeo and Juliet* as "two teenagers fall in love and then die". Both when considering Shakespeare and the drummer of *The Jam*, it is the gaps between the main plot events that provide the greatest interest.

Buckler's account of growing up in Woking during the sixties and seventies is fascinating, especially to someone who didn't. But what the young Rick Buckler and the young Jonathan Downes *did* have in common was a shared emotional involvement with music.

Music mattered to us in a way that I don't think that it did for anyone born before 1940 or after 1995. Sure, those younger and older than me can be music fans, but I think that it is seldom that they engage with music in the same way as those of us of a certain age. Rick Buckler's account of seeing Buddy Rich playing at the Royal Albert Hall, is probably the best piece of writing in the book, and his awe when he describes the minuscule set that Rich was playing is palpable.

Interestingly enough, the most engaging bits of the book, as well as the best writing are those that cover the years before, and after, those when *The Jam* were one of the most commercially successful bands in Britain.

I have tried to analyse why this is, because - after all - with most other books it is exactly the opposite. And I have given up trying. But what is certain is that, despite its flaws, this book is a heart-warming one, and one which I am very glad that I read.

MOTHER RETURNS

And so, once again it is what Frank Sinatra described as the wee small hours, and I am putting the finishing touches to my writings for this weekend's edition of the magazine.

It is Corinna that I feel sorry for. She arrived home at about a quarter to eight, late because I fell asleep and missed her message saying that she had arrived in Devon, and so dispatched Graham to find her fifteen minutes later than I should have done.

She arrived back to a cacophony caused by three cats, a kitten, two dogs and a corvid all barking/squeaking/ yowling/cawing in excitement at her arrival. Honestly, I am not exaggerating; Even the half-fledged corvid who currently is being handreared in the corner of the kitchen made the most godawful row as soon as she walked in through the door.

And it goes without saying that I missed her terribly. I was once in a relationship with a girl who was an only child. It appears that her father was so upset by having to look after himself while her mother was in hospital, that he refused to have any further children. Pah! That is despicable.

I am not one of those pathetic men who cannot function without their wives, but neither am I one of the ones who embraces the chance of personal space and freedom at every possible opportunity. But I love my wife very much and I am very glad that she is home with me once more. Tonight I shall sleep soundly for the first time in a week.

In Corinna's absence, Prudence took on the job of mothering the kitten, probably having decided that it is a puppy of sorts and conveniently ignoring the difference in species. It is very touching to see the tiny cat and the huge dog snuggled up together affectionately.

So basically all is back to normal in the Downes household, or Downeston Abbey as it is affectionately known by some of the cheekier youngsters who work here.

So mote it be.

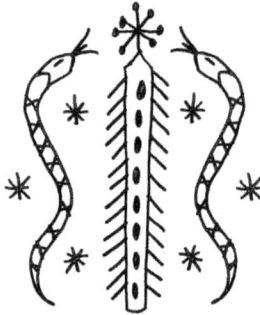

MIDSUMMER MADNESS

Welcome to another issue of what is rapidly becoming one of the world's stranger, and more diverse, magazines. Last week I got so carried away with what I was writing that I totally forgot that it was Midsummer, and it was only when my dear friends the Phillipsons wrote on Facebook that they were attending the Three Wishes Fairy Festival down in darkest Cornwall, that I remembered, and it was far too late to write the editorial/article that I had intended to write about how traditional English mysticism and the music that we write about in each issue of this magazine are inextricably linked.

However, it can wait until next year, or some other time when I feel like writing about it, because this week I want to write about something else entirely.

I have always known that my tastes were out of kilter with the mainstream. At school when my friends were listening to Mud or The Sweet I was listening to Gong. When I worked in hospitals thirty years ago my tastes stuck out like a sore thumb in a milieu where everyone either listened to the increasingly vacuous Top Ten, or West End show tunes, and this is probably the first time in my life when I can say that (if you exclude my 86-year-old mother-in-law from the equation) my tastes aren't conspicuously different from most of the other people in my life. OK Corinna likes Viking folk metal, Graham still eulogises about Hawkwind as he has any time this past forty years, and they both wince whenever I put on The Flying Burrito Brothers but on the whole my tastes don't stand out anywhere near as radically as they have at other times in my strange and interesting lifetime.

However, recently I have realised that there are some major ways in which my tastes differ from those proscribed by the tastemakers of the Rock and Roll thought police. I will give you an example.

It is the received wisdom of the rock and roll establishment that Captain Beefheart was a genius. Yup, I will go along with that. But it is also the received wisdom that in 1974 he produced a couple of all time awful records. Wikipedia repeats the party line:

"Vliet was forced to quickly form a new Magic Band to complete support-tour dates, with musicians who had no experience with his music and in fact had never heard it. Having no knowledge of the previous Magic Band style, they simply improvised what they thought would go with each song, playing much slicker versions that have been described as "bar band" versions of Beefheart songs. A review described this incarnation of the Magic Band as the "Tragic Band", a term that has stuck over the years. Mike Barnes said that the description of the new band "grooving along pleasantly", was "...an appropriately banal description of the music of a man who only a few years ago composed with the expressed intent of shaking listeners out of their torpor". The one album they recorded, Bluejeans & Moonbeams (1974) has, like its predecessor, a completely different, almost soft rock sound from any other Beefheart record. Neither was well received; drummer Art Tripp recalled that when he and the original Magic Band listened to Unconditionally Guaranteed, they "...were horrified. As we listened, it was as though each song was worse than the one which preceded it". Beefheart later disowned both albums, calling them "horrible and vulgar", asking that they not be considered part of his musical output and urging fans who bought them to "take copies back for a refund". "

Sadly for any hopes that I ever had of achieving even a modicum of hip credibility, I adore the album, and - even worse - I am afraid that it is my favourite of the good captain's records. Indeed, there is a piano phrase in *Further than We've Gone* which is guaranteed to lift my spirits even when I am in the deepest troughs of my manic depression.

Another example is Yes. This is a band who are acknowledged favourites of many of the readers of this magazine, but - again - they are a band about which there are firm opinions expressed by the rock and roll Stasi. *Tales from Topographic Oceans*, for example - a double album with only four tracks - is often cited as being an overblown, pretentious mess. *Sounds* magazine reviewed the album and live performance using the headlines "Wishy washy tales from the deep" and "Close to boredom". In his review for *Rolling Stone* magazine, Gordon Fletcher described the record as "psychedelic doodling." Guess which of their albums is my favourite?

Other records by the band that are largely disliked include Tormato and Union, and I have to admit that I quite like both of them, and certainly have had more entertainment out of both records than I have about the two mid-1980s records which were their commercial peak.

But Oasis who were always supposed to be the great white hope for the genre in the mid-1990s, and their various spinoff acts have always left me completely cold.

Every time they put out another tawdry record even more derivative than the last, the sycophantic press would hail it as a return to form, whereas I would shrug sadly and think that they sounded like a bar band in a not very good inner city pub. And when Noel Gallagher's solo album came out, and was dissected like it was a work of art equal to something by Bob Dylan at his best, I just gave up.

And I have a sneaking suspicion that I am not the only one. I don't know what this tells you about me and I don't really care, but I do know what it tells you about the rock and roll music press establishment. Like any establishment it is overdue for a revolution or at least a kick up the arse every few years, and one of the best things about the present sea change which the music industry is undergoing is that that kick up the arse is being delivered as we speak.

This magazine, however, will continue to plough its own idiosyncratic furrow, and wait and see what happens.

Welcome to the future boys and girls,

Om Shanti

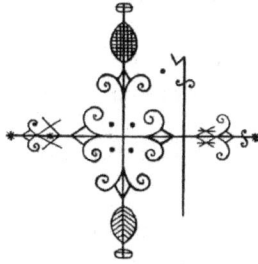

REVIEW

THE DARK NET
Jamie Bartlett

I had completely the wrong idea about this book before I read it. I assumed that it was about what has become known as 'The Dark Web', the public World Wide Web content that exists on darknets, networks which overlay the public Internet and require specific software, configurations or authorization to access. It forms part of the Deep Web, the part of the Web not indexed by search engines. The darknets which constitute the Dark Web include small, friend-to-friend peer-to-peer networks, as well as large, popular networks like Freenet, I2P, and Tor, operated by public organisations and individuals. It is, of course, about this but it is about so much more.

This is a book about all sorts of Internet subcultures, and organisations, some of which I had heard of, but not others. I had heard of cam girls, or cam whores, or whatever you want to call them, for example, but until I read this book I had no idea of the complexity or organisation of the organisations that support them, nor how much money that a bright young woman can make by getting her kit off on screen. I found the section of the book dealing with a girl called Vex, who apparently clears 40k a year doing this totally enthralling, and ended up admiring both her ingenuity and her entrepreneurial skills, but I truly hope that none of the girls in my extended family end up following her career trajectory.

I was fascinated by the section on bitcoin, and feel that this is something that I very much want to get involved with, and as an anarchist of the Penny Rimbaud/Steve Ignorant school for over thirty years now, I am intrigued to see how the powers that be in the global economy react to a currency that it looks at the moment, at least, that they cannot control. Will there be a clampdown upon it in the same way that there was on Megaupload? However from the descriptions Jamie gives in this remarkable book, it seems that those behind the idea have foreseen this possibility, and made it so decentralised that simple demolition of a website like they did to the aforementioned Megaupload and The Pirate Bay just won't get the job down, and that to obliterate bitcoin once and for all may end up just being impossible for them.

I had also heard of the TOR network. According to Wikipedia it is:

"Tor is free software for enabling anonymous communication. The name is an acronym derived from the original software project name The Onion Router. Tor directs Internet traffic through a free, worldwide, volunteer network consisting of more than six thousand relays to conceal a user's location and usage from anyone conducting network surveillance or traffic analysis. Using Tor makes it more difficult for Internet activity to be traced back to the user: this includes "visits to Web sites, online posts, instant messages, and other communication forms". Tor's use is intended to protect the personal privacy of users, as well as their freedom and ability to conduct confidential communication by keeping their Internet activities from being monitored. An extract of a Top Secret appraisal by the National Security Agency (NSA) characterised Tor as "the King of high-secure, low-latency Internet anonymity" with "no contenders for the throne in waiting", and the Parliamentary Office of Science and Technology deemed it, with approximately 2.5 million users daily "by far the most popular anonymous internet communication system."

That being said, I have tried to install it on my office PC and on my iPad but can't get it to work on either of them. I have nothing in particular that I want to hide, and will not be cruising the darkweb for illegal pornography or drugs, but the idea of a completely unpoliced portion of the Internet, something like The Walled City was to Colonial Hong Kong until the British Administration eventually tired of the continual pin pricks of lawlessness, and had it torn down in 1993 is undeniably intriguing.

The descriptions of how even illicit businesses have to operate according to market forces within a sort of *lassaiz faire* capitalism was both amusing and frightening, but excellently written and totally enthralling.

The section of the book that I found by far the most horrifying was that about 'Pro Ana' websites and other communities for the suicidal and those who self harm. Pro Ana, by the way, for those like me who had never heard of the term, is one used by people who actively promote of the eating disorder anorexia nervosa. It is often referred to simply as ana and is sometimes personified by anorexics as a girl named 'Ana'. The lesser-used term pro-mia refers likewise to bulimia nervosa, and is sometimes used interchangeably with pro-ana. It appears that Pro-ana organizations differ widely in their stances. Most claim that they exist mainly as a non-judgemental environment for anorexics; a place to turn to, to discuss their illness, and to support those who choose to enter recovery. Others deny anorexia nervosa is a mental illness and claim instead that it is a "lifestyle choice" that should be respected by doctors and family.

The scientific community, on the other hand, recognises anorexia nervosa as a serious illness. Some research suggests anorexia nervosa has the highest rate of mortality of any psychological disorder. I don't think that anyone would object to support groups for anorexia or bulimia sufferers, but it appears that the more extreme of these sites actually endorse anorexia and/or bulimia as desirable (84% and 64% respectively in a 2010 survey) and offer crash dieting techniques and recipes (67% of sites in a 2006 survey, rising to 83% in a 2010 survey), compete with each other at losing weight, or fast together in displays of solidarity, commiserate with one another after breaking fast or binging, advise on how to best induce vomiting, and on using laxatives and emetics, give tips on hiding weight loss from parents and doctors, share information on reducing the side-effects of anorexia, and suggest ways to ignore or suppress hunger pangs.

But this pals into insignificance beside Bartlett's descriptions of the communities for the suicidal where members share tips on the best way to off themselves. I have been suicidal at a couple of times in my life, one of my family members killed himself a few years ago, and others have tried over the years. But the communities described by Bartlett beggar belief.

The book also covers political extremists, transhumanists, and those who would endorse a Pol Pot-like return to an agrarian economy, and lurk in the darker areas of the internet, using their computers to berate technology, but I won't explain more. You must read the book for yourself. I think that the greatest strength of the book is that Jamie Bartlett is a man of great compassion, and writes sympathetically about even the most extreme nutjobs that he encounters. We live in extraordinary times, and anyone even slightly interested in the digital multiverse needs to read this book.

Well done Jamie.

GOOD GRIEF

In 1997, and again in 2002, when much loved public figures died, there was a great outpouring of public grief, here in the UK at least, amongst large sectors of the population. I always disliked Princess Diana intensely, and encouraged the (probably apocryphal) story that a friend of mine queued for eleven hours in order to write surreal stoned drivel in the book of condolences in Exeter Cathedral. I also got sacked from my position at the BBC for claiming (on air) that her death had been the result of a conspiracy by Interflora, who seemed to have been the only people to benefit.

Five years later when it all happened again I was less cynical, but refused to join in the grief for a lady of 101 to whom I was not related, despite the fact that she had lived an extraordinary life and achieved some extraordinary things.

Over the lifespan (so far) of this magazine we have seen the deaths of many luminaries, and tried to celebrate their lives in these pages. Two in particular spring to mind: Daevid Allen (earlier this year) and Mick Farren (in 2013). I knew both personally, and whilst neither death was unexpected, they both hit me hard.

After the magazine comes out some time on Saturday afternoon, I usually spend much of the weekend resting, and this weekend gone was no exception. Sunday afternoon, Prudence the bulldog and I had gone to bed for a post-prandial snooze, and were just drifting off into the arms of Morpheus, when Corinna, my darling and long suffering wife burst in.

"I thought that I had better tell you immediately" she said. "But Chris Squire has just died!"

Unlike Mick Farren or Daevid Allen, I never knew, or even met Chris Squire. I never even saw *Yes* live, unlike Corinna who saw them on the notorious *Tales from Topographic Oceans* tour back in 1974, but he had been part of my life - by default, which is probably not the right word - for over four decades, since an elder boy on the school bus leant me a copy of *Close to the Edge*, and I realised for the first time that there was life outside the Top 20.

I was saddened, but not particularly surprised by the news.

In May 2015, Squire announced a hiatus from Yes after he was diagnosed with acute erythroid leukaemia. Squire died on 27 June at his home in Phoenix, Arizona. It has been a quarter of a century since I last worked for the National Health Service, but I am perfectly aware what acute erythroid leukaemia is and what a diagnosis of the same in an elderly man probably means. But to have it confirmed was a shock.

But the real shock came the next day. I have always admired Chris Squire's bass playing. He always said that his two main influences were Paul McCartney and John Entwistle, and lots of people over the years have been surprised that someone could claim two such apparently disparate influences, but they always made perfect sense to me. I am a bass player myself, and the two musicians that he cited were probably my greatest influences as well.

So I have always seen Chris Squire as someone to be admired. To me, his melodic but earthy bass playing was as much part of the classic sound of *Yes* as Rick Wakeman's keyboards or Jon Anderson's voice. But I never knew quite how much loved he was.

When Diana Princess of Wales died in 1997, and when Elizabeth the Queen Mother died in 2002, there were books of condolences in public places, and veritable mountains of soft toys and wilting flowers by the roadsides, and of course nothing of the sort happened to mark the passing of an elderly rock and roll bassist. But in all the years that I have been editing this magazine (139 weeks because there have been 137 issues and two weeks on which we put out double issues) I have known such an outpouring of emotion on the internet. The Facebook groups on which I post the daily notifications of the *Gonzo Daily* online magazine each day are full of tributes to, and memories of the man. And my email inbox has been bursting with even more messages of respect and loss.

So this week as my assistant Jessica, Prudence and I have been beavering away in the converted potato shed which serves as my office, my recording studio, my video editing suite, the place where I breed tropical fish and play online video games, I have been listening to *Yes* and slowly planning how I would explain to you all why this issue of the peculiar little e-magazine which I started because it amused me, is dedicated to Chris Squire.

Because he was a great musician, the one remaining original member of the band, and the only person who had played in every one of the different line-ups, and stylistic directions that the band has taken since he and Jon Anderson first started the band back in 1968. Chris Squire always said that he had always hoped that the band that he had founded would continue down through the decades long after the original members were dead and gone. Maybe it will work out like that, maybe it won't. I, for one, certainly hope that it does. But one thing is certain. Whatever happens in the future, *Yes* will never be the same. And neither will we.

Many blessings and much love to you all.

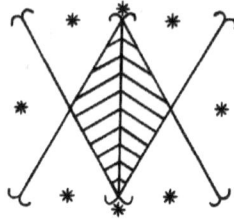

REVIEW

IN PURSUIT OF BUTTERFLIES: A FIFTY-YEAR AFFAIR
Matthew Oates

I really don't know how many books I have read over the past few years that mention the 1970 Isle of Wight Festival. It was the show at which Mick Farren and a couple of mates, under the guise of the UK White Panther Party put together an anarchic free festie on a hill overlooking the official event. It was the show at which ELP are rumoured to have got together for a jam with Jimi Hendrix, prompting nearly half a century of rumours that have categorically been denied by Greg Lake at least. It was one of the last shows Hendrix ever played before his death eighteen days later. And it was the show that a young Matthew Oates attended because he wanted to see Leonard Cohen.

For those of you who have never heard of him, Oates is somewhat of a legend amongst those of us who are interested in the long twisted saga which surrounds the sixty odd species of butterflies which are found in the United Kingdom. He is the National Specialist on Nature for the National Trust, and his biography on their website proclaims: "Butterfly expert, author, poet...Matthew Oates is something of a Renaissance Man. Celebrating 50 years of butterflying in 2013, Matthew is one of those rare ecologists with a background in the arts – his passion for butterflies matched only by that for the great English poets Coleridge and Edward Thomas.

Graduating in English, Matthew then moved into the world of nature conservation and has been at the Trust since 1990. He is particularly drawn to people's relationships with nature, places and seasons, and increasingly the impact of weather on wildlife.

Matthew is well known to the media. He's made a number of appearances on BBC Radio 4 - from the *Today* programme and *Shared Earth*, to presenting two short series: *In Pursuit of the Ridiculous* and *In Pursuit of Spring*. His TV credits include *The One Show*, *Springwatch*, *Great British Summer* and *Butterflies - A Very British Obsession*."

This book, very thinly disguised as an autobiography is nothing less than a personal look at fifty years of British butterfly reports from 1963 to 2013, based around, but not inclusive of, his own observations across the years.

He is what Bob Marley once called a "natural mystic" and his prose and poetry reflect a deep, spiritual and completely overwhelming love of the British countryside and its papilonid inhabitants, of the sort that one found in the reminiscences of 19th Century country parsons, but is increasingly uncommon in our own degenerate age.

I have always been fond of natural history memoirs, the moth collecting books of P.B.M Allan - a trilogy: *Moths and Memories, A Moth Hunter's Gossip* and *Talking of Moths*, being particular favourites - but until a few years ago I thought that this was a literary genre which had vanished forever. Then along came a book by Patrick Barkham, which resurrected the genre, but also managing to bring it up to date with such 21st Century additions as text messages, soon to be ex-girlfriends, and all sorts of other things that dear old Philip Allan would probably never have mentioned (although one of the trilogy listed above does hint at a teenage dalliance with the massively saucy daughter of a country innkeeper).

Now Matthew Oates comes along with probably the most poetic and romantic (in the literary sense) book on British Butterflies, complete with comments about Bob Dylan's *Blood on the Tracks*, which unlike so much poetry that I have read by scientists, is truly not at all bollocks! His prose even borders on the Richard Jeffreysesque, and - trust me - that is truly high praise indeed as far as I am concerned.

The tragedy of this book is that it is unlikely to be read outside the butterflying community, and that is a great pity. This is the sort of book that should be read by anybody who appreciates the countryside and the world about us, and also contains a fair smattering of social history of the British middle classes, chronicling a way of life that is unlikely ever to happen again. I truly recommend this book to everyone who reads this magazine, even the sort of person who would never consider buying a book about little fluttering insects.

Well done Matthew.

GO WELL RICHARD

A quarter of a century ago I was sitting in a pub with my friend Jane Bradley (who, herself, died twenty years ago, and is remembered on the song 'The Day we Buried Jane' on my last album). I cannot remember the name of the pub but I could take you there in a trice if it hasn't been knocked down. We were talking about feral wallabies in The Peak District, when a stocky bloke with a deep, cultured voice and an impressive beard came into the pub. Jane introduced us.

It was Richard Ingram: physicist, anarchist, social activist, potter, astronomer (the House Astronomer for Glastonbury Festival for a number of years), sometime reader of Gonzo Weekly, and speaker at the Weird Weekend. I became very fond of him over the years, and was saddened to hear over the weekend that he has died of cancer aged 68. Bless you my friend. May your spirit soar free. Because, after all, it always did.

Andy the Druid who I introduced elsewhere in this issue, writing for Chris Squire, wrote a few words for Richard:

For Richard

Birth, life, death and rebirth
In an eternal circle
Your soul a blessing to this Earth
Your passion still warming all who knew you
The wheel has turned, your soul flies free, returning to spirit
Your rebirth, that you are remembered always by those who love you

Go well Richard

And so say we all. So mote it be!

FOR FOX SAKE

Corinna sent me the following news item featuring the bass player of some half-remembered band from the sixties:

"Paul McCartney has issued a response to government proposals that could pave the way for the return of fox hunting.

On 9 July, the Conservatives published an amendment to the Hunting Act 2004 that – if passed by MPs in a vote on 15 July – would allow foxes to be hunted by packs of dogs in England and Wales, so long as it is "appropriate" for the terrain and done "efficiently" to protect other animals."

There is something distinctly surreal about politics in the United Kingdom at the moment. We are facing huge economic and social problems at home, the Eurozone is about to go tits up, and large swathes of the Middle East are under the control of Medieval brigands who post videos of their victims being crucified on YouTube, and Her Majesty's Government's primary concern seems to be the persecution of a small wild carnivore.

The story continues:

A statement from the musician, a longtime vegetarian and animal-rights activist, said that fox hunting was "cruel and unnecessary" and could cost the party support if the proposals were to go ahead:

"The people of Britain are behind this Tory government on many things but the vast majority of us will be against them if hunting is reintroduced. It is cruel and unnecessary and will lose them support from ordinary people and animal lovers like myself."

Well, despite the equally surreal concept of anyone describing Sir Paul McCartney, one of the most famous British musicians of all time, and who has twice as big a personal fortune than The Queen as "A Normal Person", it is hard not to agree with him. In fact I won't even try. That well known population biologist Roger Waters recently described foxes as "vermin" that had to be controlled, but misses the point entirely. Hunting does not "control" foxes, it merely terrorises them.

The story continues:

"His sentiments echo those of Queen's Brian May, who slammed pro-hunting activists on BBC's Newsnight on 9 July. May criticised the Countryside Alliance, calling them "a bunch of lying bastards".

"There is no justification for the hunting of foxes on the grounds of control of foxes," said May. "They breed them to hunt; it's all about people out there trying to catch foxes for fun. They like causing pain and this is what Cameron is endorsing."

Well, again I would take exception to the statement that "they breed them to hunt" although I know what he means, but the main crux of his argument is completely true. Fox hunting has absolutely nothing to do with pest control, sustainable farming or anything else. Bear baiting, bull baiting, dog fighting and cock fighting have been illegal ever since the Cruelty to Animals Act of 1835. How, in the 21st Century, can so-called civilised people possibly countenance having a wild animal ripped apart by a pack of dogs for sport? Because that is all it is, barbaric entertainment.

Sir Paul McCartney is completely correct. The vast majority of people in this country are against the idea of the ban being overturned. The people like that irritating Katie whatshername claim that this is purely a manifestation of class envy, as the *canaille* are expressing their sadness that they cannot indulge in Upper Class sporting pursuits. Once this may have been the case, but now I think that is a completely outdated concept. The people in my social circle who - like me - were born into the rural English Upper Classes are without exception Green Party voting veggie anarchists, whilst the people I know who hunt, or who are pro-hunting, are the ones who became affluent during the decade when Thatcher proclaimed that there was no such thing as society and then did her best to make that silly proclamation come true.

Those who say that the banning of hunting is an attack on the English rural way of life are as stupid as the ones who say that the Royal Family's main role is to boost tourism. If the hereditary Heads of State are only good for flogging postcards, and the English rural way of life stands or falls on ritualised animal torture, then the day we end both cannot come soon enough for me. And I am a countryman and a royalist.

Next week will see a free vote on the subject. MPs will be able to vote, allegedly without pressure from party whips, and decide the future of hunting in this country once and for all. Will our elected representatives remember that their role is to carry out the wishes of the electorate? One would like to think so.

Time will tell.

ANARCHY IN THE YEW KAY

Many years ago I first read a book that would change my life. It was called *Ismo* and it was the third in a series of children's novels by Sir John Verney, a Baronet, war hero, and celebrated painter of whom I am a particular fan. It told the story of a loose knit anarchist group with the same name as the title of the book, that both made mischief and had an on-off serious political agenda.

Verney is probably best known for his semi-autobiographical book *Going to the Wars*, which recounts his spectacularly exciting military career, but he has always been most important to me through his alter-ego, journalist and harassed father Augustus "Gus" Callendar, one of the central characters of a series of children's books which were written between 1959 and 1972. Much to my grave disappointment, they remain spectacularly obscure, and very few people have heard of them. However, they all have a worthy message to those of us of a Fortean persuasion, and have peculiarly surrealchemical plot twists and anarchistic themes, which are all the more peculiar when you discover that the author is not only a notable war hero, but also a minor Peer of the Realm.

The last three books, in particular, are very Fortean in their outlook, in that at every twist and turn of the plot you find out that, as Lloyd Pye said, "everything you know is wrong". And all preconceptions are demolished, as Verney plays surreal word games worthy of Tony Shiels upon the hapless reader. Whereas, on the surface at least, these books appear to be stuck well within the genre, which was popular 50 years ago of 'middle class children, with ponies, having adventures and thwarting the adult world', in reality these books are far more complex. Where else in the canon of children's literature do you find two novels about a mythical global anarchist group founded in Italy by an Italian aristocrat posing as a pop singer (who has always reminded me of the late Richard Chanfray, who alongside a not very successful career as a third rate Jacques Brel or Claude Francois, copyist, claimed to be the immortal and invisible Count of Saint Germain)? And, furthermore, where in the canon of children's literature do you find novels in which the concept of anarchism, at least as practised by the CFZ, is portrayed not just in a positive light, but as a jolly good idea?

I loved the idea of the non-hierarchical, mischief making anarchists, and have been disappointed all my adult life that such a group never seemed to exist in the real world. Only, of course, they have.

Anonymous (used as a mass noun) is a loosely associated international network of activist and hacktivist entities. A website nominally associated with the group describes it as "an internet gathering" with "a very loose and decentralized command structure that operates on ideas rather than directives". The group became known for a series of well-publicized publicity stunts and distributed denial-of-service (DDoS) attacks on government, religious, and corporate websites.

Anonymous originated in 2003 on the imageboard 4chan, representing the concept of many online and offline community users simultaneously existing as an anarchic, digitized global brain. Anonymous members (known as "Anons") can be distinguished in public by the wearing of stylised Guy Fawkes masks.

I have found the activities of this group utterly fascinating, even though it was only whilst reading Parmy Olson's book that I realised how many sociopolitical and conceptual links there are between the The Internet Hate Machine, and Verney's fictional activists. I read another book on the subject (*Epic Win for Anonymous* by Cole Stryker) which was, I am afraid, somewhat of a disappointment, and I intimated as much when I reviewed it in these pages. This book, however, is a far more meaty proposition.

This book purports to be the first full account of how a loosely assembled group of hackers scattered across the globe formed a new kind of insurgency, seized headlines, and tortured the feds-and the ultimate betrayal that would eventually bring them down. The author makes a concerted effort to find the truth behind the media furore and sensationalist headlines, and during her research she carried out hundreds of conversations with the hackers themselves, including exclusive interviews with various members of Anonymous and with all six core members of LulzSec, a black hat computer hacker group that claimed responsibility for several high profile attacks, including the compromise of user accounts from Sony Pictures in 2011. The group also claimed responsibility for taking the CIA website offline. Previous to these events, in late 2010, thousands of hacktivists joined a mass digital assault on the websites of VISA, MasterCard, and PayPal to protest their treatment of WikiLeaks. Other targets were wide ranging - the websites of corporations from Sony Entertainment and Fox to the Vatican and the Church of Scientology were hacked, defaced, and embarrassed - and the message was that no one was safe. Thousands of user accounts from pornography websites were released, exposing government employees and military personnel.

But it wasn't until I read Parmy Olson's excellent book that I realised that the non hierarchical, multinational, mischief making anarchist group had finally arrived. Except that - quite possibly in part because the late 1950s and the early 1960s when Verney was writing were a gentler time - they are in part, at least, a far more vicious proposition. The book reads like a thriller, as Parmy examines the motivation of the Lulzsec hackers in detail, and she is such a good writer, as one becomes emotionally involved in the affairs of these peculiar young people, one is enthralled by their exploits but feels ever more uncomfortable at the less ethical adventures that they carry out.

Verney once described ISMO as being a double edged sword. It was like electricity, he aid. It could give you a nasty shock or play you a nice tune on the gramophone. It is the same thing with the new breed of anarchic black hat hackers. Few reading this magazine would argue against the attacks in child pornographers and their website, and many would support the attacks on The Church of Scientology, or the actions in support of the beleaguered Wikileaks. Other attacks seem, however, to have been carried out purely "for the lulz" and are more or less malicious in nature.

This is a remarkable book, and by far the best piece of writing that I have read on the subject. However, it misses one enormous trick. All the way through, on of the subplots concerns a hacker called Kayla who claimed to be a teenage girl. Is he, isn't she? The conundra and conflicting pieces of evidence pile up, until the denouement that Kayla was actually an ex (male) soldier called Ryan Ackroyd who was in his mid twenties. He was sentenced to thirty months in prison, but the best is yet to come, and is not chronicled in Parmy Olson's book. 'Kayla', under his real name, is now an Associate Lecturer at Sheffield's Hallam University. Never in the whole field of human anarchoconflict, has an outlaw joined the establishment quite so rapidly.

Lulz indeed.

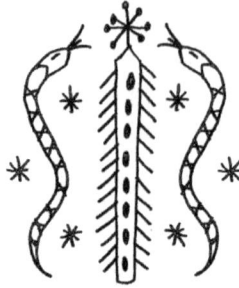

ROUTING THE ONION

After reading Jamie Bartlett's 'The Dark Net', I wanted to check out the TOR network for myself. So I downloaded the app onto my iPad and went blithely on. For those of you not aware of it, over to Wikipedia:

"Tor is free software for enabling anonymous communication. The name is an acronym derived from the original software project name The Onion Router. Tor directs Internet traffic through a free, worldwide, volunteer network consisting of more than six thousand relays to conceal a user's location and usage from anyone conducting network surveillance or traffic analysis. Using Tor makes it more difficult for Internet activity to be traced back to the user: this includes "visits to Web sites, online posts, instant messages, and other communication forms". Tor's use is intended to protect the personal privacy of users, as well as their freedom and ability to conduct confidential communication by keeping their Internet activities from being monitored. An extract of a Top Secret appraisal by the National Security Agency (NSA) characterized Tor as "the King of high-secure, low-latency Internet anonymity" with "no contenders for the throne in waiting", and the Parliamentary Office of Science and Technology deemed it, with approximately 2.5 million users daily "by far the most popular anonymous internet communication system."

I found 'The Hidden Wiki', and within less than five minutes I was directed to a UK based website purporting to sell handguns, a whole plethora of drug markets, although the only one I looked at seemed rather expensive, and a category of adult websites called 'Hard Candy', which I suspect are probably illegal pornography, but not being Pete Townshend I did not sully my hard drive by investigating any further.

I suppose that as an anarchist I am supposed to be excited at this new electronic wild frontier, but actually it scared the crap out of me.

Maybe I am less of a rabble rouser than I have always pretended.

A SLICE OF LIFE

The postman arrived, heralded by a torrent of barks from my two unruly canids, and handed me a pile of post.

I glanced through it quickly, making sure that there was nothing nasty, that I didn't owe someone enormous sums of money of which I was previously unaware, and that my recent diabetic blood tests hadn't shown up anything untoward. There was nothing of any importance; merely a couple of brochures for holidays that I would have had no intention of going on even if I could have afforded them, and a circular from the Public School from which I was expelled in 1977 asking for money for a new gymnasium. They had told me that I could never darken their doors again upon my untimely exit, but a few years ago, after I had appeared on television one too many times, and they realised that I had achieved a certain level of spurious fame, my name miraculously reappeared upon the lists of alumni, and had even appeared briefly on their website as a distinguished Old Boy until they discovered that I was an anarchist and quietly removed it again.

But there was also a jiffy bag with a Norfolk postmark. I tore it open to find a pristine copy of the debut album by Steve Ignorant's Slice of Life. 3 BLOODY HELL IGS! I DIDN'T EXPECT THIS I don't mean that I didn't expect the album; I knew that Steve had posted me a copy, and I was looking forward to hearing it, but I was not prepared for the remarkable suite of songs that I heard earlier today.

First the back-story for those who are unaware of it. Steve is best known for having been the lead singer of the anarchopunk band Crass from their inception in 1977 until the band split in 1984. He had co- founded the group with drummer Penny Rimbaud, and his Touretty vocals had been the principal selling point of the band to many of their followers. A few years ago he assembled a band and conducted a world tour in which he had played the songs of Crass live for the very last time. The DVD of the final night of this tour has just been released on Gonzo.

When the tour was over, Steve assembled an a acoustic band with several members of his touring group, and started doing acoustic shows. This debut album from the new band has been a long time in coming, and has been eagerly awaited by many of Steve's fans, but I don't think that anyone was expecting such a revelatory album. First of all, it is - indeed - acoustic, but whereas I assume that most people were expecting acoustic guitar strummety strums, with a 4/4 beat, the album is nothing like that. Indeed, it is almost 4 jazzy in places, and far more subtle musically than I, for one, had expected.

It is a matter of record that Steve has always been a massive David Bowie fan. Indeed the name for his first band came from a line in the song 'Ziggy Stardust' in which Bowie sang "The kids was just Crass".

When I met his collaborator (the words backing singer seem woefully inadequate to describe her input) Carol Hodge (aka Gonzo Multimedia recording artiste Miss Crystal Grenade) in the foyer of Manchester Museum of Natural History last year, she told me that the band had been including a cover of David Bowie's 'Sweet Thing', originally from The Thin White Duke's dystopian fantasy 'Diamond Dogs'. I searched on You Tube, and eventually found a live rendition, which worked surprisingly well. So I was mildly expecting a bit of a Bowie vibe about the Slice of Life album. I was right, there is. But it is not at all the type of Bowie vibe that I was expecting.

During the 1960s from about 1964 onwards, Bowie (under a number of different names) had been experimenting with a number of different guises in an attempt to find one which would attract the record buying public.

One of these was to emulate his hero Anthony Newley with a series of clever songs which bordered on the cerebral at times, and which sounded for all the world as if they had come straight from the original soundtracks of the more intellectual end of West End musicals. This phase of Bowie's career culminated with a short movie called 'Love you till Tuesday' which I rather liked, although I was in the minority.

When Bowie finally achieved global megastardom in about 1973 his previous record company realised that they were sitting on a veritable goldmine and rereleased his late 1960s output, often with deliberately misleading cover artwork in a quite successful attempt to sell these loss makers to the legion of new Ziggy fans who now thronged in every High Street in the land. I don't know whether the teenaged Steve Williams (in his pre-punk days) had bought any of these albums like The World of David Bowie, and Images, but I would wager a fair sum that he had heard at least one of them back in the day.

I am not for one minute suggesting that Steve ripped off this peculiar time in his hero's history, but in my humble opinion his mellifluous range of influences led him unconsciously in a parallel direction. For this remarkable record also sounds like excerpts from the artier end of West End musicals. Forget *Cats* or *Starlight Express*, if anyone made a musical of *A Kind of* Loving or *Room at the Top*, I have a sneaking suspicion that it would sound like this.

The next big surprise is a compositional one. Steve has always been publically unimpressed by the more avant garde areas of Crass' output, which is why the bits of musique concrete that are found throughout this album are such an impressive surprise. However, unlike some of the more outré examples of the mother band's output, these examples work perfectly, and give the impression of a sort of radio play, in which Igs acts not only as a narrator, but as a chorus in the style of the formal ancient Greek drama, or Shakespeare's *Henry V.*

I had got the impression that Steve had decided to put his rabble rousing days behind him, but some of the songs on this album, especially one of the spoken word pieces is as politically spot on as anything he has ever written. However, times have changed, we have all grown older and what Steve has to say now makes the point to people of his (and my) generation far more succinctly than a photo collage of Margaret Thatcher eating a turd. I have always thought that Steve Ignorant had the greatest pop sensibility of any of the erstwhile members of Crass.

Songs like *Do the owe us a Living?'* and *Banned from the Roxy* may well have been scabrous rants, but they had a classic pop song structure like the best of things which came from the pen of Phil Spector. Indeed I have spent much of the last three decades vaguely planning to do a cover version of the first of these in the style of The Ronettes singing *Be My Baby.*

However this new album takes it all a step further; sonically, musically and lyrically the songs are meticulously crafted, and Steve reveals himself not only to be a songwriter who deserves far more recognition than he has garnered in his career so far, but also to be a poet of no mean ability.

By anyone's standards this is a remarkable album. It is a career best so far for Steve (notice that I say SO FAR, for I am by no means convinced that his best work isn't yet to come) and it is the best post-Crass work to come yet from any of the quondam members. Go out and buy it.

Do we owe him a living? I should coco.

TALIBANAND TILLERMAN

I have spent much of the time since the last issue came out listening to one particular album; *Tell 'Em I'm Gone* by a bloke called Yusuf Islam, released under the nom de guerre of Yusuf. I hope that you will forgive me if I sound too much like Sherlock Holmes, but this record does have more than a few aspects of interest.

First of all, for those of you who ware not aware, Yusuf previously operated under another *nom de guerre* - Cat Stevens, and as such had a very successful musical career in the late 1960s and early 1970s as a predominantly acoustic balladeer, with such classic albums as *Teaser and the Firecat, Tea for the Tillerman* and my personal favourite, *Catch Bull at Four*.

He was born Steven Demetre Georgiou in 1948 to a Cypriot family living in London. Forgive me for the history lesson, because I think that this is important. Whereas nowadays, multiculturalism, especially in the big cities, is seen as an established way of life, it was not so back when Steven Georgiou was a boy. But Cyprus, a large island in the Eastern Mediterranean had been a British possession since the 1880s and was to remain so until young Steven was 12. The island was dominated by its ethnic Greek population, who even now comprise 70% of Cypriots, and Steven's father was from this part of the island's population and was a practicing member of the Greek Orthodox Church.

It was just past the zenith of Stevens' career when the Greek government sponsored a coup d'etat in Cyprus. Enosis has been part of unofficial Greek foreign policy for centuries. It is the sociopolitical movement to make places with a Greek majority population in political union with Greece itself.

During the past the same term was used in various times and places to denote movements among Greek populations remaining outside the boundaries of the Kingdom of Greece as originally created in 1830, who aspired to be incorporated in that kingdom.

Movements calling for Enosis were popular in Crete, the Ionian Islands and Dodecanese, culminating with their achieving their aim and joining Greece. At the conclusion of World War I, Greece attempted to annex portions of Western Anatolia at the invitation of the victorious Allies of World War I, particularly British Prime Minister David Lloyd George.

The attempted Enosis failed, however, when the new Turkish Republic prevailed in the resulting Greco-Turkish War of 1919–1922, after which most Anatolian Christians who had not already fled during the war were forced to relocate to Greece in the 1923 population exchange between Greece and Turkey.

Cat Stevens continued making music for a few more years after the Cypriot Enosis, but following a near-fatal swimming accident in 1976, he converted to Islam the following year.

There were two final Cat Stevens albums, but after *Izitso* in 1977, which was broadly ignored (although I, for one liked it a lot) he withdrew from the music business, and changed his name to Yusuf Islam.

• **FALLACY #1**
It has often been claimed that Yusuf withdrew from the music business because he was forbidden to be a pop star under his new religious regime. What apparently actually happened was that when he became a Muslim in 1977, he said, the Imam at the mosque was told that he was a pop star, and he told Yusuf that it was fine to continue as a musician, so long as the songs were morally acceptable.

But Yusuf says he knew there were aspects of the music business, such as vanity and temptations, that did go against the teachings of the Qur'an, and this was the primary reason he gave for retreating from the spotlight. But in his first performance on the television show Later... with Jools Holland, 27 years after leaving the music business, and in other interviews, he gave different reasons for leaving:

"A lot of people would have loved me to keep singing", he said. "You come to a point where you have sung, more or less ... your whole repertoire and you want to get down to the job of living. You know, up until that point, I hadn't had a life. I'd been searching, been on the road."

It should be remembered here that there was a long and well-attested history of pop stars from western countries adopting exotic eastern and middle eastern religions. George Harrison had become a Hindu, Pete Townshend had become a follower of Meher Baba, as had Ronnie Lane, and Richard Thompson, who also appears on this new record by Yusuf, had also become a Muslim. At the time, Cat Stevens' actions seemed a perfectly "normal" thing for a pop star to do, and no-one batted an eyelid.

One should also remember that in the late 1970s, there was no real public consciousness of Islam, and - despite the predations of the Palestine Liberation Front - no real public antagonism against it, in the same way as the actions of the IRA had not caused any great backlash against Roman Catholics except amongst Glasgow Rangers supporters.

Here, may I point out that I am not taking sides, making any political or religious statements, or doing anything except for pointing out what I believe are interesting sociopolitical and religious/cultural aspects to one of the better albums that has been released in the last few weeks. I am a pantheistic Christian anarchist with no real affiliation to any established church.

My father was an Islamic scholar, my brother is a C of E vicar, and at a wedding in Lancashire, I recently gave the Catholic bride to be married to her Muslim husband. I truly have no axe to grind, and my interest here is purely wearing the mantle of Rock and Roll archaeologist.

The proverbial shit hit the fan in 1988 when Salman Rushdie's fourth novel, *The Satanic Verses* was published. Again, please do not read any of my comments on this book to assume any sociopolitical or religious position of my own, but I found it to be a load of pretentious tosh, and almost unreadable. If a death sentence had been passed upon him by campaigners for readable English literature I would not have been overly surprised, but in the event it was the universally feared Ayatollah Khomeini, then the head of state of post revolutionary Iran, who stated:

"We are from Allah and to Allah we shall return. I am informing all brave Muslims of the world that the author of The Satanic Verses, a text written, edited, and published against Islam, the Prophet of Islam, and the Qur'an, along with all the editors and publishers aware of its contents, are condemned to death. I call on all valiant Muslims wherever they may be in the world to kill them without delay, so that no one will dare insult the sacred beliefs of Muslims henceforth. And whoever is killed in this cause will be a martyr, Allah Willing. Meanwhile if someone has access to the author of the book but is incapable of carrying out the execution, he should inform the people so that [Rushdie] is punished for his actions.

Rouhollah al-Mousavi al-Khomeini. "

The irony was that I severely doubt whether Khomeini, or the 7,000 protesters who marched in Bradford, or the 10,000 people who protested in Islamabad had actually read the bloody thing, and it is even more amusing to find out that Islamic scholars who actually read the bloody thing were less critical. Other Islamic scholars outside of Iran took issue with the fact that the sentence was not passed by an Islamic court, or that it did not limit its "jurisdiction only [to] countries under Islamic law". Muhammad Hussan ad-Din, a theologian at Al-Azhar University, argued "Blood must not be shed except after a trial [when the accused has been] given a chance to defend himself and repent". Abdallah al-Mushidd, head of Azhar's Fatwā Council stated "We must try the author in a legal fashion as Islam does not accept killing as a legal instrument".

Bizarrely, Western commentators were more negative about Rushdie and his book. Among authors, Roald Dahl was scathing and called Rushdie's book sensationalist and Rushdie "a dangerous opportunist". John le Carré thought the death sentence to be outrageous, but he also criticized Rushdie's action: "I don't think it is given to any of us to be impertinent to great religions with impunity". But is was poor old Yusuf that suffered most.

In 1989 I was in tour with Steve Harley, and every night he sang Cat Stevens' song 'Father and Son', prefacing it with (and I am paraphrasing, because I lost my bootleg tapes of the tour years ago):

"This song was written by a man who, when he was young, had great wisdom, but has now been perverted by RELIGIOUS FUCKING DOGMA" But what had Yusuf Islam actually done?

- **FALLACY #2**
Cat Stevens went on UK Breakfast TV to call for the death of Salman Rushdie. Well he didn't. After all these years it is uncertain what actually did happen, but that most certainly didn't.

He has always claimed that when onstage at Kingston Uni, and asked about the *Satanic Verses* affair, he was put in a difficult position as a relatively recent Islamic scholar. In an interview with *Rolling Stone* eleven years later, he claimed:

"I'm very sad that this seems to be the No. 1 question people want to discuss. I had nothing to do with the issue other than what the media created. I was innocently drawn into the whole controversy. So, after many years, I'm glad at least now that I have been given the opportunity to explain to the public and fans my side of the story in my own words. At a lecture, back in 1989, I was asked a question about blasphemy according to Islamic Law, I simply repeated the legal view according to my limited knowledge of the Scriptural texts, based directly on historical commentaries of the Qur'an. The next day the newspaper headlines read, "Cat Says, Kill Rushdie."

I was abhorred, but what could I do? I was a new Muslim. If you ask a Bible student to quote the legal punishment of a person who commits blasphemy in the Bible, he would be dishonest if he didn't mention Leviticus 24:16."

And on one of his own websites he wrote:

"I never called for the death of Salman Rushdie; nor backed the Fatwa issued by the Ayatollah Khomeini— and still don't. The book itself destroyed the harmony between peoples and created an unnecessary international crisis."

From reading transcripts of TV appearances at the time, it would appear that if the transcripts are correct that Yusuf made some unfortunate statements at the time, which could well be open to a sinister interpretation. But that is actually irrelevant as far as the main thrust of this editorial. No doubt I shall receive letters from readers giving a different account of what happened at the time, but the important thing is that for the past twenty-five years Yusuf has taken the position that he never stated that Rushdie should be executed, and certainly never called for it to take place. The last part of the back-story that needs to be told is that, much to the delight of fans all over the world, Yusuf started making secular records again back in 2006 (he had released several Islamic albums, at least one of which appeared on Voiceprint, the precursor to Gonzo Multimedia) and there was a follow up in 2009.

Both albums were everything that one would have wanted from a Cat Stevens record in the 21st Century, and fans across the globe (me included) were happy.

The second of these albums included a cover version of Eric Burdon's *Don't let me be Misunderstood*, but other than tapping our toes to it, nobody gave it a second thought. Now, that brings the story up to date.

I have always been very wary of the breed of musicologists who read more into supposed clues in the music than is actually there. At the lunatic fringe of this movement one can find people like A. J. Weberman, who made all sorts of extraordinary claims about Bob Dylan's state of mind and motivation from clues found in his lyrics and in his garbage. Another example would be the American DJ who claimed that Paul McCartney was dead based on a series of unlikely clues found in Beatles song lyrics and LP covers. But the more respectable end of academia has also fallen for it. One famous academic whose name I forget, but it might have been Wilfred Mellors, claimed that the positioning of a flower bed on the cover of the

Beatles's Sgt Pepper album was a deliberate attempt to show the widening gulf between the band and their audience (the band are standing behind the flower bed).

I always thought that this was nonsense, and when - many years ago - I helped a friend with his essay on the cover, I/he was reprimanded severely for not having mentioned this. Not that I had not mentioned Mellors' claim, but that we had not repeated a claim which by then had become canon. So I am very aware that I may fall into the trap of doing exactly the same thing with this album, but it seems to me that Yusuf has put so many clues and subtexts within this record that it really cannot be coincidental.

But shall we get the big question out of the way first? Is it any good? Well, yeh, of course it is.

I really don't think that the man is capable of making a bad record, and this is a pretty damn good one. His once angelic balladeer's voice has acquired a slight bluesy roughness that comes with age, and it suits the new music perfectly, because this new music is a return to his bluesy roots. The young Steven Georgiou, like his contemporaries in 'Swinging London' will have been enthused by the sounds of working class bluesmen from Chicago and all points south.

The music had reached its apogee in the '40s and '50s and by the time it became the inspiration for a whole generation of peacock painted white youths across the Atlantic, the men who had made it were getting on a bit, and the king of them all, who had - according to the lore of the blues - sold his soul to a cornuted fellow in return for being the gift of being the greatest guitar player of all time had been dead for a quarter of a century. But even in his poppiest early days I don't think that this taste for the blues had ever shown itself before, but he was friends with, and toured with, Jimi Hendrix, and his most famous records were produced by an ex-Yardbird, and maybe some of the DNA rubbed off. Because this album is an unashamed blues album and none the worse for that.

But what are all these clues that I have been alluding to for the last few pages? Let's look at a list of them in some vague order.

1.   The album is co-produced by Rick Rubin, who is admittedly the go-to producer for singer songwriters of a certain age who wish to revitalise a career. He most notably worked his magic on Johnny Cash for the 'American Recording' series, but also worked with Neil Diamond, Mick Jagger and a fistful of others. However, for someone determined not to be viewed as a militant Islamist, the choice of a Jewish producer is a good, but brave, one.

2.   It could have been argued that choosing to adopt Islam was a particularly rebellious move for a Greek Orthodox Cypriot boy. Following the attempted coup described above, the Turkish Cypriots rebelled and the Island was partitioned into Greek (Christian) and Turkish (Moslem) areas, a partition that remains today. What is little known is that 98 square miles of the island remain under British sovereignty, but that is another story. However with this album he seeks to make peace with both the Greek and Christian parts of his ancestry; he sings about the death of the Greek philosopher Socrates in 388BC, but attributes to him one of the last sentences attributed to Jesus. Just like Socrates, the man from Greece Fell down on his knees Said, Lord! Forgive them please Forgive them please And he spoke no more And the cup spilled out on the editing floor

3.   It is this song *Editing Floor Blues* that is one of the two pivotal ones of the album. It plays games with the format of Howling Wolf's classic *Killing Floor* and the more recent song *Cutting Room Floor* by I the Mighty which asks

> *"If hell broke out in the White House,*
> *how long would it take for word to carry here?*
> *Would it stay hush hush till the weather changed,*
> *till the sun warmed the snow and fears?"*

Both songs are subtly referenced, but the most important verse is:

> *"One day the papers rang us up, T'check if I said this?*
> *I said, "Oh boy! I'd never say that!"*

Then we got down to the truth of But they never printed that! Somehow his cover version of *Why Must I be so Misunderstood* five years ago begins to make a little more sense.

4.   *Editing Floor Blues* is the polar opposite/alchemical sister of the opening number *I was raised in Babylon*, which tells the story of a fictionalised youth at the hub of another empire in what is now Iraq, several millennia before his upbringing as a wild colonial boy in what was then still the hub of the greatest empire that the world has ever seen.

In *Editing Floor Blues* he sings:

> *I was born in the West-End*
> *In the summer of '48*
> *Above a small Cafe*

In the other song he relates:

> *I used to serve the Empire*
> *On which the sun set, never Oh!*
> *Now times have turned*
> *We thought our white skins would save us – then we got burned*

Bloody hell, this is getting heavy!

5.   The new album is a canny mix of cover versions - one each from Jimmy Reed and Leadbelly, which underline his blues cred, and one each from Edgar Winter and Procul Harum, plus a nod to Rick Rubin's legacy with the second version of *You are my Sunshine* that he has produced, the other being by Johnny Cash. and sung as a lament to June Carter.

But whereas Cash's motivation was clear, and Brian Wilson put it into a peculiar mournful minor key on \SMiLE, this version makes it into a pure chugging blues. You are my sunshine? Who is his sunshine? God? If so, it appears that his love affair has brought pain as well as joy.

Perhaps I am reading too much into this, but it seems to me that the whole record is about his relationship with the Imperium of religion, and - presumably - in particular Islam. In his slightly recast version of Leadbelly's *Take this Hammer* he sings:

> *Take this hammer,*
> *carry it to the captain*
> *Tell 'em I'm gone*
> *and If he asks you was I runnin'*
> *Tell 'em I was flyin'*
> *Tell 'em I was flyin'*

and finally

> *If he asks you was I laughin'*
> *Tell 'em I was cryin'*

Leadbelly spent the years between 1918 and 1925 in prison for murder, and it has often been assumed that this song is one that he composed during his years on the chain gang. It does not take too big a paradigm shift to see that Yusuf has changed it into something else. The Jimmy Reed song goes:

> *Well, I'm gonna get me a boss man*
> *One's gonna treat me right*
> *Work hard in the day time*
> *Rest easy at night*

Just who is Yusuf's big boss man?

6.   The rest of the album has similar lyrical concerns, even on the songs he wrote himself. On *Gold Digger* he adopts the persona of a downtrodden South African mine worker, and on *Cat & the dog trap* he sings:

> *There was a time*
> *When I was bolder*
> *I'd chase the heels*
> *Of any stranger*
> *About to learn*
> *About to learn,*
> *ohhhh Cat's In a cage*
> *Chained to a stone*
> *Empty bowl by his side*
> *Just an old fish bone*
> *Dreams of home*

These are not the words of someone who is entirely happy with the place that his life choices have taken him

7.   One of the most impressive collaborations on the album is with the Tuareg rebel musicians Tinariwen.

Tinariwen was founded by Ibrahim Ag Alhabib, who at age four witnessed the execution of his father (a Tuareg rebel) during a 1963 uprising in Mali. As a child he saw a western film in which a cowboy played a guitar. Ag Alhabib built his own guitar out of a tin can, a stick and bicycle brake wire. He started to play old Tuareg and modern Arabic pop tunes. Ag Alhabib first lived in Algeria in refugee camps near Bordj Badji Mokhtar and in the deserts around the southern city of Tamanrasset, where he received a guitar from a local Arab man. Later, he resided with other Tuareg exiles in Libya and Algeria.

In the late 1970s Ag Alhabib joined with other musicians in the Tuareg rebel community, exploring the radical chaabi protest music of Moroccan groups like Nass El Ghiwane and Jil Jilala; Algerian pop rai; and western rock and pop artists like

Elvis Presley, Led Zeppelin, Carlos Santana, Dire Straits, Jimi Hendrix, Boney M, and Bob Marley. Ag Alhabib formed a group with Alhassane Ag Touhami and brothers Inteyeden Ag Ablil and Liya Ag Ablil in Tamanrasset, Algeria to play at parties and weddings. Ag Alhabib acquired his first real acoustic guitar in 1979.

While the group had no official name, people began to call them Kel Tinariwen, which in the Tamashek language translates as "The People of the Deserts" or "The Desert Boys." The Tuareg people fused their traditional animist religions with Islam centuries ago, but their portmanteau religion has brought them into conflict in recent years with some groups of fundamental Islamists.

It appears to me that Yusuf's choice of collaborators on this album is interesting, not just for musical reasons. One has a Jewish producer, a band of Malian guerillas, and probably the best known Muslim guitarist in western music. Add to that a collection of songs which reference freedom, rebellion, oppression as well as his own Greek and Christian upbringing.

To put the final touches to this smorgasbord of cultural influences, the final song *Doors* has the structure of a Christian gospel song complete with church organ, and intones: "When a door is closed somewhere, there's a door that's opening".

8.   Then let us go back to the opening track again for some very revealing words. He sings:

"They used to call us civilised – but those days are gone",

and goes on to say how he loved to march with the 'Sultan', stressing the past tense. Past Imperfect I believe.

9.   Finally (in fact it's not finally, because there are dozens more examples that I could cite, but I don't want to over-egg the pudding of this particular argument), this is the first album of his to have been credited to Yusuf/Cat Stevens. Even his website credits both names. But the truth is, that this record is not by either of them. It is by Steven Demetre Georgiou, and it is quite possibly the most important, and the most personal record that he has ever produced.

CONCLUSION
So where am I leading with all of this?

I believe that Yusuf is as scared as the rest of us about the state of the world at the moment, and - like any intelligent human being - can see that whatever the outcome of the current events in the Middle East, it is unlikely to be good for anyone.

I am sure that he is a devout Muslim, and a decent and God-fearing man, but I think that the events of twenty years ago, are still catching up with him and that he now realises that there are powerful factions within Islam who have a different agenda to the one of love, peace, humility and family values that he has espoused all his life.

I don't for one moment suggest that he feels that he has backed the wrong horse all these years, but I think he - like me - can foresee a situation whereby moderate Muslims across the globe are becoming tarred with the same brush as the lunatic butchers of ISIL, and he wants to try and do something about it. I don't know whether he did make the comments attributed to him all those years ago. I suspect that he might well have done, but that he immediately regretted it, and has been searching ever since for a way to redress the balance.

In an immensely brave move he has tried to pull together all the disparate aspects of his life and career, to try and show - by example - that most Muslims are as appalled by the events in the Middle East as the rest of us. He is, deliberately, setting himself up as a target for every one of what Roy Harper called "the nutters of God" who disapprove of his actions to take a pop at him, in a vain attempt to lead by example and to deflect the horrible backlash which is looming against his people, when those who tar all Muslims with the same ideological brush wreak what they see as righteous revenge and start a race war. I may be right. I may be wrong.

But this album moved me immensely and I felt moved to spend most of the day writing this when I should have been doing a hundred and one other things. But I am the editor, and I am allowed to do what I want.

So there

THE UNSPEAKABLE IN PURSUIT

I am writing this under very unusual (for me) circumstances. I am alone. Or rather, I suppose I should qualify this by saying that I am the only human being in the house. There are various ghosts and a multifarious selection of animals, both tame and wild, but I am - at the moment, at least - the only human, and I am enjoying every moment of it.

Don't get me wrong. I love my family and my extended family very much. But sheer solitude and silence (except for an amorous pair of *Testudo graeca* banging their shells together in a large vivarium on the sitting room floor, and the snuffling sounds made when Prudence the bulldog x boxer bitch who looks more like a pygmy hippo than a dog) is both nurturing and oddly comforting for me. It is certainly a novelty, because I am usually surrounded by people.

We are living in strange times. And the big question that I want answered is whether they have always been as strange as this? If so, is it only the ubiquity of information via the Internet that is actually making things seem weirder?

Look at this week for example. SNP leader Nicola Sturgeon has told David Cameron he is "not master of all he surveys" after her party forced a delay in a planned fox-hunting vote. Ministers shelved Wednesday's vote on relaxing hunting laws in England and Wales after the SNP said it would vote against the changes. The party had previously said it would not vote on issues affecting England and Wales only. Mr Cameron said the SNP's position was "entirely opportunistic". Downing Street said it was "disappointing" that the vote had to be postponed, and said new proposals on the Hunting Act would be introduced "in due course".

Even Cameron's own cabinet are not wholly behind him. At least two Cabinet Ministers and an estimated forty Tory MPs were preparing to vote against the repeal of the ban, and it seems that whatever happened the ban would have stayed in place. There is also widespread anger about possible plans to rewrite the Hunting Act so that hunting could be reinstated "through the back door", and if Cameron decides to follow this route then I have a sneaking feeling that once again he will have a monumental fight on his hands.

So why is he doing this? It has only been a matter of weeks since he surprised everyone by being re-elected with a majority amidst a torrent of old-Etonian jokes, and columnists hinting at ex-public schoolboys and their predeliction for what I believe Swinburne called 'The English Disease'. In that few weeks he has apparently been doing his best to alienate as much of the electorate as possible, and I truly wonder why.

I am not trying to turn this magazine into a political rag (as one reader accused me a year or so ago) and the main crux of this magazine is and always will be music, books and the like. But I have never known a political *cause célèbre* like the current crises surrounding hunting and to a lesser degree the general culture of austerity. At least not one that has attracted so many A-List music personalities to it. And furthermore, A-listers like Brian May who are not known for making political music. (That is, unless I am missing some rampant subtext within *Bohemian Rhapsody*).

May, who set up Team Fox to fight the repeal of the law, was cautious about celebrating victory. He told Express.co.uk: "It is a victory for Team Fox and all our supporters who have emailed and campaigned with us. This is an abject humiliation for the Government. After tampering with democracy and trying to dupe the public they have been caught out.

"This was hunting by any other name. We have won the battle and we are committed to the war. We stand strong and firm in our commitment and beliefs along with 80 per cent of the population. Fox hunting is cruel and needs to remain in the history books."

Paul McCartney issued a statement: "The people of Britain are behind this Tory government on many things but the vast majority of us will be against them if hunting is reintroduced. It is cruel and unnecessary and will lose them support from ordinary people and animal lovers like myself."

Morrissey wrote: "Often the excuse of 'culling' is tagged on to the argument of legalized killing of beings, yet as we all know, motorized vehicles manage the business of 'culling' foxes and badgers quite well without messengers of death on horseback. Wildlife (that is, freelife) has its own methods of balancing nature – foxes and owls and birds of prey tending to help themselves to whatever crosses their path.

The countryside, quite remarkably, does not need the Hunting Act to be repealed. You would need to be mindless to believe that it does. People who hunt are under delusions of possession and property and divine right, and their debasement of human standards is always evident in their outrage at ever being questioned about their activities. Meanwhile, the Hunt Saboteurs (who are always termed 'extremists' by the Daily Bra – as if opposing brutal killing is an extreme emotion) are themselves symbols of freedom. Hunt Saboteurs do not kill. High Court judges on horseback, dressed in blood-red outfits, are the ones who kill."

And continued: "I apologize very deeply for my support over the years for the group Roxy Music. I had no idea until very recently that their singer Bryan Ferret is also an avid hunter, and is now managed by his Lord of the Hunt son, Odious Ferry."

Right on Mozza.

Then there was an interesting piece in today's *Metro*:

Are the public more concerned with the well being of animals than they are those with disabilities? That's what this artist wants to know, is it because disabled people aren't cute enough to care about? She is pretty annoyed that people are more concerned that the Conservative government might be legalising fox hunting, rather than the cuts they've already served up to disabled people who depend on welfare.

To vent her frustration, she's created some artwork to express her feelings in a positive way. (Take note trolls). Sharing her work online, she captions the image: 'Great that so many people oppose fox hunting, would be nice to see the same outrage over treatment of the disabled and vulnerable in society.' Metro.co.uk got in touch with the artist – who wishes to remain anonymous – to find out exactly what motivated her to create the illustrations.

She told us: 'I think reintroducing fox hunting would be horrific and unnecessary. It does feel like they [the Tories] have brought this back now to detract from all the other stuff they're up to.'

One certainly does begin to wonder. And so conspiracy theories come away from the lunatic fringe and into the mainstream, cos you cannot get much more mainstream than the *Metro*. Like I said, we are living in strange times. Strange days indeed (most peculiar Mama).

REVIEW

CALLING ME HOME: GRAM PARSONS AND THE ROOTS OF COUNTRY ROCK
by Bob Kealing

As regular readers of my inky fingered scribblings here and elsewhere will know, I have been an avid reader of rock and roll biographies for over forty years, and that most weeks I review one in these hallowed pages. This week is no exception.

I have been a fan of Gram Parsons for well over a decade, ever since discovering in about 2001 that I liked country music a heck of a lot more than I had always said that I did (if that makes any sense). I have listened to as much of his officially released oeuvre (and, for that matter, his unreleased) as I have been able to get hold of, and I think that he rivals Scott Walker, Tom Waits and Elvis Presley for the title of my favourite male vocalist.

But until I read this book I had not realised what an insufferable prick he was.

This isn't the first book about Parsons that I have read. My lovely wife gave me a copy of *Twenty Thousand Roads: The Ballad of Gram Parsons and His Cosmic American Music* by David N. Meyer, and whilst it didn't pull any punches, it still managed to sanctify the boy with the voice of an angel. This book tells much the same story, but loses the glitz and gloss that Meyer, and I suspect other biographers had sprayed all over Parsons' rather unpleasant and tawdry life story. And what's more it does so without going into any ghoulish details about Parsons' sordid death, and doesn't even repeat the story of his junkie childhood friend Margaret Fisher trying to revive the dying Parsons by inserting ice cubes into his rectum.

No. In the most unsensational way possible, Bob Kealing tells the story of a spoiled rich boy who manipulated his way through life, making and breaking friendships as it suited him and pissing over even his most loyal friends with gay abandon, and getting away with it purely because of his not inconsiderable charm. In fact, reading between the lines of this well researched little book, it could well be argued that the only true friendships that he ever had were with Phil Kauffman and Emmylou Harris. And that the ultimate tragedy of the Parsons story is that he and Harris were falling in love with each other at the time of his death, and that had he survived that fateful trip to the *Joshua Tree Inn* then they would not only have got together, but as a result he might actually have achieved the sort of redemption that only occurs in the lyrics of the best country and western songs.

Another important point about this book, and something which I think makes it a far better book than *Twenty Thousand Roads*, if not as entertaining a read, is the almost sociological analysis he gives of the youth centre scene in the Florida of the late 1950s and early 1960s. Sometime last year I reviewed a fascinating DVD about Duane Allman and the early days of the *Allman Brothers Band* which was kindly sent to me by Rob Johnston from Chrome Dream, and between that DVD and this book a fascinating picture emerges of a rural social network which has very little comparisons in British history - the nearest possibly being the Merseybeat scene in Liverpool, although this was, of course, entirely rural. The most important revelation is perhaps the role that these networks played in breaking down racial barriers in the beleaguered south. the author really needs to be congratulated for such a thorough piece if research.

This is not to say the book is perfect. It could have done with a little more editing. For example it claims that Dr Sam Hutt is the stage name of some dude called Hank Wangford, and there is a paragraph about the musical scene in the early 1970s with "Beatles splinters" or something of the sort which actually makes no sense whatsoever. But I am nitpicking. These errors are as nothing to some of the boo boos I have made during my professional career.

Also, strangely this book has had the opposite effect on me to many rock biographies. On many occasions in these pages I have written that so and so's biography of someone has made me listen to albums that I would not otherwise have heard, and in the case of this book that simply isn't so. I had listened to everything I could by Gram Parsons well before I read this book, and as a result of reading *Twenty Thousand Roads* I had even devoured the music of people like *The Louvin Brothers* whom I would not have encountered without reading it.

But as a result of this book my playlist has hardly changed at all. (There is one exception, an album that I actually didn't know existed before, but I digress). The fact that I have read a whole series of anecdotes about Parsons which make uncomfortable, if not unpleasant, reading makes no difference at all to the fact that this nasty little man had the voice of an angel and made some of the greatest music that I have ever heard.

WHAT'S A FOOT?

Yesterday was a strange one even by my standards. I went to a routine chiropody appointment at Bideford and District Hospital, where I used to live over a third of a century ago when I was a young Nursing Assistant.

Everything went normally until they found a big dark mark on the sole of my left foot and discovered that I had an abscess that was ulcerating quite nastily. If they had not caught it and treated it in time then things could have got very unpleasant and I might even have had my foot amputated!

Just the news one needs on a Thursday afternoon.

But apart from that it has been a relatively ordinary week. Last week was my darling Corinna's birthday and despite my best efforts half of her presents singularly failed to arrive on time and dribbled in throughout this week, which is weird.

I have always liked Richard Thompson, but his new record 'Still' is the one that is closest to my taste for many years. The gently understated arrangements and old fashioned production with wide stereo separation make this an elegantly elegiac album, which actually sounds in part like The Beatles circa *Abbey Road* whilst still being unmistakably Thompson. Both his remarkable songwriting and guitar playing skills are showcased, with the chord patterns taking cheekily unexpected paths and switching playfully between major and minor keys and different genres at will. Bloody hell this man is a true guitar God. And the further he gets away from straight rock and roll the better he is. And the thing that distinguishes guitar masters like Thompson and Johnny Marr from the self indulgent widdley woo brigade who shred themselves round in circles like headless chickens trying to show off, is that real guitar heroes make it all seem so effortless.

NOT THE BEST GIG

Over the years during which I have been working as a rock and roll journalist lots of people have asked me to choose the best gig that I ever saw. That is impossible, but I can narrow it down to the best three (Ian Dury, Glastonbury 1985; Pink Floyd, Earls Court 1995, and Steve Harley and Cockney Rebel, Glasgow, 1991 with an honourable mention to The Who, Royal Albert Hall

2000), but this week I was contacted by a *Gonzo Weekly* reader who asked me something that I have not been asked before. He asked me what the *worst* gigs I had ever seen were, by an act that I had expected to be good.

I am glad that he included the caveat there, because this excludes things like school plays, crap bands in pubs, or support bands low down the bill on festival bills that consisted of three roadies and a stoned drongo on drums. I remember a band called *Glass Pierces Flesh* that I saw supporting a mate's band back in the day, and not only could none of them actually play their instruments but all their songs were about seven minutes of feedback and screaming. There was another band whose name I cannot remember after all these years whose act consisted of them ripping a pig's head (that had thankfully been removed from the pig by a local butcher) apart whilst the lead singer recited a list of prostitute's adverts from London telephone boxes against a wall of feedback. And I remember one band which supported my own ensemble once, whose stage act involved the lead singer having sex with a cream cake (don't ask).

But we can ignore all the above mentioned sonic atrocities and concentrate on bands that really *should* have - by all expectations - been good. And whilst, from a journalistic point of view, that might seem to be a straightforward proposition, like Oscar Wilde said "the truth is never pure and rarely simple" (or it might have been the other way around, and I cannot really be bothered to look it up).

However, although I am a journalist who does his best to adhere to the best traditions of Her Majesty's Press, I am also very much aware that I work for a record company, and edit a magazine which deals with a wide range of different musical artists and styles, and I would hate to find myself in the position that XXXXX artist signs to Gonzo and I find myself interviewing somebody that I have slagged off in print. But then again, none of the acts on the list are currently (or as far as I am aware have ever been) signed to Gonzo, although bizarrely one of them is actually featured this week, and another one has been featured (both in articles by Doug Harr) in the past.

But I am not saying that any of these three acts are always terrible live. Only that on the night that I saw them I found their performance attitude or whatever not to my taste.

But enough of the caveats. On with the article.

1. *Simple Minds* Exeter University, 1982

I had really been looking forward to this gig. I had bought the album *New Gold Dream* and danced enthusiastically to the two singles that been released from it. But Jesus they were terrible. the support band China Crisis were excellent, but after they finished their set....nothing. The main band were - if I remember rightly - an hour or so late, and when they finally came on they were taciturn, robotic and completely unengaging. And everyone I know who went to the gig agreed with me.

Now, in the interests of freedom of speech and all that jazz, I know people who went to see the band on the same tour and LOVED them. So, it seems that Exeter on a cold autumnal night was just a fluke. But that is one evening I will never get back again.

2. *Steeleye Span* (I think) Cropredy, (I also think) 1990

In the interests of what I believe is called Full Disclosure and Plausible Deniability, or at least I think that these are the expressions used whenever a self-styled whistleblower decides to release information appertaining to the one world government's UFO programme which is done in conjunction with some bunch of skinny looking alien dudes from Alpha Centauri, I have to admit that I was very drunk and probably very stoned at the time. The summers of 1989 and 1990 were the ones during which my not very good relationship with my employers at the Exeter Health Authority finally went monumentally tits up and my career as a nurse came to an end. I had two very nasty breakdowns on top of each other and self-medicated to a ludicrous extent.

So I cannot be sure exactly when and where I saw them. But I remember seeing *Steeleye Span*, a band who I have seen both before and since, and enjoyed massively, and thinking they were bloody awful. They were out of tune, out of synch with each other and gave every impression that they would have rather been anywhere else in the universe than playing for us on the night that they did. It goes down in the annals of my personal experience as one of the most dramatic feet of clay experiences of my life. sad but True.

3. *The Divine Comedy*, somewhere in Bristol, 1999.

Oh dear. I have a very soft spot for the work of Neil Hannon, and feel that he would be at his best in some louche supper club, with scantily clad chanteuses and the smell of opium in the air. or possibly as a sideshow at Hendon Regatta, whilst the audience ate strawberries and cream and wore straw boaters.

But whatever way one imagines seeing this charmingly erudite and classy ensemble, it is not on stage at a run of the mill rock venue, quite possibly attached to an institute of higher education, painfully loud and coming on with Neil Hannon drawling "'Ullo Bristol, are you ready to have a good time?" As if he was David St Hubbins and his band were *Spinal Tap*. The band played well enough, but they were a rock band, this was a rock concert, and it was at a rock audience in a rock venue, with the smell of cigarette smoke and pints of chemical lager served in plastic glasses. It would have worked perfectly well for *Whitesnake* but for *The Divine Comedy* it was a ridiculously bad error of judgement.

So there you have it. I still have records by all three bands, and listen to the second two at least reasonably regularly. But will I ever travel further than say Bideford (nine miles away) to see them? Unlikely.

I should probably give a dishonourable mention to *Twisted Sister* who Corinna and I saw supporting Alice Cooper about a decade ago. They were completely terrible, and Dee Snyder should win an award for the most uses of the word 'fuck' per sentence, but then again I never liked them anyway which takes them slightly out of the remit of this list which is bands who should have been good but weren't rather than a band that were never gonna be to my taste in a month of Sundays.

Now, at the risk of sounding like a post-psychedelic Esther Rantzen, what about you? What are the worst gigs from your memories of gig going? Yes you, the *Gonzo Weekly* readership. I am throwing the gauntlet out into readershipland....

Om Shanti

DOUG

Last Sunday Corinna and I drove to Barnstaple in time to meet the 7:10 train which - amongst a myriad of other people - contained our very own Doug Harr, who had come to spend a couple of days with us. As you will read in this issue, Doug was in the UK to see Camel and various other bands at the Ramblin' Man festival in Kent, but that is by the by. The *real* issue here is that Doug and I have known each other for two years, we have been working together closely for all of that time, and for someone who lived almost four decades in a world without an Internet, it seems absolutely extraordinary that we have developed such a close relationship, but that last Sunday was the first time that we had actually met in the flesh as it were.

We only actually spent one afternoon and two evenings together, but Doug confirmed in person what I had always suspected; that he was and is a jolly nice chap, and furthermore one that I am happy to have had stay with us. If I had known that his lovely wife Artina was back in California I would have had him stay here, but we have no spare room since Mama-in-law has taken up semi-permanent residence in what was once my library, and he would have to had fought the dogs off the sofa.

We took him on a brief whistlestop tour of rural North Devon. He was *au fait* with Kipling, although he had never read *Stalky and Co*, so we took him to Westward Ho! And showed him the block of houses (now, expensive apartments) of which the great man wrote:

> *Western wind and open surge*
> *Took us from our mothers,*
> *Flung us on a naked shore*
> *(Twelve bleak houses by the shore!*
> *Seven summers by the shore!)*
> *'Mid two hundred brothers.*

Then we took him to the Pebbleridge. I was appalled about twenty minutes ago when I went to Wikipedia to see if I could actually find some facts about this enormous bank of pebbles, at least 125,000 years old, which stretches for about three miles along the North Devon coastline. All I knew about it was what I remembered my Mother telling me when I was a boy, and remembered a schoolteacher telling us when - as part of a school mathematics project - we had to calculate the number of pebbles in the ridge. (I vaguely remember the number four billion, but after over forty years I don't remember, and truthfully don't care that much.)

However, imagine my horror to find that there was no article about the Pebbleridge, no article about Kipling's *alma mater* whereas there are dozens of articles about Pokemon, and more than a few about scatological sex acts. Truly this is a world which I understand less and less as time goes by.

128

So I told Doug what I remembered my Mother telling me about the Pebbleridge all those years ago, and Mama-in-law and I decided that discretion was the best part of valour and stayed in the car as Graham and Doug climbed up the Pebbleridge to have a gander at the grey Bristol Channel, whereupon the wind was so strong that Doug promptly slipped down the side of the ridge, luckily without hurting himself.

Then we did what Graham and I have done any time this past thirty years and with Doug and Mother in tow went down the pub where lager was consumed in some quantity and I introduced Doug to lager and lime, in the English style, rather than with a bottle of Corona and a wedge of green citrus fruit. A convivial time was had by all and we went home to where Corinna had prepared a gorgeous vegetarian meal whose name I can never spell.

So what is the moral of this story?

OK, Wikipedia is embarrassingly slewed towards the more bollocks end of popular culture, but I suspect that we all knew that already. I am sure that the Head Wiki-Pedos would claim that if I wanted to see articles about things that I consider to be of cultural importance, then I only have to write them myself, but after years of trying to do just that I have given up in that direction. The articles about my day job at the Centre for Fortean Zoology and CFZ Press have been eroded so much by various vicious edits, that I have lost interest in trying to fix them. And when I tried to repair a completely erroneous claim about me in my own page, it took two years and I was banned once.

But we know Wikipedia is almost fatally flawed even though many of us still use it far more than we admit that we should, and there is no point in discussing it here.

No, the important thing is how well Doug got on with a bunch of people that he had never met before, quickly becoming like one of the family, purely because of a bond formed by working together unpaid on this very magazine. There are people all over the world who read these pages, comment on them, and who have bonded together into a quasi-family that nearly three years ago when Rob Ayling first asked me to write a record company newsletter and I - for my sins - started to argue that I thought it would be much better if we published a magazine instead, I would never have dreamed of.

I have been wanting to produce a magazine like this ever since I was in my early twenties, but only now has the technology caught up with me. And all this time, I have always daydreamed about my conceptual magazine being the hub of an international group of friends and colleagues, but if I am truthful to myself, I never really thought that it would happen.

So peculiar hippy fairy tales do sometimes happen. And thanks for coming such a long way to visit us Doug.

Here endeth the lesson for today,

REVIEW

THE MISFIT ECONOMY: LESSONS IN CREATIVITY FROM PIRATES, HACKERS, GANGSTERS AND OTHER INFORMAL ENTREPRENEURS
by Alexa Clay and Kyra Maya Phillips

This book turned out to be completely unlike what I had been expecting. I had thought it was going to be how underground groups like Black Hat Hackers had formed their own neologistic economy on things like the Dark Net, but it wasn't anything at all like this.

It told the story of how one woman started a course of entrepreneurship for American prison inmates, many of whom - having had pre-existing successful businesses as drug dealers, for example (successful that is, until they got caught) - were already in the prime mental state to make a success of their new careers. However, it turned out that this particular woman's lust for glory was curtailed because of her lust for convicts.

It told the story of a group of moderately successful Somali Pirates and a group of people selling unpasteurised camel milk, as far as I can tell without any real scientific evidence to back it up, that it has extraordinary medical and curative powers.

It told the stories of people in China who made a great deal of money by producing bootleg versions of other people's clothes, electronic goods, and in one extraordinary section, buildings and even an entire city, basing their whole raison d'être on copyright theft.

This is a very peculiar book, because it brings out all sorts of totally mixed emotions in your truly. part of me just gets angry at the continued celebration of Capitalism and Consumerism which in my humble opinion are to of the things which are doing the worst damage to society. However, I find the ingenuity of some of the people described both admirable and fascinating.

I was very impressed by the story of the entrepreneurs who predated the Fair Trade movement. Tyler Gage, for example, who spent a long time working and living with indigenous peoples in Ecuador, and - horrified by the depredations that conventional economics were wreaking upon the rainforest - started a cooperative business to import a beverage made from a forest tree into urban America where it became a qualified success, bringing a new prosperity to the area and slowing if not stopping the depredations of the logging industry.

Stories like this are fascinating, as are the descriptions of new types of Industrial Democracy where workers band together to start new forms and modes of business. But the chapters which conclude that Pirates, Gangsters and Drug Dealers are actually good and self actualised capitalists tell me nothing that I have not always suspected.

I am not stupid or naive enough to think that human beings should survive without money. That would be completely unrealistic, and I cannot actually envisage how such a process would take place unless we all became part of a Huxleyan New World Order. But our species is not going to survive for as long as the individual lust for money and 'things' is what consumes us. In short, for as long as we are nothing but consumers in a Gadarene rush towards an undefined precipice over which lies a Malthusian nightmare.

The positive and uplifting thing about this book is that it does put forward a few scenarios whereby this horrific future may be avoided. The terrifying thing about this book as it portrays a future society run by people with the mindset of pirates, gangsters and drug dealers. Hold on, isn't that what we have already?

BACHELOR BOY AND THE WRONG FISH

Basically, my lovely wife Corinna who is the reason that I get out of bed in the mornings, has been away since Tuesday, visiting my eldest stepdaughter Shoshannah up in the Midlands. Now, I am not one of those pathetic men who cannot function without their wives. For example, one previous inamorata of mine was an only child precisely because her father had sulked so much when her mother had gone into hospital to give birth that he refused to ever go through the stress and privations of wifelessness again. Well, I always thought that was completely pathetic and was just another reason (of many) for me to dislike the spineless little oaf, but I will be the first to admit that I do not enjoy being in a wifeless condition.

This is partly because there are various creatures who are imprinted on her, the noisiest of which is a large crow which lives in the kitchen and makes loud and unpleasant forlorn noises whenever she is away. But there is also a small kitten and an extremely flatulent dog who also miss her nearly as much as the crow, and wander about the house in a miserable manner squeaking and farting as they go.

But Graham (my partner in crime for the past quarter century), and my elderly mother-in-law and I muddle along quite happily together, and sit around eating takeaways and drinking wine and watching *Star Trek* dvds and generally living a respectable bachelor existence, or at least a far more respectable existence than I did back in the days when I was a bachelor. However, that is another story altogether.

For Corinna is not just my wife she is my helpmeet and we do all sorts of the stuff that we do together. And that stuff includes working on this peculiar little magazine, which - as I so often write - I started for fun, and which I never imagined would end up taking over my life the way that it has. So, to cut a long story short, until about eight this evening I was not only in a condition of wifelessness, but had no-one to physically put the magazine together with, because although I collaborate closely with Doug Harr it is perforce done using the magickal interface that is Facebook Messenger.

I had a very peculiar thought earlier this evening when I realised that one of my minor ambitions within the world of music can now never be realised. Yes, the recent death of *Yes* bassist and co-founder Chris Squire means that I can now never josh him about the unscientific presentation of one of his songs. The *Fragile* album from 1970 was split into two halves.

Fragile is formed of nine tracks; four are "group arranged and performed" with the remaining five being "the individual ideas, personally arranged and organised" by the five members. Squire reasoned this approach was necessary in part to save time and reduce studio costs, as money was used to purchase keyboard equipment for Wakeman. According to Bruford: "There was this endless discussion about how the band could be used ... I felt we could use all five musicians differently ... So I said - brightly - 'Why don't we do some individual things, whereby we all use the group for our own musical fantasy? I'll be the director, conductor, and maestro for the day, then you do your track, and so on.'" Wakeman commented on the album's structure. "Some critics thought this was just being flash. The thinking behind this was that we realised there would be a lot of new listeners coming to the band. They could find out where each individual player's contribution lay."

Squire's solo track was called "The Fish (*Schindleria Praematurus*)". Michael Tait, the band's lighting advisor recalled Anderson called him "at ten o'clock one night from Advision and said, 'I want the name of prehistoric fish in eight syllables. Call me back in half an hour'". Tait subsequently found *Schindleria praematurus*, a species of marine fish, in a copy of *Guinness Book of Records*. Howe performs his solo guitar piece "Mood for a Day" on a Conde flamenco guitar. "Heart of the Sunrise" is a track where Wakeman's classically trained background came into play; he introduced the band to the idea of recapitulation where previous segments in music are revisited.

This story has been repeated many times over the years. I just pinched the gist of it from Wikipedia, changing only a few words here and there, but the interesting thing is that people have copied Tait's testimony over again, even assuming that the placoderm prehistoric fish on the cover for *Tales from Topographic Oceans* was this species. Well, it ain't. Four of the fish are like an unholy cross between a perch and a salmon, and the one at the bottom is indeed a placoderm. But it is not *Schindleria.*

Placodermi (from the Greek πλάξ = plate and δέρμα = skin, literally "plate-skinned") is an extinct class of armoured prehistoric fish, known from fossils, which lived from the Silurian to the end of the Devonian Period. Their head and thorax were covered by articulated armoured plates and the rest of the body was scaled or naked, depending on the species. Placoderms were among the first jawed fish; their jaws likely evolved from the first of their gill arches.

For years I, too, assumed that *Schindleria praematurus* if it indeed existed was a placoderm, as I took Tat's testimony at face value. But it isn't. It isn't even an extinct fish from deep in the aeons of prehistory.

Schindleria is a genus of marine fish. It is the only genus of family Schindleriidae, among the Gobioidei of order Perciformes. The type species is *S. praematura*, Schindler's fish. The Schindleria species are known generically as Schindler's fishes after German zoologist Otto Schindler (1906–1959), or infantfishes. They are native to the southern Pacific Ocean, from the South China Sea to the Great Barrier Reef off eastern Australia.

The infantfishes are so called because they retain many of their larval characteristics (an example of neoteny). Their elongated bodies are transparent, and many of the bones never develop. *S. praematura* reaches a length of 2.5 cm (1.0 in). All of the Schindleria species are reef fishes. They may be among the most common fish of the reefs, based on the results of plankton tows, but because of their transparency and small size, they are infrequently seen in life. A recently described species, the stout infantfish, *S. brevipinguis*, (pictured above) was briefly the world's smallest known vertebrate at 8 mm (about one-third inch), smaller even than the dwarf gobies, until the new record was set by the 7.9-mm *Paedocypris progenetica* in early 2006 and supplanted by the 7.7-mm frog *Paedophryne amauensis* in 2012.

I have even kept a species of infantfish which I caught as a child on a small coral reef on the southern shores of Po Toi island, Hong Kong. But why was it in the *Guiness Book of Records*? After all, even though brevipinguis was briefly considered the world's smallest fish it was not even discovered until a decade after *Tales from Topographic Oceans* had been released. So that remains a mystery.

But what was it about the song that I truly would have taken issue with Chris Squire about if we had ever spoken? Quite simply the nomenclatural illiteracy if the title "The Fish *(Schindleria Praematurus)*". The specific part of any binomial nomenclature is not capitalised unless it refers to someone's proper name which praematurus doesn't as any fule kno. And it should have been *italicised.*

Shame on forty one years of sleeve designers and editors for not picking that up! And sadly I couldn't find a picture of *Schindleria praematurus* for you to see. Every time I entered the words into a search engine all I got was pictures of a bloke with a bass guitar.

Pah!

REVIEW

NEMO: River of ghosts
by Alan Moore

I didn't need Pop Will Eat Itself to tell me that Alan Moore does indeed know the score. Back in the dog days of 1988 when I was going spectacularly insane as my career as a nurse was going slowly and inexorably down the pan, I was on night duty, and on the recommendation of my friend Jane Bradley, sadly dead these twenty years after being hit by a car on the M5 as she drunkenly tried to cross the road, I bought a copy of a book called *Watchmen* co-authored by this dude Alan Moore. And it was one of the great epiphanetic (if that is a word, which my spellchecker says that it isn't) books of my life. because it was the first time that I realised that comic books could be great literature.

It wasn't actually the first time that I had encountered Alan Moore. Back when I was a student, and devoured comic books, I had followed a story arc written by Moore for the sadly under-appreciated British comic *Captain Britain.* This was the legendary Jasper's Warp story which told how Captain Britain and his sidekick Jackdaw have various weird encounters, including fighting a monster made out of junk and a group of insane Alice in Wonderland-themed villains called The Crazy Gang and the mysterious Saturnyne and her henchmen, the Avant Guard.

During the course of his adventures he discovers he is on an alternate Earth called Earth-238 which is under the control of Sir Jim Jaspers, the leader of The Crazy Gang and a powerful mutant with the ability to warp and change reality. Captain Britain discovers that Jaspers was a British MP who had been in charge of regulating and eventually eliminating the superheroes of Earth-238.

To carry out this massacre of this world's superheroes, Jaspers had created The

Fury (whose name is another reference to Alice in Wonderland), an incredibly powerful creature able to destroy any super powered person with the exception of Jaspers himself.

Jaspers had become insane, a side-effect of his reality warping powers, and altered this Earth to fit his own insane ideas, hence why Captain Britain had not recognised this world. After seeing The Fury kill Jackdaw and Saturnyne flee this Earth, Captain Britain is confronted by Jaspers and is killed by The Fury.

And that is just how it starts. This was back in 1982, and the paranoid CRASS obsessed 23 year old Jon Downes found the idea of an insane time shifting Tory MP just to his taste. But I digress even worse than usual. To cut a long story short ever since then I have read everything I can by Alan Moore, and what a long strange trip its been.

The *League of Extraordinary Gentlemen*, (the books not the execrable film) tells how the year is 1898, and Mina Murray is recruited by Campion Bond on behalf of British Intelligence and asked to assemble a league of other extraordinary individuals to protect the interests of the Empire: Captain Nemo, Allan Quatermain, Dr. Jekyll and Hawley Griffin, the Invisible Man.

They help stop a gang-war between Fu Manchu and Professor Moriarty, nemesis of Sherlock Holmes. Following this they are involved in the events of H. G. Wells's The War of the Worlds. Two members of the League (Mina Murray and Allan Quatermain) achieve immortality, and are next seen in an adventure in 1958, which follows events that take place after the fall of the Big Brother government from Nineteen Eighty Four.

Following this Mina and Allan team up with fellow immortal Orlando and are shown in an adventure which spans a century, from 1910 to 2009, concerning a plot by evil magicians to create a Moonchild that might well turn out to be the Antichrist. During this adventure Captain Nemo's daughter, Janni Dakkar, is introduced, and some of her adventures are chronicled subsequently.

This current book is the third and final of the *Nemo* trilogy and follows on from *The Roses of Berlin*, which I enjoyed immensely.

However, unlike most reviewers I found this the weakest, and most insubstantial, of the series. Captain Nemo's elderly and senile daughter Janni who was first seen as a fifteen year old swimming naked diving for pearls in the incredibly erudite *Century Volume One* which presented a gloriously arcane alternate version of

Berthold Brecht's *Beggar's Opera* takes her intrepid crew up the Amazon to find an enclave of Renegade Nazis, and a reality where the plots of *The Boys from Brazil*, Charlie Chaplin's *The Great Dictator*, and *She who must be obeyed* are thrown into a blender and served up in one gloriously psychotic multicoloured cocktail.

I am not saying that it is a bad book. Far from it. And, I truly think that Moore and O'Neill are incapable of putting out a BAD book, but it is nowhere near as good as they are capable of.

At their best they are cerebral, erudite, anarchic, childish and incredibly entertaining. *League of Gentlemen: The Black Dossier* for example is up with *Watchmen* and *From Hell* as being not only amongst the best books that either man has written but up there amongst the best graphic novels ever created.

Sadly, none of the *Nemo* series hit those heights, and this is probably the weakest of the three. However it would be churlish if I didn't admit that it gave me a very entertaining ninety minutes for seven quid, and there is very little that you can say that about these days.

EQUAL TO THE LOVE YOU MAKE

And in the end, the love you take blah blah blah.

I never did understand what McCartney's coda to the last proper song on *Abbey Road* actually meant. I have a sneaking suspicion that like so many of McCartney's songs it actually didn't mean very much. Poor Sir Paul. because he was in a band with someone who really COULD write nonsense down and get away with it he thought that he could get away with writing bollocks down just because he had the God-given gift of being able to write music that could make you cry.

My brother is a Church of England clergyman, and my father was a lay preacher, and so I wanted to follow in the family tradition and preach a sermon to end this week's issue of the magazine. And my chosen text was the final lines of *The End* by The Beatles. Until I looked at it and found like so many things in life, when you look at them too hard they end up not actually making much sense. The more you look at it, the more meaningless it is. McCartney said, "I wanted [the medley] to end with a little meaningful couplet, so I followed the Bard and wrote a couplet." In his 1980 interview with *Playboy*, John Lennon acknowledged McCartney's authorship by saying, "That's Paul again ... He had a line in it, 'And in the end, the love you get is equal to the love you give,' which is a very cosmic, philosophical line. Which again proves that if he wants to, he can think."

But Lennon misquoted the line; the actual words are, "And in the end, the love you take is equal to the love you make." What Lennon quoted actually is both cosmic and philosophical, where the words sung by McCartney are neither, although they do rhyme and scan better. Of course I know vaguely what he meant. It is the basic golden rule which is the basis for many world philosophies, what Dickens called "do as you would be done by", but it was seldom expressed as clunkily as it was by McCartney when he tried to provide an epitaph to the band that he was to publicly leave in April the next year.

And why am I writing about this now? It is basically that as Corinna writes her bits, I am sitting at my iPad in my favourite armchair, as Prudence farts and snores in the corner, trying two write a nice piece of valedictory prose for this issue and McCartney's line came into my head. Has it got any real significance to anything else in this magazine, or indeed to wrapping up this particular issue? Not really. But as Paul McCartney discovered back in 1969 when he was trying to pen a suitable valedictorian message not just to the *Abbey Road* album but to the career of The Beatles as a whole, sometimes things don't actually have to make any sense to be totally appropriate for the job.

Night night and God bless,
Om Shanti
Jon

CHUCKY AR SOMETHING

This weekend is the sixteenth annual Weird Weekend; a gathering of freethinkers and

Forteans that I first invented on a drunken evening towards the end of 1999, when me and Graham and our old friend Nigel were (and this is a totally true story, I promise) in a bar owned by one of the Aldershot Pub Bombers.

Now although I am not necessarily a pacifist, and can easily envisage a time when I would take arms in defence of my family and my beliefs, if not necessarily my country, I have been interested in Irish history for some years. I am in a peculiar position here; I was one of the last generation of children born and brought up within the British Empire, and I truly think that in most of its facets the British Empire was a force for good, and a lot better than most of the alternatives. However, I will be the first to admit that the way we treated our closest colony across the Irish Sea was often shameful.

So, there I was with Graham and my old mate Nigel Wright at a thinly disguised Sinn Fein benefit gig in North London, waiting for a rather nifty band called Athenrye to come on stage. I was working for a very short-lived Sunday newspaper called *The Planet on Sunday* and I had slightly mischievously chosen the latest live album by *Athenrye* as one of my records of the year. For some reason I think that I had expected the audience to be an Irish version of the people who go to see Leon Rosselson or someone singing songs from the General Strike, or other ditties about the Communist Party. But the audience were a bunch of crew-cutted young Irishmen, mostly suited and booted to kill, and I was scared shitless.

Although the band could not have been nicer to us, it was also somewhat distressing to find that we were the only English people in the audience. The night before Graham and I got happily and cheerfully drunk - oblivious to the fact that Nigel was getting ever more frightened and that the toughest and most sinister members of the audience paid no attention to the fact we knew all the words to the songs and were beginning to look (as Nigel said later), as if they were planning to forcibly remove us and probably our kneecaps.

Then it happened. The band were halfway through a particularly stirring number which exhorted the British Army to "go home", before they made them. The melodies stopped, and soon all there was in the crowded room, were 250 tough young men - some wearing black balaclavas and with suspicious-looking bulges in their coat pockets - dancing stationary, and bobbing up and down on to the martial drumbeat and the rhythmic bass guitar. The drums continued, and the crowd began to chant "I - R - IRA - below the British scum away", and then at that point Graham and I began to get nervous. And then the chanting stopped - as the drums and bass continued, Terry Manton the lead singer approached the microphone.

"You know that all British journalists are lying scum", he started, and my heart dropped. I looked around me nervously, hoping that although some of the crowd knew that I was English, that none of them knew that I was a journalist. Then Terry continued:

"But there are a few British journalists who have deep inside them beating hearts of bold Fenian men. There are three of them here in the audience tonight - Jonathan Downes, Graham Inglis and Nigel Wright. This song is dedicated to them and to the *Planet on Sunday* - it's called *S.A.M Missiles in the sky*"

I gave an audible gasp of relief, I looked at Graham and he was grinning back at me. When the song finished, Graham and I left the dancefloor and returned to our seats to find ourselves being treated like heroes by a group of very violent looking young men. They all bought drinks for us, and at least two convicted murderers shook us by the hand.

I found out later that my review of the album, together with a photograph of me and Graham surrounded by a group of men wearing balaclavas and presenting the closed fist salute of the Provisional IRA appeared on a number of republican websites and may well have appeared in *An Poblacht*.

Although it would be amusing to find out what of the elderly, and rather inept managing editor of the *Planet on Sunday* would have thought about having his eminently dull, but respectable newspaper cited as being recommended reading for the young terrorist, we soon realised that we had - by our naivety and stupidity - not only put ourselves in a potentially life-threatening situation, but had also laid ourselves open to some gravely serious repercussions from the British Government.

There was one - mildly curious and slightly Fortean - repercussion from this unfortunate incident. A UFO researcher called Barry King, had for some years, been circulating an irregular (and almost illiterate), newsletter which contained lists of UFO researchers whom he claimed the British Government had opened files on. In common with most people within the UFO community (at least those with any sense), I had always felt that Barry was an amiable but harmless fruitcake. In April 2000 - four months after our unfortunate run-in with the boys from the old brigade - my name appeared on that list for the first time. I am certain that there is nothing that I have ever written or investigated within the world of UFOs, which could possibly lay me open to any form of government investigation. However, it is almost certain that being a journalist on a national newspaper with known terrorist connections would mean that there would be a number of files on me. The fact that Barry King included my name on his list four months after my only overt involvement with terrorist politics indicates that perhaps he should be taken more seriously in future.

To be quite honest, my involvement with the Provisional IRA began and ended with being bought a drink by one of the Aldershot pub bombers. But something important and lasting did come out of that very weird weekend. Nigel and I had been the guests if various regional UFO and Paranormal groups over the year. We had just released our book *The Rising of the Moon* and had toured quite intensively to promote it. We had enjoyed the regional conferences and conventions (I am not quite sure of the difference even now) massively, and we decided that it was time we threw one of our own.

REVIEW

SAGA VOLUME 1
by Brian K Vaughan and Fiona Staples (Artist)

As I explained last week, when we looked at the slightly disappointing latest instalment of the *League of Extraordinary Gentlemen* series, I have been an avid reader of comic books most if my life, but after reading *Watchmen* in about 1988, I realised that they could be great art as well as great fun. Whether this series, which I am awesomely unhip in not having heard of until last week, is art or not remains to be seen, but it is certainly great fun.

This is, apparently a massively hip series. But being a fifty six year old hippie with an impressive display of chips on his shoulder, I don't think I ever was hip, except for a few months in 1980 when I had heard of *Joy Division* when nobody else had. And I am certainly not going to pretend that I had ever heard of *Saga* except totally by accident when I was looking for something else online. I would love to rewrite history and say that I was looking for the holiday company of the same name which caters to folk like me and the Mrs. who have achieved our half century, but it was actually a dull quest for stuff about Norse folklore, trying to find a suitable name for Corinna's pet raven, which turned out not to be a raven at all.

I guess that this is where I ought to let y'all know the premise of this series that I am praising so highly. To quote from those jolly nice fellows at Wikiwotsit:

"*Saga* is an epic space opera/fantasy comic book series written by Brian K. Vaughan and illustrated by Fiona Staples, published monthly by Image Comics. The series is heavily influenced by *Star Wars* and is based on ideas Vaughan conceived both as a child and as a parent. It depicts a husband and wife from long-warring extraterrestrial races, Alana and Marko, fleeing authorities from both sides of a galactic war as they struggle to care for their daughter, Hazel, who is born in the beginning of the series, who occasionally narrates the series as an unseen adult.

The comic was described in solicitations as "*Star Wars* meets *Game of Thrones*," and by critics as evocative of both science fiction and fantasy epics such as *The Lord of the Rings* and classic works like *Romeo & Juliet*. It is Vaughan's first creator-owned work to be published through Image Comics, and represents the *Saga* is an epic space opera/fantasy comic book series written by Brian K. Vaughan and illustrated by Fiona Staples, published monthly by Image Comics. The series is heavily influenced by *Star Wars* and is based on ideas Vaughan conceived both as a child and as a parent. It depicts a husband and wife from long-warring extraterrestrial races, Alana and Marko, fleeing authorities from both sides of a galactic war as they struggle to care for their daughter, Hazel, who is born in the beginning of the series, who occasionally narrates the series as an unseen adult.

The comic was described in solicitations as "*Star Wars* meets *Game of Thrones*," and by critics as evocative of both science fiction and fantasy epics such as *The Lord of the Rings* and classic works like *Romeo & Juliet*. It is Vaughan's first creator-owned work to be published through Image Comics, and represents the first time he employs narration in his comics writing first time he employs narration in his comics writing."

The interesting thing about this comic is not actually the plot, entertaining though it is. It is the characterisation, and the situation - unusual in this genre - where all the major protagonists have aspects to their characters that are broadly sympathetic. And it is the nuances and subplots that are admirable here. I have only read the first volume so far, and although I have ordered the next two or three, only Volume Three has arrived so far and I - surprisingly - have enough self control not to read them out of turn.

The art is also above average, and neither skimps or dwells on the nastier aspects of the story. Izabel is the ghost of a teenage girl from the planet Cleave who was killed by a landmine. She manifests as a reddish torso with her intestines hanging out from under the hem of her T-shirt.

The comic also addresses some uncomfortable subjects. Sophie, a rescued child prostitute, for example. Vaughan has stated that Sophie, whose first appearance Staples initially refused to draw, was created to illustrate the horrific effects of war, and as a critique of the sexualized portrayal of Princess Leia as Jabba the Hutt's slave in the film Star Wars: Return of the Jedi, explaining, "That's that character at her least sexy. There are slave girls in the world and they don't look like Princess Leia in a bikini."

I will be interested to see how this series pans out. At the moment it looks very promising indeed. Watch this space.

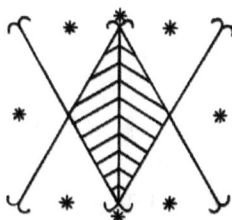

REVIEW

HACKER, HOAXER, WHISTLEBLOWER, SPY: THE MANY FACES OF ANONYMOUS
By Gabriella Coleman

I have always been interested in civil disobedience on the Internet. This goes back to the late 1990s when, after having read a particularly salacious article about a teenage hangout called *Habbo Hotel*, I went in, and almost immediately was greeted by a bunch of grey coloured characters all called Geno, with a string of numerals after each name. They were wandering about, muttering nonsense about the light being grey, and gave all the appearance of being members of some peculiar cult. I was intrigued and spent some time watching them, before I realised that these people were actually doing their best to be as collectively annoying as possible; subverting Ghandi's idea of non-violent protest into something both irritating and hilariously funny. I kept an eye on the cult of Geno for a year or so until they went the way of all flesh, and certainly all internet memes, and disappeared.

It was nearly ten years before I heard of Anonymous. There was an irritating bloke who used to work for me, whom I disliked intensely. However, he introduced me to *Encyclopaedia Dramatica*, which in turn introduced me to *4Chan*. I hung around there occasionally, as, indeed, I have occasionally ever since and found the anarchic humour interspersed with psychosocial violence and pictures of naked young women a bit too rich a mixture for my liking, although - in my defence - I am about three times as old as the average *4Chan* reader. The board /b/ was often described as the asshole of the Internet, but it was from here that the phenomenon of Anonymous first emerged. I watched its emergence with mild interest, but it was only with the massively amusing campaign against the Church of Scientology that I began to take any real interest.

I have been interested in the concept of cyber insurgency for a long time, and so, in recent months, I have read a lot about Anonymous, LulzSec, and other online insurgency groups. This book is unique in that it is written by an anthropologist, and furthermore the anthropologist widely considered as the world's expert on Anonymous. She is described as:

"Enid Gabriella Coleman (usually known as Gabriella Coleman or 'Biella') is an anthropologist, academic and author whose work focuses on hacker culture and online activism, particularly Anonymous. She currently holds the Wolfe Chair in Scientific & Technological Literacy at McGill University, Montreal, Quebec, Canada. Nathan Schneider writing in the Chronicle of Higher Education named her "the world's foremost scholar on Anonymous".

After completing her high school at St. John's School in San Juan, Puerto Rico, Coleman graduated with a Bachelor of Arts in religious studies from Columbia University in May 1996.[She moved to the University of Chicago where she completed a Master of Arts in socio-cultural anthropology in August 1999. She was awarded her Ph.D in socio-cultural anthropology for her dissertation *The social construction of freedom in free and open source software: Hackers, ethics, and the liberal tradition.* in 2005."

This is not the most entertaining book on the subject. In my humble opinion that honour goes to Parmy Olson's book *We are Anonymous* that I reviewed in these pages a few weeks ago. But it is certainly the most erudite. Back in the day, I read Julian Dibble's book *My Tiny Life* and I wrote a lengthy (5000 word) piece for a long defunct magazine called *Parascience* on what I called 'cybersociology'. That was back in 1998 or 1999, and the ubiquity of online social networking has changed immeasurably since then, and the work that Biella Coleman and others do on the emerging cultural anthropology of these groups is fascinating.

Olson wrote about her ambivalence about the moral compass of Anonymous:

"In some cases, yes, I think it has in terms of some of the stuff they did in the Middle East supporting the pro-democracy demonstrators. But a lot of bad things too, unnecessarily harassing people -- I would class that as a bad thing. DDOSing the CIA website, stealing customer data and posting it online just for shits and giggles is not a good thing."

It is hard not to agree, although I am afraid that I have a sneaking suspicion that had some of the events of the Arab Spring NOT taken place, the current horrors in the Middle East, with burnings, beheadings and crucifixions becoming commonplace for the first time in centuries, might not have come to pass. Whereas Olson, at least in writing, identified with the main protagonists of LulzSec, and spun an adventure yarn worthy of Frederick Forsyth, Biella Coleman is far more objective, not to say ambivalent about the people she portrays. She gives a thorough overview of both people and events, and goes a long way towards explaining why and how the hell these people do what they do.

The most important thing that comes out of this book, however, is that although it is undeniable that some Anonymous have done nasty things to people who may or may not have deserved it, all the major arrests and persecutions of Anonymous and other hacktivists have been for doing good things. Biella quotes one such convicted hacktivist as complaining that when government agencies have used destructive DDoS attacks against him and his comrades there was no comeback, whereas he was convicted and imprisoned for doing exactly the same thing.

With the possible exception of the Middle East insurgency programmes, and my comments upon those are basically just my innate paranoia speaking, the hacktivist campaigns covered in this book have done nothing but good. Which has to lead us to the question: Why have they been so severely persecuted by the powers that be?

Gabriella Coleman should be congratulated for having produced such a thorough and intellectually weighty tome, which for the first time, does real justice to its complex, and much misunderstood, subject.

BOYS FROM THE COUNTY HELL

Just when you thought that it was safe to go back in the water.

As many if you will know, I was badly screwed over by some so-called friends who were tenants of mine in the house that I own in Exeter. As a result, I was told by those jolly nice people in Exeter City Council that I was unable to rent it out until I had a lot of work done to it. Work that I am afraid that I cannot afford. In the interim my tenants moved out and left the place looking like a pigsty.

So, ever since the end of last July I have had to leave the property empty, having little bits and bobs of work done as I can afford to do so. I am now five hundred quid a month worse off, and have been struggling.

This morning I received a bill for Council Tax for the property ever since it became empty. Not only do I have to pay out over eighty quid a month, but I have a bill for arrears of over six hundred quid. This is truly not fair.

However, it appears that there is nothing that I can do about it. I am not posting this just in order to bellyache about it all, but so anyone who finds themselves in the same position as I do can be warned that the *Boys from the County Hall* will be screwing you in every way that they can.

STAIRWAY TO...

Last week one of the presents that I had for my 56th birthday was the latest album by Robert Plant. It was one of the few new records that I wanted to check out that wasn't available streamed, so like the latest Bob Dylan album earlier in the year I was forced to get a hard copy, and because I am more than averagely skint since the disaster with my buggered hard drive earlier this year, I was forced to do what I did as a teenager, and wait until my birthday came around in order to listen to it.

Then, the universe being run according to Sod's Law, on my birthday we had a house guest with a sleeping disorder, so I wasn't able to listen to it at the volume which I thought that it deserved, so I had to wait until Tuesday. Then, on Tuesday I found there was a problem with the hifi and that it would only play through one channel.

The next day, Graham had a quick look at the aforementioned hifi and found that a wire had come loose, probably because of the predations of Squeaky Biscuit the kitten, who is living proof that one should never name kittens after one of the Manson Family, and within a few minutes of him fiddling around, the hifi was working fine.

So that evening, together with some brandy that I had been given to celebrate the anniversary of my arrival on the planet, and a bottle of Diet Coke from the Village Shop, I sat down to listen to it some eleven months after it was released, I sat down and listened to *Lullaby and the Ceaseless Roar* and I tell you what, it was well worth the wait.

Yes, it's a bloody good album, but that is not really the point of what I want to write about this evening. Well, it is, and it isn't. The album is a gorgeous mix of western rock, African textures, and hiphop rhythms, with the odd *je ne sais quoi* that he got from his tenure within country music that is almost impossible for me to pin down.

As I sat back and revelled in the textured sound of the multinational band, playing intelligent and sophisticated music and at the top of their game, I realised again why Robert Plant no longer wants to play with *Led Zeppelin* and why he is quite right to do so.

"You're going back to the same old shit," he says.

"A tour would have been an absolute menagerie of vested interests and the very essence of everything that's shitty about big-time stadium rock. We were surrounded by a circus of people that would have had our souls on the fire. I'm not part of a jukebox!"

And when a reporter from *Rolling Stone* pointed out that most of his peers were happy to do just that, Plant commented vituperatively:

"Good luck to them, I hope they're having a real riveting and wonderful late middle age. Somehow I don't think they are."

It is hard to imagine the Robert Plant of today going back again to the place where he was when, at the age of 32, *Led Zeppelin* quietly disbanded in the aftermath of John Bonham's death.

Bizarrely it was all about the timing. The series of tragedies which had rocked his life in the mid-1970s had already caused him to turn his back on the excesses of the rock and roll oeuvre. The previous year the low key *In through the Out Door* album, which many people do their best to ignore, hinted at an interesting new direction for the band, and furthermore, one in which squeezing lemons until the juice ran down one's leg, and giving un-named nubiles every inch of his love, were less obviously on the agenda.

The band had always been musically highly sophisticated and it is interesting to wonder upon the directions that they might have taken had Bonzo not choked to death that fateful night. Page and Plant have done various things together over the years, and I do hope that Page takes up Plant's offer to do something acoustic with his old singer in the future. But unfortunately I think that it is increasingly unlikely that they would do so, and even if they did it would NOT be Led Zeppelin, nor should it be.

Of the three surviving members of the band, Plant is the only one who has had a truly satisfying solo career, and it is one which - bizarrely - gets more satisfying with each successive album giving the lie to the oft quoted adage that rock and roll is a young man's game. And I truly wonder if the album he released in September 2014 in a parallel universe as one quarter of Led Zeppelin would truly have been any more satisfying?

We shall never know.

Om Shanti.

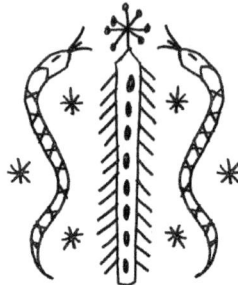

REVIEW

RINGO: WITH A LITTLE HELP
by Michael Starr

As regular readers of this magazine, and particularly the book reviews, will know,

I have been collecting books about the Beatles since the mid 1970's and have even written a volume on the subject myself. It never ceases to amaze me how many new volumes are published each year, and that most of them contain information of which I, as a devotee, have been previously unaware the band were only a functioning unit for about 10 years, and were only famous for 7 of those. How can 7 short years have inspired so many thousand books and so many million words?

But now get this. This next thing is really weird. In all my years of reading books about the band, the book that I am reviewing here this week, is - I think - the first time that I have ever read a book dedicated purely to their drummer.

As many of you will know in my other life I am a zoologist, more accurately a cryptozoologist. Over the year I have amassed a vast collection of books on the subject and allied subjects these include a number of books by a man called Ivan T Sanderson (January 30, 1911 – February 19, 1973). He was a biologist and writer born in Edinburgh, Scotland, who became a naturalized citizen of the United States. Sanderson is remembered for his nature writing and his interest in cryptozoology and paranormal subjects. He also wrote fiction under the name Terence Roberts.

In 1956 he wrote a book called 'follow the whale' which has been widely sited within the cryptozoological community for its mentions of Sanderson's belief in the possibility primitive ancestors of whales may have survived into modern times.

He wrote: "Perhaps there are Acrodelphids still cruising the oceans; Zeuglodonts browsing in lakes, lochs and fjords, the ancestors of these in tropical rivers, and even some 'First Ancestors' [Archaeoceti] on their banks."

However, sadly for the cryptozoological community, this was about the only reference to their favourite discipline in the book but, there is another, and far more important, object lesson to be learned within its pages.

The book is a history of the whaling industry, among other things, and each section is based around one of the historically important centres of said industry. Now, this is where it gets interesting. Those of us in the western world were brought up with a map of the world centred on western Europe. This is largely because during the great ages of exploration it is the voyages of western European explorers that are seen as important.

But that is neither true nor fair. The voyages of exploration carried out by ancient Arabs and Chinese are at least as important, and certainly as impressive. And they pale into insignificance besides the remarkable Diaspora of the peoples of the Pacific. But the maps were made by Englishman, Frenchman, and a Dutchmen and so years after the European empires had faded from the world of view, maps of the world still are centred upon Western Europe. Sanderson, however, prefaced each section of his book with a world map centred upon the place he was writing about, and – at first – the resulting map is almost unrecognisable.

So it is with this book. When the other three Beatles, who usually grab the limelight, are reduced to mere bit-part players, the story of the band is completely different. I had never thought about the pressure on Ringo as a musician, for example, when – as the band's music got more complex, and technically demanding – the drumming remained much the same. Jon and Paul could experiment with backwards tapes, orchestras, and strange electronic effects, whilst George could fanny about playing the sitar and becoming a Hindu to their hearts' content, poor Ringo laid down his 'four to the floor' rhythm in the straightforward manner that he had always done. He then had to sit around for months whilst his bandmates pursued their own arcane directions. No wonder the poor bastard was the first to quit the band (although he was tempted back a few weeks later).

This book is full of fascinating vignettes that I simply hadn't heard of before, and I am happy to say that they are presented in an eminently readable and literate style. I enjoyed this book massively, and look forward to reading anything by this author that may find itself upon my ever more voluminous and ever-growing reviews pile.

Ringo's life would actually have been pretty extraordinary even if he hadn't been the most famous drummer in the world. The fact that he survived a succession of near-fatal childhood diseases and emerged unscathed apart from a taste for the sauce and a predilection for bad puns is extraordinary enough. I think it is testament both to his own strength of character, and his extraordinary supportive family that he survived at all.

And this book introduces, almost for the first time into the cultural pantheon of the characters crawling about the pages of one's Beatles library, some extraordinary characters, not the least being Ringo's own biological father in a clear and dramatic contrast to John Lennon's dad. Mr Starkey senior always behaved like a perfect gentleman after his divorce from Ringo's mother, and never tried to take advantage of his son's unparalleled fame and fortune. If

Lennon's father had done likewise, then possibly the history of the four most famous pop musicians that the world has ever seen, might have panned out very differently.

FOREVER AUTUMN

There is something particularly horrible about the way all sorts of people from all parts of the political spectrum have seized upon a photograph of a drowned child and used it to make whatever political capital their own inclinations demand. If it wasn't so horrible it would be amusing in a particularly ironic sort of way.

As we blunder into the season of mists and mellow fruitfulness, the big guns are beginning to release their records. David Gilmour is hardly the most prolific of artists, for example. This new record is only his fourth solo album in thirty seven years, and has - apparently - been nearly two decades in the making, with at least one song dating back eighteen years to when it was written with his wife Polly Samson.

He says:

"This one [Rattle That Lock] has been going on for a while. The Endless River interrupted the making of this album. This album has been slowly snowballing, gathering speed and momentum as it goes along from a very slow, leisurely pace seven, eight years ago to now, when it's been like an avalanche, really."

It is not out for another week or so, and little magazines like this one (OK we get 1,500+ readers each issue, but we are hardly a threat to Q or Mojo) are not in a big enough league to be sent review copies of such stellar releases, so although we are all looking forward to it, we shall have to wait a while longer before we write about it.

The big release that we have heard for the first time this week is *What the World Needs Now* by Public Image Limited which is a total stonker, oozing scabrous rage and sly humour in equal proportions. It is another self-funded record on their own label, and for some reason I find the fact that both this and its predecessor a few years ago were recorded at Steve Winwood's studio monumentally amusing. I am quite perturbed by the reviews that I have read which seem to treat it as the natural follow up to *This is PiL* which was undoubtedly the well crafted proggy, dancy, Shamanic head trip that they all describe. But this record - the most enjoyably bilious that Lydon has ever produced outside the *Sex Pistols* - is by no means just part two of the previous record like some of the reviewers have implied.

Caroline Sullivan in *The Guardian*, for example, writes:

"it's noticeably similar to 2012's *This Is PiL* – and for a truly engaged evisceration of the establishment, you'd currently do better with Sleaford Mods."

I truly wonder whether we were listening to the same record! This is the most Tourettesy (if that is a word, which I strongly suspect that it isn't) that Lydon has been since he sang *Bodies* back in the year that two sevens clashed. And it is the funniest. *This is PiL* was a remarkable record in which he and the band set out their stall as accomplished elder statesman of a movement that they themselves invented. *What the World needs Now* is the sound of Lydon reminding us all that he is still rotten at heart, and that the world needs him now more than ever. "What the world needs now is another fuck off" indeed.

However, back to the records which are released by such big league players that little league magazines like this one are unlikely to get a look in.

Keith Richards also has only released a handful of solo records, but of the four bits that I have heard so far of this new record, one *Robbed Blind* sounds the most warmly human and approachable that he has ever been. OK this is the human riff, a scary dude, and do we want him to sound human and approachable? Yes, I think we probably do. Four tracks have been streamed on Spotify and I am happily listening to them as I write. Sadly, however, the other three sound just like you know who, without ol' rubber lips on vocals, and the hopes that he was finally going to release a solo album which lives up to the promise shown by those legendary bootlegged sessions from Toronto in the late 1970s, when he covered Merle Haggard songs and other slices of bona fide Outlaw Country recede like the early morning mist.

I have always preferred the country side of The Rolling Stones to the riffy crotch-thrusting aspect, and it would be wonderful to have Keef make a whole album of this sort of material. just check out his duet with Marianne Faithful on *Sing me Back Home* if you don't know what I mean.

A new album by *New Order*, most tellingly their first without Peter Hook is also imminent but I am getting bored of writing that we are not important enough to get review copies of such things, although - I have to say - that I haven't asked for any of the records listed in this editorial. Life is too short, and I will get hold of copies soon enough.

One thing that is weird, however, is the new Prince album HITNRUN, his second with 3RDEYEGIRL. It came out last week, but at the moment is only available via a streaming service that I have never heard of, and which one cannot get for free. I am not one of these people who objects to paying for music. I pay the maximum streaming fee for Spotify, and I would have happily signed up for this new bunch if I could have figured out how the bloody hell to do so. I don't mind paying out an extra tenner a month to these jokers, but the instructions made no sense whatsoever, and I got punted from pillar to post across Facebook, until I just gave up.

So there is more than a little about which we should all be reasonably pleased this autumn in the music business. But what is really weird is that I was intending to finish this editorial off with a look at what was going to be released during the last quarter of the year, and when I looked at the 2015 Albums page on Wikipedia I was surprised to find out that although there is a whole slew of records that interest me coming out now give or take a week or two, during the final quarter of the year there is practically nothing to which I am looking forward. OK there is a new album by Joanna Newsom, and much though I admire her peculiar artistic resolve, someone once described her as sounding like an injured lizard on helium, and it is hard not to agree with them.

Ho hum!

REVIEW

TIME AND TIME AGAIN
by Ben Elton

A year or so ago, when the phrase "guilty pleasures" was one of those irritating social memes which turned up everywhere, a bit like those bloody 'Keep Calm and Carry On' slogans, which were funny the first time that you saw one, and basically get more and more irritating the more you see, someone included in their 'Guilty Pleasures' the novels of Ben Elton. Why he felt that he had to pretend to feel guilty about reading them I don't know, because I have always found them massively entertaining, and have read all but one of them, most of them repeatedly.

Last year he published his fifteenth novel, and Corinna was kind enough to give it to me as a birthday present. As usual I devoured it in under 48 hours, and found it interesting enough to want to discuss it in these pages, the book review column of which is usually reserved for books of musicology.

This is his second novel to venture into the events of the First World War, although in this book he does so only tangentially. The premise of the book ventures vaguely into science fiction territory as time travel, albeit only one way, it the central premise of the book, in which the main protagonist seeks to prevent the carnage of the First World War, by changing history just that little bit.

One of the reasons that I don't like reviewing novels is that whereas you can quite happily discuss the content of a non-fiction book, because they are basically used for reference, and a detailed review can sometimes be the deciding factor in helping someone decide whether or not to buy the damn thing, there is something unethical (at least to my mind) in revealing plot twists of a non-fiction book, which is - after all - only ever going to be read for pleasure by someone whose main rationale for reading a novel is usually to find out what happens in the plot and how the story pans out.

So I am not going to even attempt to describe any more of the plot because I do not want to spoil it for you.

I always remember when I was reading one of Ben Elton's novels on a long and tortuous train journey from Norwich to Exeter. I had been appearing on 'The Sunday Show' in the summer of 1999 when they wanted me - as editor of a vaguely New Age magazine called *Quest* - to talk about the spiritual aspects of the forthcoming Millennium. I was in a bad mood that day. "There aren't any", I said, and went on to blast the mass media for building up a whole hoo hah which contributed towards Millennial cults and all the other bollocks that was going down at the time. It was my first and only time on a religious TV show.

But just before I boarded the train to go home, I bought a copy if Elton's *Blast from the Past* in the railway station bookstall, and read it all the way home. It was totally gripping, and as I told Graham when I telephoned him from Taunton to tell him that the train had broken down and all the toilets had overflowed, so we were gonna have to wait for a replacement, I was three quarters of the way through the book and I had absolutely no idea what was going to happen. In fact it wasn't until about five pages before the end that I guessed what the denouement was going to be, and I still consider that book to be one of the best fivers I have ever spent.

This book isn't quite as gripping as *Blast from the Past* was, but it is certainly up there with his best. After a string of relatively lighthearted books (a murder mystery set within Friends Reunited, and including some of the most graphic sex scenes I have ever read in a mainstream novel, and books set in a Big Brother type reality TV show, and a Pop Idol type talent show, which actually featured Prince Charles of all people) his writing has taken a more sombre turn over the past few books.

This one is set in 1914, and the one before was set in the Germany of the late 1930s with a Jewish family as the central protagonists, but this is no bad thing.

His more serious writing may be less frivolous but it is certainly hardcore, and is paving the way for a time when accusations of Elton being a guilty pleasure, will be a thing of the past.

IMAGINE NO HYPERBOLE. I WONDER IF YOU CAN.

It was interesting that Lauren Oyler writing in *Vice* magazine says: "Yesterday marked the 44th anniversary of the release of John Lennon's goody-goody solo album Imagine, on which he softly bleats for world peace and borderless harmony. Described by Rolling Stone as Lennon's "greatest musical gift to the world," the song of the same name fantasizes about a mankind without qualities of evil and suffering, such as possessions, greed, hunger, and war. Perhaps a less ambitious dream would be of a world in which people are not as monstrous as John Lennon." She then goes on to describe a druggy philanderer who cheated on his wife and smacked his young son for bad table manners.

Oh bollocks. Context my dear, context. None of this is news. Writing in *The Lives of John Lennon* well over twenty years ago, Albert Goldman wrote all this and more, and the account written by his mistress May Pang would make your hair curl. Particularly when he was drunk he was a very nasty piece of work, which is something that he admitted. "That is why I am always on about peace, you see. It is the most violent people who go for love and peace" he said.

As for smacking his son, it was fifty years ago, in a time where most people still believed in corporal punishment, and as for him having a 'God Complex' because he believed that because he was on a macrobiotic diet that smoking would not cause him to die of cancer, is one to condemn everyone who has non-standard health fads? If so, then practically everyone that I know would have a 'God Complex' and I truly do not believe that I am surrounded by deities.

Yes Lennon was a violent twat at times, but a monster? No. Hitler, Stalin and The Moors Murderers were monsters. Jimmy Savile was a monster. Lennon was just a deeply flawed human being who wrote some marvellous and inspirational music.

But Imagine is cod-utopian bollocks and always has been. Slainte…..

REVIEW

GO SET A WATCHMAN
By Harper Lee

This book presents me, the reviewer, with a paradigm which I have come across time and time again during my long and chequered career as a rock music scribe, but one that I don't think that I have ever actually encountered before as a book reviewer.

I have mentioned before how, when reviewing a work of fiction, I am placed in a very difficult position whereby I don't actually LIKE giving away what are called 'spoilers' in the current vernacular, because unlike the non fiction books which I usually review, which are basically reference works, people read novels almost entirely to find out where the story path leads, and most reviews, will - perforce - spoil that for people. So, if you are reading this hoping to find out the story line of this long awaited book, then I am afraid that you are very much out of luck, because I intend to do nothing of the sort.

I am probably wrong in describing this book as being 'long awaited' because, until a few short months ago, nobody even knew this book existed. Nelle Harper Lee, is revered as the author of *To Kill a Mockingbird*, one of the greatest novels of the 20th Century. She never published another one, and always said that she would never do so. However, with Lee now in her dotage things may be considerably different. Lee's sister and protector from public scrutiny, who died in November 2014, wrote in 2011, that Lee "can't see and can't hear and will sign anything put before her by anyone in whom she has confidence." And Marja Mills, a lifetime friend describes Lee as "in a wheelchair in an assisted living center, nearly deaf and blind, with a uniformed guard posted at the door" and her visitors "restricted to those on an approved list."

In 2014, Lee's lawyer re-examined Lee's safe-deposit box in 2014 and found the manuscript for *Go Set a Watchman*. It is, depending on who you believe, an early draft of her better known book, or the third part of a trilogy of which *To Kill a Mockingbird* is the third, and part two was never written.

In February 2015, the State of Alabama, through its Human Resources Department, launched an investigation into whether Lee was competent enough to consent to the publishing of *Go Set a Watchman*. The investigation found that the claims of coercion and elder abuse were unfounded, and, according to Lee's laywer, Lee is "happy as hell" with the publication.

So the first controversy appears to have been dealt with. The second concerns the character of Atticus Finch, the much beloved father of the protagonist of both books, portrayed in the iconic film by Gregory Peck.

An early review by Michiko Kakutani in *The New York Times* described Atticus' characterization as "shocking", as he "has been affiliating with raving anti-integration, anti-black crazies, and the reader shares [Scout's] horror and confusion". Other reviewers howl in pain and talk how Atticus' character had crumbled as he got older, ignoring the fact that he is NOT a real character but a literary one, and as this new novel is nothing more than an early draft, (most people agree on this now) that it would be more truthful to say that Atticus improved as Lee improved as a writer and more and more polishing was done. The third, and by far the most interesting controversy involves the only spoiler I am going to give. Neither Jem or, more importantly, Dill are in the novel, although they are referred to occasionally. Like Lee, the tomboy Scout of *To Kill a Mockingbird* is the daughter of a respected small-town Alabama attorney. Scout's friend, Dill, was inspired by Lee's childhood friend and neighbour, Truman Capote; Lee, in turn, is the model for a character in Capote's first novel, published in 1948.

Although the plot of Lee's novel involves an unsuccessful legal defence similar to one undertaken by her attorney father, the 1931 landmark Scottsboro Boys interracial rape case may also have helped to shape Lee's social conscience.

And herein lies the mystery. It has been suggested over the years that not only was Capote the inspiration for Dill, but that he helped Lee with the writing of the novel. In this new book neither Dill or Capote are to be found, but the oft voiced complaint that this novel is not as magickal as the one published in 1960, is purely because it is set well over a decade after the events chronicled in *To Kill a Mockingbird*, and the wide eyed innocence of Scout's childhood has been replaced by the knowing cynicism of her adult years.

I think that I am far more forgiving of this book and its undoubted flaws because I come from a music industry background, and we are used to people releasing albums of demos and rehearsal tapes either as bootlegs or as adjuncts to the more accepted canon of an artist's work. Of course *Go Set a Watchman* is nowhere near as good as *To Kill a Mockingbird*. But then again nobody with any sense would have expected it to have been so. But it is a hell of a lot better than anyone could reasonably have suspected and provides a fascinating adjunct to the better known work.

REVIEW

GREAT WHITE WONDERS
By Clinton Heylin

When I was younger, rock bootlegs were of intense interest to me. There was something intensely alluring about them; being able to listen to music that 'The Man' didn't want you to have, was a heady experience. The fact that most of this music was bloody awful didn't really matter.

I spent my formative years living here in North Devon, and whilst I am sure that if I had been hip enough, there would have been somewhere in the region that I could have bought such sought aft rarities as *Sweet Apple Trax* by The Beatles, or *Electric Lycanthrope* by Little Feat, I - who wanted to be hip, and indeed acted as if I was hip, but was actually painfully shy and naive - had no idea where to go. i did, however, have a book called *The Bootleg Bible* that I had bought on a rare visit to one of the grown up and freaky record shops in Exeter, and this rather badly written and cheaply printed tome kept me happy for many long years.

The first bootleg that i ever bought was in 1983. I was in the process of doing my training to be a Registered Nurse for the Mentally Subnormal (as it was called in those days) and I was doing a placement with the Community Mental Health Team in Torbay. I was temporarily without a car, so at the close of play each day I would walk about half a mile from the Community Team offices to the bus station, where I would catch a bus back to the Nurses Home at Starcross Hospital where I lived for many years.

In those days I had no difficulty in walking so I would explore some of the less trodden roadways off my main path, and in one of them I found a second hand shop which sold guitars and musical instruments as well as the normal tat that one finds in some places, and outside, without any great display of its importance was a box of C60 cassettes with photocopied covers. Amongst them were *Lie* by Charles Manson and *Cocksucker Blues* by The Rolling Stones.

I bought both of them.

For those not aware of the latter title, here is a brief resume. *Schoolboy Blues* is a 1970 song by the Rolling Stones, commonly recognised by the name *Cocksucker Blues*. It was written by Mick Jagger to be the Stones' final single for Decca Records as per their contract. The song is a parody of Dr. John's *The Lonesome Guitar Strangler*, released on his 1969 album *Babylon*, however its context and language were chosen specifically to anger Decca executives. The track was refused by Decca, although promotional 12" singles of it were pressed in the US.

The song was only officially released later by Decca in West Germany in 1983, where it accompanied a four-LP compilation entitled *The Rest of the Best* as a bonus single. That version was withdrawn and the boxed set was re-released without the single. Bootleg singles of the song have been issued, and one of these, together with an early version of Brown Sugar allegedly featuring Eric Clapton and/or Ron Wood had been taped by person or persons unknown, and together with some rather nondescript live material from 1970 had found its way onto a tape that I bought in

1983. The story of this noisome little ditty, and a hundred others are here in Clinton Heylin's remarkable history of the Bootleg industry. Of course, like everything else, the advent of cheap digital technology changed the game for everyone, and - although I haven't been to a record fair in years - I am certain that the serried ranks of bootleg tapes that I and my compadres sold back in the day are now replaced by serried ranks of home made compact discs, although the advent of illegal file sharing has - I am sure - affected the trade in illegal music as much, or more, as it has the trade in legitimate records.

The legitimate music market has also changed, with all sorts of gems that would otherwise have only been heard in bootlegs, coming out either as bona fide releases in their own right, or as extra tracks on deluxe reissues. Bands like Yes for example have released several packages of material that are basically official bootlegs, the 14 CD Progeny, which contains seven complete shows from 1972, being a good example.

The first rock bootleg is often claimed to be something called *The Great White Wonder*, featuring unreleased 'Basement Tapes' material by Bob Dylan. It was released in July 1969, by two Loas Angeles businessmen called Ken and Dub, and was the first of many releases on their Trademark of Quality record label. Clinton Heylin tells their story, and the stories of those who came afterwards with dispassionate good humour, and often produces a totally gripping narrative worthy of a novel by Frederick Forsyth. This book came out a long time ago, but it is absolutely essential for those of you who are interested, not only in Rock and Roll history, but in the way that the mainstream can be so radically influenced by those standing in the shadows. A totally gripping book, and one that I strongly urge you all to seek out and buy.

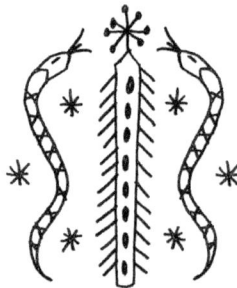

CARLOS CASTANEDA TERRITORY

I was actually doing quite well this week until I received a letter from Exeter City Council this morning. In July last year I was informed that I would have to do a lot of expensive work on my house in Exeter before I would be able to let it to tenants. The fact that a lot of the damage that had been done had been done by the tenants that I had there at the time was irrelevant, and so I was forced to evict them. As I could not afford to do the repairs, I let the house stand empty until I could raise the funds. A couple of months back I was told by Exeter City Council that I was liable to pay Council Tax on the empty property, and I have now been informed that I have to pay 150% tax as of next year. This is, to my mind, completely bloody outrageous, and I intend to be as obstructive and difficult over the affair as I possibly can be. However, as the old saying goes, you can't fight City Hall, and I don't fancy my chances that much.

But it has been a strange week overall. On Monday I was well into Carlos Castaneda territory being off my tits on Gila Monster saliva. The Gila monster (*Heloderma suspectum*), is a species of venomous lizard native to the southwestern United States and northwestern Mexican state of Sonora.

A heavy, slow-moving lizard, up to 60 cm (2.0 ft) long, the Gila monster is the only venomous lizard native to the United States and one of only two known species of venomous lizards in North America. The hormone exendin-4 occurs naturally in its saliva. Exenatide, a drug that is a synthetic form of this, led to healthy sustained glucose levels and progressive weight loss among people with type 2 diabetes who took part in a three-year study.

For the first couple of days I felt very peculiar. I was in a very odd, semi-psychedelic place, and it is nowhere near as much fun as you may have imagined. Many apologies to Steve Ignorant. I was supposed to be telephoning him on Monday but instead I was in a rocky cave picking scorpions off my skin, while a scarlet sun shone down on the desiccated earth. Well, very nearly.

ANARCHY, PEACE AND FREEDOM

I often write about how my life is particularly weird at any point, but today is different, my life is fairly ordinary today. I have to go for a doctor's appointment this afternoon, followed by nurses doing something arcane with my veins. Once upon a time the world seemed to make some sort of sense to me, but, as I get older, it just seems to be more illogical and more unfair.

Take this for example. A friend of mine, who is part of my extended family, paid £45 less than she should have done to Torridge District Council for her Council tax monthly payments. By the time the mess was sorted out she was five days late, and she found that the whole affair had been put into the hands of bailiffs who then threatened to kick her door down if she didn't pay the entire year's tax, including monies which were not yet due, in full. Luckily we were able to help, but on behalf of all the poor victims of vile tactics like these I think that I am going to make a stand, and take this outrage as far as I can.

It is time to man the barricades, comrades.

But this is only one of many similar stories which I am hearing, if not everyday, then every week. Whereas one upon a time those put in power over us at least gave the appearance that they cared about the welfare of the people of whom the ruled. That pretence seems to have gone out of the window, and it appears more and more that the only thing that motivates them is screwing as much money out of the populous as they can possibly manage.

I am currently reading a fascinating book which gives a remarkably complex overview of the legacy of the punk rock movement. It is a fascinating tale, and one of the most morally and spiritually uplifting books that I have read in a long time. Of course, a large proportion of it is centred around the events that have taken place within the community who have lived at Dial House in Essex since 1967. Of course the best known members of this ever shifting population are Crass, but the open house community has been responsible for dozens of other art and social projects over the years. Penny Rimbaud once wrote that after he had first formulated the open door policy at Dial House, he had naïvely expected other such institutions to spring up across the country, and was saddened and disappointed when they didn't. I have a lot of people who come and make music or work on community projects based around my house in North Devon but it is a constant struggle to try and maintain my own boundaries and head space, and the idea of doing a Dial House style community actually completely freaks me out.

Because, there is a serious dichotomy between what is, and what should be.

In Amsterdam in about 1966 the revolutionary anarchist group Provo instituted a scheme whereby they left bicycles painted white around the city, and made it known that they were for public use. People could pick one up, and use it to ride from their location to their destination, and then leave it for somebody else to use. I think that is a beautiful and noble idea. However, when somebody in Exeter tried the same thing about 25 years ago those bicycles which were not stolen were found thrown into the canal.

It is heartening to read about community gigs when punk bands would come together to work on a major event like a festival or a concert that they could not have managed by themselves. Again, I have personal experience of some events like these where various band members just got drunk and wrecked the place and ruined it for everyone else. It is weird reading this book, when so much of my personal experience of human beings seems to be that if – in any given situation – they can behave badly, cruelly, selfishly or destructively they will often do so.

Of course this is not always true, and like the compilers of this magnificent book (which I shall be reviewing properly in the next few weeks) I have experienced some remarkable and heart warming incidences of human kindness and generosity over the 56 years I have been on this planet. But, sad to say, I have learnt over the years that one had to legislate for the inevitable outbreaks of HAS [Human Assholism Syndrome].

I do find it heart warming (and I realise, with a jolt, that I have used the work 'heart warming' far more then usual in this editorial) that the musical genre which kickstarted so much creative socio-political altruism – Anarchopunk - is still surprisingly popular amongst people of a certain age. When I was about 20 years old there was a small gaggle of Teddy Boys who used to hand around one of the pubs on Bideford quay every weekend. Being a young brash 20 year old I thought that these ageing toughs with their blue suede brothel creepers and their drape coats were a peculiar anachronism in the brave new world of the 1980's; middle-aged men brought together by their memories and a jukebox full of the music they loved.

I think that the little ghettos of anarchopunks that exist around the Western world have more relevance to the world today than did the Teddy Boys of my youth. Because it's not just about the music. The philosophy that so many of us picked up in the early days of Thatcherism is as valid now – if not more so – then it was back then. These lessons have truly stayed with us all of our lives, and magazines like this and organizations like my day job at the Centre for Fortean Zoology are testament to the fact that the hippies sometimes now really do wear black.

Love and peace,

THE BLOOD MOON

Once again it has been one of those weeks reminiscent if the chorus of the Grateful Dead song *Trucking* from the *American Beauty* album, because it truly has been a long, strange trip. Last weekend all my more cosmic friends were massively excited because of the eclipse of what was being referred to as a 'blood moon' in the early hours of Monday morning. Now, for some reason, astronomy has never been one of those subjects that has interested me overly, and I have a sneaking suspicion that whilst there may well be come connection between our individual body chemistries and the positions of the heavenly bodies at the time of conception, or maybe (as the astrology dudes and dudettes would have it) the time of our birth, I think that an awful lot of the stuff people talk about these things is probably nonsense.

Then again, that is what I thought about a lot of things that I have since discovered to be fascinating. For example, I invited Jaki Windmill to the Weird Weekend this year to talk about Astroshamanism, because she is a friend of mine and I thought that the WW punters would be interested, which by and large they were. But I was certainly not expecting to be taken into the weirdest out of body experience that I have ever had without chemicals, so my mind is far broader as I get older. So, surprising even myself, I found myself up at 4:00am with a small bottle of good brandy which the Grande Fromage gave me last Christmas, in my hand, leaning on my walking stick out on the road outside my house as I gazed up into the night sky at what was undoubtedly one of the most extraordinary celestial objects that I have ever seen. The moon was not blood red, but it was a sort of grey and pink, not as in the jolly colours of the first Caravan album, but more like the appearance of a blood blister or a great boil just about to burst. I have read about the moon looking "liquid" but this was the first time that I had ever seen it for myself as it hung in the sky looking like an immense globule of frogspawn. I could hear other people around the village out and about, presumably watching the sky for their own arcane reasons, and I could even hear the farm labourers bringing home the last of the harvest. And I could hear what sounded suspiciously like chanting from the village green outside the church at the top of the little lane which runs past my house. But I was not in the mood to join them, and preferred my own company as I stood in the moonlight, singing Daevid Allen's *Selene* from *Camembert Electrique* under my breath and swigging from the bottle of brandy, which is so much better than the usual gutrot that I get from Tescos that I am forced to treat it with a great deal of respect. After about ten minutes I went back to bed, and bullied my long suffering wife into going outside to pay her respects to Our Lady of the Night. And that was even before the events of Monday started properly. On Tuesday Jessica was ill, and I gave a guitar lesson to a young lady of Gothic persuasion, on Wednesday we took delivery of a batch of baby millipedes from West Africa, and late on Thursday night my dear wife and dogs pushed me out of bed onto the floor.

What a long strange trip indeed.

THE MORE YOU SEE

I have never been a particular fan of television, or visual media at all really, preferring things you can read and things that you can listen to, to things that you can passively watch. However, like in so many other ways the advent of my iPad, combined with the new high speed broadband which has finally made its way to the village has changed my life, in that new temptations in the shape of online movies, and BBC iPlayer conspire to rob me of my sleep.

The other evening, for example, I had intended to go to sleep early. Corinna and I had been out at a Pagan gathering in Bude, for a lecture on shamanism by my old acquaintance Julian Vayne from Barnstaple Museum. We got back in the middle of a vile rainstorm, and by the time we had done the things that we needed to do, I (for one) felt that discretion was the better part of valour.

A night or so before I had watched an entertaining documentary on indie music, which seemed to be trying to combine the story of the original punk DIY ethic with the story of the commercially successful independent labels like Andy Miller's Mute. I am not sure that this approach was altogether successful, but there were entertaining contributions from Genesis P Orridge and my personal hero Bill Drummond, both of whom may be as mad as a bagful of cheese, but are both massively entertaining and interesting characters, so I don't consider that this was a waste of sixty minutes of my life. But I couldn't remember whether this was part of a series or whether it was a standalone documentary (I still don't know, but I tend to think the latter) and so I was poking about on iPlayer to see if there was a second episode that I could watch when I found a documentary on Joy

Division, that I truly couldn't remember whether I had seen before. And having seen it, I am in the peculiar position of still not knowing. The BBC website describes it thus:

"On June 4 1976, four young men from ruined, post-industrial Manchester went to see a Sex Pistols show at the Manchester Lesser Free Trade Hall. Inspired by the gig that is now credited with igniting the Manchester music scene, they formed what was to become one of the world's most influential bands, Joy Division.

Over thirty years later, despite a tragedy that was to cut them off in their prime, they are enjoying a larger audience and more influence than ever before, with a profound legacy that resonates fiercely in today's heavily manufactured pop culture. Featuring the unprecedented participation of all the surviving band members, this film examines the band's story through never-before-seen live performance footage, personal photos, period films and newly discovered audiotapes.

A fresh visual account of a unique time and place, this is the untold story of how four men transcended economic and cultural barriers to produce an enduring musical legacy, at a time of great social and political change."

Some of the clips were, of course, familiar to me, and having read Hooky's autobiography, in which many of the anecdotes presented in the film were put word for word, but I don't remember the whole epic story having been presented for me in quite such a lucid manner before. But the thing which was most notable for me was how timeless the music is. I am a fan of music from all sorts of eras, but most of what I listen to is broadly rock music dating for about forty years from the mid 1960s. However, although I still get great pleasure from listening to The Beatles and The Rolling Stones, for example, in many ways the music that they made - insanely great though it is - was firmly of its time. Whereas, the music of Joy Division, is truly that very rare thing...timeless.

I think that it is possible that no matter how hard various bands have tried, from Factory wannabies like Crispy Ambulance, to New Order themselves, nobody has ever managed to sound exactly like Joy Division. Lots of bands have sounded like The Beatles, although very few have managed to reach their stellar heights of songwriting prowess, and nobody in such volume, but Joy Division were not only the first band to sound like that, but the only one ever to manage it. The interesting thing for me was to watch the documentary immediately after watching Julian Vayne talking about shamanism. It was Annik, Ian Curtis' mistress who described him as being 'shamanic' on the documentary, and once one heard the story of how this essentially ordinary, quiet and polite chap from Manchester, not only channelled a hitherto untapped vein of cultural mores going back to J G Ballard and William Burroughs, but in doing it became an epileptic, and a manic depressive who very soon took his own life.

Now I am not an epileptic, but I have known people who were, both in my private life and during my career as a nurse for what were then known as the Mentally Subnormal. But I am, as many of you are aware, bipolar or manic depressive. Russell Hoban, in his classic novel *Turtle Diary* notes that shamans were the odd ones, the epileptic and the sick, and whilst I have never noted any spiritual aspects to those whom I have known whose cerebral cortex has laid themselves open to tonic clonic epileptiform seizures, and the people I know who have claimed shamanic status have not been epileptic, this is a well known paradigm in the surprisingly large body of literature on the subject.

Denise and John Carmody, for example, in their text *Ways to the Center: An Introduction to World Religions* , offer the following omnibus definition of a shaman:

> One who is a specialist in ancient techniques of ecstacy. The shaman normally is a functionary for a nonliterate community, serving as its healer, intermediary with the gods, guide of the souls of the dead to their rest, and custodian of traditional tribal lore. The typical shaman comes to this role through either heredity or having manifested idiosyncratic traits (epilepsy, sexual ambiguity, poetic sensitivity, dramatic dreams). Psychologically, shamans depend on an ability to function in two worlds, the ordinary reality of daily life and the extraordinary reality they encounter through their ecstatic journeys. As well, they serve their tribe as a defense of meaning, by incarnating a contact with the powers thought to hold the tribe's destiny (Carmody & Carmody 1989;33).

Ian Curtis certainly ticks many of the right boxes. But then again it could be argued that so did Martin Hannett, their visionary and barking mad record producer. It all depends whether you look for a mystickal element to the creative process. I will admit that I quite often do, although like all my religious beliefs it is something that I don't tend to talk about very often.

So, I stayed up until four watching the documentary, and then making notes on it, and trying to work out whether Ian Curtis is/was/might have been a shaman, and if so does it matter? And then I realised that the same questions could be asked abut the granddaddy of modern rock music, Robert Johnson, or at least about the myth that surrounds him to this very day. And then, after sneaking downstairs for a cheese sandwich and having an intense cuddle with a small grey kitten, I started asking myself whether it mattered anyway. And then I fell asleep with the question unanswered....

I wish that I could think of a cute and clever way to wrap up this editorial, but I can't. So I will leave you with a sleeping fat man in the arms of a tiny grey kitten called Dotty, and remind you that it was the ancient Chinese philosopher Lao Tzu who said that "The more you see, the less you know", and I think I got that from the liner notes of a Crass album back in the day.

REVIEW

THE TRUTH OF REVOLUTION, BROTHER: AN EXPLORATION OF PUNK PHILOSOPHY
edited by Robin Ryde

Last week I got a life changing new book. Some years ago, Corinna bought me a copy of Bill Drummond's book *17*, and I found it so enthralling and inspiring that I keep it on my bedside table, and dip into it randomly at regular intervals, always getting something out of it. I think that this book may just have found itself a stylistic companion.

This is what the publishers say:

"*The Truth of Revolution, Brother* is a unique exploration of the philosophy of punk, based on the ideas, beliefs and lives of the people that created the movement. The punk explosion of the late 70s and early 80s changed the face of music, art, and fashion. But it didn't stop there. Punks were onto something really important. They had a unique view on an alternative way of living. *The Truth of Revolution, Brother* is the result of a year spent with some of punk's most influential figures. From legendary British anarchos Crass to US stalwarts Fugazi and Dead Kennedys; first generation figures the Adverts to contemporary carrier of the flame Jeffrey Lewis, this groundbreaking book investigates the approaches and life choices made by the people associated with this most misunderstood genre. The result is truly life-affirming. From the fields of Essex to Iceland's corridors of power; the West Country to Washington DC, 30 interviews gently reveal a host of strategies for living that are more meaningful now than they were back in punk's heyday. Unique testament is mixed with thoughtful analysis and original art to create a true punk one-off. 30

original interviews, including Jello Biafra, Penny Rimbaud, Ian MacKaye, Gee Vaucher, Steve Albini, Vi Subversa, Little Annie, Mark Stewart, Tim Smith, Steve Ignorant, Jón Gnarr, Einar Örn Benediktsson and many more."

Like so many major projects, this was funded by a kick starter campaign which allowed the authors to spend far more time and effort on the project than, possibly, they would have done otherwise. I do, by the way, have the considerably cheaper paperback copy, although I think that I shall probably put the 32 quid hard back which includes a series of full colour plates of original art work on my Christmas list.

It is surprising, or at least I think it is, that although punk was a relatively diverse movement, covering everything from art school aesthetes to drunken thuggery, how much of the philosophy contained within this remarkable tome resonates perfectly with the way I have chosen to live my life, the idea that freedom must come responsibility and that anarchism is not working towards a state where everybody can just do what they want, and that chaos and anarchy are two different things. While reading this book lines of lyrics from my own juvenilia came back to haunt me…

"Anarchy doesn't mean chaos, we need to show that we don't need, establishment peaks to rule our lives, we just need room to breathe."

Although I hope that I would express it a little bit more elegantly now, my own political views have changed little since I wrote that back in 1982.

I was surprised at how many of the interviewees I had met over the years, and there was even one person whom I had been to school with. Perhaps less surprisingly, there were even more people on the list who had been in my record collection back before I sold it all to pay for my divorce nearly 20 years ago. This is a totally inspirational book on punk as a force for good.

There are, of course people who both then and now feel that punk was something else entirely; a public custard pie fight? An excuse for a ruck? And these people are the ones who object to this book now. As Jed Babey writes on 'louder then war':

"The book has come in for an unfair amount of criticism on 'social media' as there are a substantial proportion of the older punk generation who do not believe that punk and philosophy go together at all … or at least can be best summed up in slogans. Slogans short enough to fit on a button badge: I'm A Mess. Contained in song-titles and lyrics: 'I Wanna Be Me', 'It was easy, it was cheap, go and do it!' 'One Golden Rule – No Rules At All', and so on. But then there was the magic word 'Anarchy'… which some people took very, very seriously indeed."

But punk *was* a broad church. That is what made it so exciting and interesting. These days, younger members of my extended family grate me because I don't know the difference between Speed Metal, Death Metal, Black Metal and a dozen other arbitrary musical delineators. Would they believe that the umbrella of 'punk' would include acts as diverse as Crass, Joy Division, Swell Maps, XTC, Vice Squad and the Sex Pistols? It is this very diversity which made it interesting at the time and which makes the music and philosophy relevant today.

It would be churlish to point out the flaws in the book, so I won't do it. I will leave that to those who are less interested in the community and socio-political aspects of the punk movement than I am. I am sure that men of my age throughout history have looked back at their lives in their early twenties and realised that what they did then shaped the rest of their years upon this planet. Take my late father for example. Those were the years that he spent in the Merchant Navy being torpedoed by German submarines. Take my ex-secretary; those were the years that she was dancing around a field off her tits on Ecstasy. And take my assistant Jessica; she hasn't got to that part of her life yet so she doesn't know what it has in store for her. Me? I spent it earnestly reading and re-reading the liner notes of *Christ the Album* and other pieces of agit prop that emanated from an old farm house in rural Essex, revelling in the new ideas that had been given to me and using them to formulate my own philosophy.

I love this book. And I truly cannot think of another book published this year that I can recommend more to the readers of this magazine.

WORTH THE CANDLE

This week an American God botherer claimed that the world was going to end, and various political pundits including some surprisingly heavyweight ones were suggesting that Russia's involvement in the Syrian conflict, and the rumoured advent of Chinese military action in the area, was heralding a new World War.

Well, at the time of going to press neither of those things had actually happened although the political situation in the Middle East remains precarious. Once upon a time when I was younger, so much younger than today, the world appeared to make so much sense. Now, it doesn't. And I don't know whether that is because we truly are living in remarkably dodgy times, or whether they were actually always this dodgy, and either, as a young man I took these events in my stride or, as a young man with the arrogance of youth, I didn't actually notice.

That is what this magazine is for. Music has always been important to me and has provided a soundtrack to my life, my hopes, my fears, and aspirations for four and a half decades. Now, well into what I believe it is politically correct to refer to as my third age, I am trying to put together a magazine which ticks the boxes for me that other music and lifestyle magazines do not. There have been changes with this issue and there will be more changes in the future. I hope that you like the advent of Paul "Mr Biffo" Rose and Mac Malloney as regular contributors. We are planning to start streaming another philosophically Fortean radio show, this one presented by my old mate Richard Freeman, via Gonzo web radio in the next few issues. There are other editions in the pipeline, and whilst not all of my plans will come to fruition, I am sure of that, I am certain that some of them will. And assuming that the world doesn't come to an end and that World War Three does not burst upon us like avenging furies of Ancient Greece then I am sure that this magazine will only get bigger and better.

Thanks for staying with us. I know that it is a bumpy ride at times but I hope that you agree with me that, to use a term beloved of my friend and colleague Graham Inglis, the game is truly very much worth the candle.

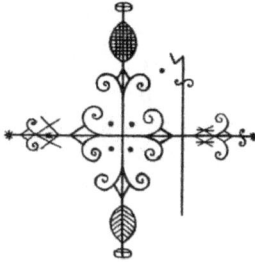

REVIEW

TRANSMETROPOLITAN VOL 1: BACK ON THE STREET
by Warren Ellis

This sounded so good. In fact it sounded red hot! A comicbook named after a song by The

Pogues, which featured a protagonist based very loosely upon Hunter S Thompson, in a dystopian hellhole which makes the universe of Blade Runner look like something out of Enid Blyton.

I was also interested when I read that the story has transhumanist themes. I became mildly interested in the concept of transhumanism when I read one of Dan Brown's novels which featured the subject as a subplot, but I first came upon the concept when I was a boy in Hong Kong and was allowed free rein to wander about the Victoria Central Library, where I came upon all sorts of things which stimulated my young psyche.

Transhumanism (abbreviated as H+ or h+) is an international and intellectual movement that aims to transform the human condition by developing and creating widely available technologies to greatly enhance human intellectual, physical, and psychological capacities. Transhumanist thinkers study the potential benefits and dangers of emerging technologies that could overcome fundamental human limitations, as well as the ethics of using such technologies. The most common thesis is that human beings may eventually be able to transform themselves into beings with greatly expanded abilities as to merit the label posthuman. Everything I heard about this comicbook made me think that it was going to be smashing. It tells the story of a retired journalist called Spider Jerusalem who lives at some unspecified point in the future, which is rumoured to be the 23rd Century. He is a sarcastic, drug-addicted, foul-mouthed, troubled, bitter, but brilliant gonzo journalist with a deep-seated hatred of authority, political corruption, and dogs. Almost always drawn wearing a set of stereoscopic sunglasses with one lens red and the other green, and is most often compared to you know who. No, not Lord fucking Voldemort.

One of Spider's most apparent character traits is his heavy drug use, which he makes no attempt to conceal. In addition to being a chain smoker and heavy drinker, Spider uses an extensive and bewildering variety of drugs ranging from mild stimulants, intellect enhancers, and mood-altering drugs to cocaine, heroin and rare, exotic, futuristic drugs. As is common in his society, Spider is resistant or immune to many forms of drug addiction, as well as lung cancer. Spider is well known for his foul language, especially when combining the word "fuck" with other words to make new and amusing insults. Spider is easily angered, his displays of temper ranging from mild verbal outbursts to violent physical assault. However, despite his temper and contempt for the City as a whole, Spider is often seen to treat innocents (particularly children) with kindness and care. Spider's past is not well known, though characters like Mitchell Royce and Spider himself have referred to past memorable incidents such as the enfant terrible (a French child assassin from the Anglo/Franco war) and the Prague telephone incident (in which Spider caused six politicians to commit suicide using just a phone). There are also hints at his childhood and early ambitions—"I wanted to be a sniper when I grew up. Didn't everyone?"—and his parents' growing madness.

He claims to have worked as a prostitute at some point in the past, and as a stripper at 8 years old. He grew up on the City's docks with drunken parents as an only child. His father drove a city bus and his mother was a housewife who cooked lizards for breakfast, lunch, and dinner every day. He returned to the docks as an adult to see that everyone was gone and the docks were abandoned and vowed to never forget his childhood there.

He is forced out of retirement for financial reasons (don't I know *that* feeling) and seeks work with his former editor in 'The City'; a dystopian bed of horrors, where sexualised images of Nazi Germany are the order of the day, and a cult called The Transients, led by a geezer called Fred Christ are trying to alter their DNA so much as to become a completely new species. He also has a Janus Cat, a term coined by my friend Dr Karl Shuker to describe cats suffering from Diprosopus (Greek διπρόσωπος, "two-faced", from δι-, di-, "two" and πρόσωπον, prósopon [neuter], "face", "person"; with Latin ending), also known as craniofacial duplication (cranio- from Greek κρανίον, "skull", the other parts Latin), an extremely rare congenital disorder whereby parts (accessories) or all of the face are duplicated on the head. Jerusalem returns to work for his old partner and editor Mitchell Royce, who now edits The Word, the City's largest newspaper. His first story is about an attempted separatist secession by the Transient movement (people who use genetic body modification based on alien DNA to become a completely different species, forced to live in the Angels 8 slum district). Fred Christ, pays to incite a riot and provoke the police, who use it as an excuse to clear out Angels 8. However, Jerusalem publishes a story revealing the truth and the brutal methods of the police; Royce publishes it live all over the city, and the public outcry forces the police to withdraw. Spider is brutally beaten by police on his way home, but defiantly says that he's here to stay. The first year of the series is a set of one-off stories exploring The City, Spider's background, and his often tense relationship with his assistants/sidekicks, Yelena Rossini and Channon Yarrow (referred to as his 'filthy assistants'), who become his full-time partners in his journalistic battles as the series progresses.

So, what's not to like? The trouble is that I am finding it extremely hard to answer that question. I'M the first to admit that I am a lover of comic books, and at their best I believe that they can be great literature. Even when they don't reach the hallowed heights of *Watchmen* when series like *Preacher* and *Saga* are good, they can be very good indeed. The problem with this series, and here I have to admit that I have only read the first volume, is that it just doesn't have that spark of greatness which propels it out of the class of being perfectly respectable (if you can, indeed, count something full of jokes about cannibalism and extreme sex as being 'perfectly respectable') into being something outstanding. Close, but no cigar, as somebody or other would have said. The are some good, and amusing, ideas, but they are too clumsily executed for my taste.

However, the premise is promising enough for me to have decided to buy a few more of the series and start again when I have the time, the money or the inclination, which I am afraid to admit is nit going to be any time soon. I truly do hope that when I do investigate the series again that I find it more impressive than I have this time around.

GONE TROPPO

As those of you who come to the magazine via our presence on Facebook, which (unless I have been seriously misreading the stats, which is always possible, because I am somewhat of a dunce at this e-marketing lark) is about half of you, will know, on Saturday afternoons we send out notifications to about forty different newsgroups using the Gonzo Jon FB account. We have a form letter that we send out, which lists the people featured in the magazine this week. Someone commented last week that it seems that "Yes fans had better watch out every week", and they completely missed the point. Yes and Hawkwind are featured EVERY week precisely because of their importance to the musical community that this magazine serves. So there!

Another band who turn up more in these pages than one would normally suspect from a band who broke up very nearly half a century ago is The Beatles, and their various spinoffs. The big music news in the last week is that the George Harrison back catalogue is now available for streaming, and when I read that, as I subscribe to a premium streaming service, I will give no prizes for guessing what I did.

The last time I indulged in a big glut of George Harrison listening was in 2002 round about the time that my mother died. I was lying in bed at seven in the morning when the telephone rang. It was my father, his voice thick with grief, to tell me that she had died about twenty minutes before. We were hardly on speaking terms at that time, so we didn't say much, but I found great solace in the music of my favourite Beatle. In fact, and I don't think I have ever told anyone this before, the first thing I did after my Father got off the 'phone was to listen to the title track of George's first proper solo album.

Now the darkness only stays at nighttime,
In the morning it will fade away
Daylight is good
At arriving at the right time
It's not always
Going to be this grey

All things must pass,
All things must pass away
All things must pass,
All things must pass away

I was quite familiar with his better known albums, but over the next few weeks I investigated the other records in his canon of work, and found some gems that I had missed out on before. Now I am doing exactly the same thing again.

One album that I completely missed out on when it came out was *Gone Troppo* (1982). I had missed out on it so soundly, that the sad truth was that I didn't even know that it existed. By 1980, Harrison had been finding the current musical climate alienating. His commercial appeal had dwindled, with 1981's *Somewhere in England* failing to go gold (despite featuring the John Lennon tribute hit, *All Those Years Ago*). With one album left on his current recording contract, Harrison decided to get it over with and recorded *Gone Troppo* (an Australian slang expression meaning "gone mad/crazy") and released it without participating in any promotion.

And pretty well everyone hated it. Even I hated it. Probably I was put off by the synth laden opening track which showed the quiet Beatle doing his best to sound contemporary. And believe me those of you who are too young to remember 1982, the stuff that was in the charts at the time was largely terrible, and whilst the glossy analogue synthesiser sounds of the time have their devotees, I am not one of them. And the opening track still sounds pretty awful.

But, and I am not sure why, I listened to *Gone Troppo* today for the first time since I had decided that it was basically bollocks thirteen years ago. And guess what. If you ignore the opening number it is not basically bollocks after all. It is a beautifully understated, mostly acoustic album on which Harrison sings some utterly gorgeous songs which are very unjustly overlooked.

Even at the time some reviewers had liked it. Among contemporary reviews, *Billboard* said of *Gone Troppo*: "Harrison's sunny lyricism shines brightest when least encumbered by self-consciousness, and here that equation yields a breezy, deceptively eclectic charmer."

People magazine's reviewer wrote: "Because of his forays into the mystical, Harrison's penchant for whimsy often gets overlooked. But here the zany side gets no short shrift." The reviewer admired "lovelies" such as *Wake Up My Love* and *Dream Away*, and described *Gone Troppo* as a "vinyl postcard" offering "flashes of brilliance".

I am really not sure yet, although I think that *India* which I first heard on a Beatles bootleg of some of the material that they wrote during their massively fruitful sojourn in Rikishesh in early 1968, where - if they didn't actually get the spiritual solace that they were looking for - they write some excellent material including most of what ended up on *The White Album*, later in the year.

I am just having to deal with the peculiar paradigm shift of having changed my mind so dramatically about the record in such a relatively short space of time. I don't know whether it says more about the human condition in general, me in particular, or the vagaries of George Harrison's guitar playing.

Seriously, from a psychological point of view I find the fact that I can change my viewpoint so strongly quite an interesting phenomenon, and as anyone who has ever followed my chequered career here and elsewhere will know, I rather like interesting phenomena.

FRIENDS IN LOW PLACES

A couple of weeks ago I was writing some blurb to go with my new novel, which was published a couple of weeks a go and which I am rather proud of. In it I stated that I thought that I had invented a new genre. 'High Fantasy' is a well known genre of literature in which a book is set in an imaginary country like Narnia or Middle Earth complete with unicorns, dragons, dwarves and any other inhabitants dreamed up by the author. 'Low Fantasy' is apparently what happens when a book is set on Earth involving " non-rational happenings that are without causality or rationality because they occur in the rational world where such things are not supposed to occur" I believe that I have invented a new genre: 'Low-life Fantasy'.

The vast majority of my book and indeed my previous novel *The Blackdown Mystery* (1999) is largely set in mental hospitals, and disused industrial estates, and the characters are mostly homeless, disabled, substance abusers, and/or on benefits a friend of mine read what I had written and was appalled. "In the current climate you can't talk about people being on benefits" he said, adding that it would adversely affect my sales. I have been thinking about this ever since. And I will say this now. Some of you already know this, and some of you don't. I am seriously ill and in receipt of two non-means tested state benefits, and whilst I can write amusing bollocks about cryptozoology or obscure rock musicians I am in no state to hold down anything approaching a proper job. There are aspects of my physical condition about which I am embarrassed, but I am not at all ashamed of being in receipt of money from the state.

Although I can no longer walk unaided, am in constant pain and I am as mad as a hatter I am more than slightly worried by my impending interview with the DWP doctors. Yes, next Wednesday at ten o'clock I will be up in front of the medical examination board who wish to discover whether I am a parasitic enemy of society or not.

One hears all sorts of horror stories about people who are terminally ill or in an even more grievous condition then me being told that they are fit to work. I would therefore, like all you people out there in readership land to keep your fingers crossed for me next Wednesday morning, and hope sanity will prevail.

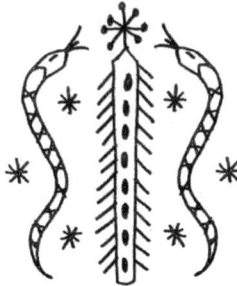

ONE MILLION MOMS MEET SATAN

Fridays is magazine day here in the potato shed, and I would love to imply that this means that there are dozens of busy figures bustling around earnestly, but firstly there just wouldn't be enough room for dozens of figures doing anything, and secondly Fridays is one of the days that my delightful assistant Jessica is NOT in the office with me, so I sit in the potato shed, Corinna sits at the Dining Room table, and we do our own bits and bobs independently of each other until we are close to finishing. Usually I try to get the bulk of what I have to do finished on the magazine earlier in the week so that all I have to do on the Friday is a sort of colour by numbers job, but this has been a very non-standard week (think Doctors, Mothers-In-Law, and teenager sitting the daughters of two friends of ours because it is Half Term, and they—quite properly– do not want to leave their offspring wandering about town unsupervised.

So Wednesday was pretty much a complete write-off, and Thursday was taken up by a visit from an ex-Conservative Town Councillor and an internationally famous author of Children's books who spent the afternoon bickering in the quondam potato shed whilst I was desperately trying to fix my email client. Oh yes, and Tuesday was a full moon.

So this week, with the ironic exception of the end bit (I really need to come up with a better title for that, but 'Valedictory Message' sounds far too pompous) which tells the story of my peculiar Wednesday, and this week's instalment of the story of Xtul, which just seems to write itself and beam itself unbidden upon my iPad, everything else is being written as we speak on the Friday afternoon.

I suspect that tonight is gonna be a late one.

A few weeks ago in the Strange Days column which appears in this magazine on the weeks that there have been enough strange items of news to make it worthwhile, we gavce a brief mention of an American TV show called *Lucifer* which has caused more than a few ripples across the pond.

It tells the story of Lucifer Morningstar: The Lord of Hell who is bored of his life, abdicates and becomes a consultant for the Los Angeles Police Department (LAPD) while running his own nightclub called Lux. Among other powers, he has a supernatural awareness of any person's sins and can compel them to speak the truth. He enjoys using these abilities to expose sinners in public. According to those jolly nice fellows at Wikipedia it is a loose adaptation of the comic book character created by Neil Gaiman for the comic book series The Sandman and its spin-off comic book series Lucifer written by Mike Carey, both published by DC Comics' Vertigo imprint.

Well, I like Vertigo Comics pretty well as much as I used to like the more arcane music put out on the Vertigo record label back in the day, and so it was pretty much a given that I would watch the show. However, it doesn't air until next year, but the pilot has just been broadcast on the Fox Network.

I managed to find a hooky copy of the pilot online, so—on Tuesday night, when my mind was pretty well frazzled by the full moon– I went to bed with some diabetic chocolate and a small bottle of vodka and settled down to watch it.

And you know what? It was complete bollocks!

It was entertaining enough in a corporate, American cop show kind of way, but the thing that I find most amusing is the knee jerk reaction it has brought out in people.

An advocacy group called One Million Moms (which probably means there are about four of them and they are blokes) has launched a petition against the show.

"The program previews mischaracterize Satan, depart from true biblical teachings about him, and inaccurately portray the beliefs of the Christian faith. By choosing to air this show, FOX is disrespecting Christianity and mocking the Bible," added the petition.

They obviously have not seen the show. Lucifer Morningstar is depicted as such an egregious jerk that the idea that watching this television show could turn people into Satanists is utterly ridiculous. Mind you Messrs Bush and Blair and Cameron are living proof that some people are stupid enough to believe any old tosh, and so perhaps the million moms have a reason to be worried after all!

REVIEW

DEAD BOY DETECTIVES VOL. 1:
SCHOOLBOY TERRORS
Toby Litt

As regular readers may have noticed, I am in somewhat of a comic book mood at the moment. I make no apologies for this, merely stating it as fact.

The Dead Boy Detectives were created by writer Neil Gaiman and artists Matt

Wagner and Malcolm Jones III in *The Sandman* #25 (April, 1991).

The characters are the ghosts of two dead children, Charles Rowland and Edwin Paine, who rather than enter the afterlife stay on Earth to become detectives investigating crimes which involve the supernatural.

Edwin Paine was murdered at his boarding school in 1916, after which he went to Hell, where he was stalked by an unseen menace through a long corridor for several decades. During the Seasons of Mist storyline, published in December 1990, Hell was emptied of its residents. As a result of this, the boarding school was overrun by the souls of its past teachers and pupils who have escaped Hell. Charles Rowland was the sole living student at the school during these events, as all the other students had gone home for the holidays. A few of the teachers who stayed behind were supervising him, but one by one they fell victim to various horrors. Paine aided Rowland in avoiding most of the dangers, such as a murderous gang of students. Ultimately, however, Rowland did not survive. He next appeared as a ghost and decided to forego going to the afterlife with Death in preference for prospective future adventures with Paine.

They have their own, sadly short lived, comic series now, which—as far as I am aware—has lasted just about long enough to fill to trade paperback sized graphic novels, before being cancelled because of low sales.

This is a great pity because the first graphic novel, at least, is remarkably good, and features the eponymous pair, alongside a live girl who is the daughter of an insanely irritating conceptual artist and her irritatingly bearded husband who looks like the sort of person I used to hang out with about a quarter of a century ago. The girl—with the brilliant name of Crystal Palace Von Hovercraft—is both a technical whizz and an obsessive devotee of various online Manga based online games and the attendant cosplay culture.

This could have been so bad. But it's not. It is very very good, and the authors deftly weave surprisingly intricate plots and marke the characters three dimensional enough for the reader to actually care about.

Toby Litt is best-known for writing his books - from *Adventures in Capitalism* to (so far) *King Death* - in alphabetical order; he is currently working on "M." His story 'John & John' won the semi-widely-known Manchester Fiction Prize, and his story 'Call it "The Bug" Because I Have No Time To Think of a Better Title" was shortlisted for the notoriously lucrative Sunday Times EFG Private Bank Short Story Award.

BACK IN THE DSS

Wednesday was like something out of Kafka. And no, I don't mean that I woke up this morning and found that I had mysteriously metamorphosed into a giant beetle. Graham and I arrived at the ever-so-dilapidated building which houses Barnstaple's Job Centre and the Committee of Affairs, or whatever they call themselves now, but as we have mislaid the letter they sent me I can't be sure. We were 10 minutes earlier, but the front door was locked. Leaving me leaning on a lamppost like a bipolar George Formby, Graham went in search of another point of ingress, a process which took two or three minutes. He took me in through this side door, and the waiting room was deserted apart from a visibly upset Black Country lass of uncertain years who was waiting for her sister to be interviewed. There was no staff of any kind visible.

For what seemed like ages, but was probably only about 20 minutes, Graham and Josef K, I'm sorry, me, waited. The automatic door from the outside into this peculiar ur-space from the outside world was obviously faulty, and kept on opening and shutting irregularly but over and over again. We tried to make cheery conversation for the sake of the Black Country lass who was by now really quite upset because her sister and husband had been in an interview which should have lasted 10 minutes for over an hour.

Eventually her sister and husband reappeared through one of the doors. Something was obviously wrong, and they bustled outside pushing her sister in the wheelchair.

Then it was time for me.

Would I be able to wait for two or three hours? They asked. Two of the doctors were off sick. "will they be claiming incapacity benefits" I sniggered, and Graham glared at me. Apparently, my levity went unnoticed, and I was told that they would make me a new appointment in a few months time.

Seriously for a second. The receptionist from the Job Centre couldn't have been kinder or more caring. The same can truly be said about the nurse that I saw back in June. But I had worked myself into quite a heavy state about it all. Not that I think that I am in any way fraudulently claiming benefits, or because I have anything that I should be ashamed about. But these days there are so many horror stories going around that I cannot help but be influenced by them. Thank you to everybody who had sent their good wishes. Just be aware that we are going to have to do the whole thing again after Christmas.

Peace…

NELSON AND THE FAIRIES

One of my favourite authors is an American thriller writer called Nelson DeMille who may not be familiar to many of the people who read this magazine. Some of you will, no doubt, be shocked by this revelation. DeMille is a fairly gung ho Republican whose ethos would seem to be quite far removed from the anarchist ethos of what I write for this magazine, and indeed, how I live my life. But he does write cracking stories!

Probably my favourite of his books is one called *Word of Honour* which tells a very interesting and morally intriguing tale. The main protagonist is a wealthy businessman who, at some time during the late 1980s, is on his way to work. Sitting opposite him that morning on the train, is an acquaintance who is reading a book about the Vietnam War. The main protagonist asks his acquaintance, jocularly, weather the book gives him an "honourably mention". His acquaintance looks at him grimly and passes him the book. The protagonist looks at the passage that his acquaintance points out. It turns out that this book was written solely to indict the protagonist for war crimes he and his men allegedly committed two decades earlier.

It is an insanely good book with some of the most gripping court room scenes that I have ever read. The most important aspects of the story are the moral and social ones. The protagonist is by now forced back into the army against his will, and facing criminal charges against the United States army code of justice for which he could face not only a court marshal, but a firing squad. The really gripping meat and potatoes of the tale is the effect that all of this has on his relationship with his hippy pacifist wife, his son and his social circle. It is totally gripping.

The relationship between the protagonist and his defence attorney is explored in detail, but there is one passage which always sticks in my mind.

The crux of the court case, and therefore of the book, are the rules of evidence as defined by international law. But the defence attorney explains that eye witness testimony is actually highly subjective, and he tells the protagonist about a famous Japanese play called *Rashōmon* which tells the story of an incident which led to the death of a Samurai told from the point of view of the man who killed him, several witnesses, and even the ghost of the murdered man. They all tell completely different versions of the events and each of them draws a completely different conclusion about the moral impact and interpretation of events. Ever since I first read the book the best part of 30 years ago, I have found this a fascinating concept, and I have often tried to give differing perspectives of events on things I have written, and so it is this week in this magazine. Although, I have to admit that some of it, at least, was not intentional.

The Pink Fairies are arguably the most important band from the counterculture of the late 1960s and the early 1970s, and last week they played two shows; one in London and the other in Wolverhampton.

The London gig was particularly important because it was at the venue where dear Mick Farren died two and a bit years ago. I, as I will readily admit, have a memory like a sieve and commissioned two separate authors from the editorial scene to cover the London show. Both of them duly submitted their copy a few days ago, leaving me with an editorial red face, so it seemed the perfect time and place to invoke the *Rashōmon* clause. However, there would be no point in me writing this magazine and putting in the man hours I put in each week if I am not going to be honest about it. It would be easy to pretend that I did it on purpose but I didn't. But it has all worked out rather nicely: as well as John and Jeremy's accounts of the London show, we have a selection of photographs taken by Pink Fairies biographer Rich Deakin at the Wolverhampton show. Well done to everybody involved, and a slightly embarrassed apology to my two authors.

In other PF news, I haven't heard the new album yet, but everybody who has tells me that the forthcoming, and very long awaited new album, is an absolute corker. Already it looks as if it is going to be one of the cultural highlights of 2016.

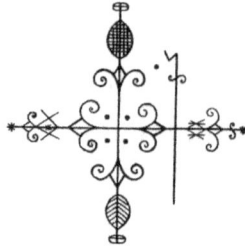

REVIEW

BECOMING THE BEACH BOYS, 1961-1963
by James B. Murphy

One of my favourite rock music biographies is *Heroes and Villains* by Steven Gaines, which tells the extraordinary story of The Beach Boys in all its glorious psychodrama. Whilst the essence of the story is no doubt true, upon reading this latest volume, one realises that a lot of the details so lovingly recounted by Gaines are not actually completely true. This is by no means a reflection upon Gaines, but more a fact that he never had the resources or the tenacity of the author of this book, who - despite being a professional vet rather than a writer - has done an absolutely awesome job of research, unparalleled within Beach Boydom.

This book is a labour of love from an obsessive fan. And I truthfully don't think that it could be anything else. Because it is only the obsessive fan who has the time, the energy, or the inclination to write such a complete piece of rock and roll archaeology as this. Because even though the world has changed massively in the past few decades, and the popular music of the fifties, sixties and seventies, is taken seriously as a cultural phenomenon, it is only the obsessive who will put in the hours of legwork necessary to come up with a book which covers the intricacies of every matrix number, inlay stamp, and change of artwork of every promotional only picture disc.

Does that make it sound boring? Well, I am sorry if that is the case, because I truly do not mean to do anything of the sort, because I, for one, found it totally enthralling. But it is enthralling in a totally different way than Gaines' book.

For *Heroes and Villains* tells the human story, whereas this is a book about the hardware and software of The Beach Boys, rather than the emotional impact of, and on the flesh and blood participants in the great game. Take the final days of David

Marks with the band, for example. The way that Gaines tells the story, one feels terribly sorry for the young man who almost overnight found himself ousted from his place in America's greatest rock and roll band. This book, however, portrays Marks as an irritating little shit, who even years later, was massively unprofessional and just laughed at the whole affair.

In fact, the more that I think of it, the more I realise that the emotional impact of Gaines' book is almost entirely missing in this one; it describes - in minute detail - the parabolic rise and fall of Brian Wilson's first love affair, from apogee to perigee, but does so in clinical terms, which throw extraordinary light upon the compositional skills of the young genius songwriter, but have little or no emotional impact upon the reader.

It is probably the first Beach Boys book ever, not to dwell on the parenting atrocities committed by Murry Wilson, but I believe that it is the first book that I have read that explains exactly how Wilson Senior lost his eye. It is also interesting in the way that it goes in great detail into the familial antecedents of even quite minor players in the drama, casting quite a lot of light upon the social structure of California in the 1950s and 1960s.

It also is almost unique amongst such books, in hardly mentioning Brian's much touted mental health difficulties, although - it should be pointed out, I think - Brian was probably saner during the three year span covered by this book, than he was at any other time during his subsequent career.

It also goes into more detail than I have ever read elsewhere of the extra curricular recording projects, not only of the uber-talented Brian Wilson, but of other members of the band and their coterie. Even David Marks, often considered to be a complete also ran in Beach Boy circles, had several side projects on the go at various times. This, I think is important, because, whereas the story as told in the more established Beach Boy biographies implies that Brian was bursting with talent that he was forced into indulging in various side projects, the fact that even such Beach Boy collaborators as Gary Usher and Roger Christian had a plethora of different things going on, places that concept into a severe perspective.

Another thing which has been presented in Gaines' biography in particular, was that Brian Wilson had a whole series of collaborative "best friends". This present book insinuates that they were not necessarily any way near as linear as has been previously shown.

In short this is a text book rather than a conventional biography. This is not because the author is a dry or dull writer, far from it. But he is intent on cramming in as much information as he possibly can into his magnum opus, and this is no bad thing. As a reviewer, and - indeed - as a Beach Boys fan, I hope that he continues to follow the story over the five decades that follow. This massive tome only covers the first thirty six months of the band's career. Can you imagine what the story of the rest of it will be like if he chronicles it in such obsessive detail?

Unfortunately, however, it will take at least another ten volumes of this size if he is to do so. But, I would probably go out and buy them if he did.

THE ROOTS OF GONZO

My first attempt at writing a music magazine happened in the mid 1970s when, together with a couple of me ne'er do well friends, I did something that was supposed to be a newsletter for kids using the school library, but actually turned into a load of surreal bollocks interspersed with me ranting on about Gong. Then after I was politely moved to another school I did much the same thing a few years later, but this time with rude poems about the government, and drug references galore (especially peculiar since at that time my actual experience with illegal drugs was zilch). I got expelled from that school after five issues, and it was 1984 before I did another fanzine. *Back to the Basic* lasted one issue, then I got married, and did my best to forswear childish things.

Then in 1988 I tried again. My wife and I were already publishing fan magazines, so we decided to have a bash at publishing a general rock music magazine. *ISMO* was named after the eponymous anarchist group in a novel of the same name by Sir John Verney, an author of whose writings I was and am very fond. For those of you not in the know here is a *Kirkus* review which tells you absolutely nothing about the book:

> "What have we here--an incredibly involved mystery? a philosophical manifesto? a hall of mirrors, reflecting the inconsistency, the inconstancy of good and bad? Observing, occasionally participants, are February Callender, more baffled than in her earlier involvements, her younger sister Gail, a charming idealist, their older brother Friday, ""an eager Rupert Brooke-ish

sort of young man."" Around them swirls a fantastic set of characters who are forever changing identity as they tumble over each other from Yorkshire to Florence, recherche references to Simone Martini and Jean-Paul Sartre, and ismo--""a new movement...a new technique of cooperating...the potential conscience and sense of humor for the whole world."" Ismo gives its adherents a secret language, a secret sign, a sense of shared power, an opportunity for harrying pomposity, for challenging tyranny--and it may be turned on its own tail. The super-plot involves three versions of a famous painting--which is authentic?--and the use made of ismo to spirit them across Europe. But the grand ironic achievement of ismo is the affair of President de Gaulle's trousers.... There are parts here for Margaret Rutherford and Alec Guiness and especially for Peter Sellers (who is invoked appropriately). This literate imbroglio is Older than it looks, is a very special sip of international expresso, is a puzzlement for a purpose. In the words of the most enigmatic conspirator: ""What is it, to understand? To enjoy is more important."

This review may tell you nothing about the book but it also tells you *everything*. Because the whole story works on so many different levels that the experience of reading it is different every time. But I digress, because I am supposed to be talking about my career as a rock and roll lifestyle magazine editor rather than my favourite surrealistic children's book.

So, back to the narrative. *ISMO* lasted for about ten issues, the issues getting better, and selling fewer each time, and - because we were in those glorious pre-internet days when "upgrading one's software" meant buying a new packet of letraset - the gaps between issues became longer and longer until I gave up. Post Internet and post divorce from my first wife, I tried to run it as an internet magazine for another five or six issues, but this again fizzled out as my day job running the Centre for Fortean Zoology became more onerous.

One thing I didn't mention is that the big interview in issue one of *ISMO* was with the legendary Daevid Allen. He played a show at Exeter Arts Centre in the spring of 1988, and we went to see him at the shared house where he was staying the next day. It was then that we met Rob Ayling, and the two of us became friends, a relationship that lasts to this day.

In 2000 I became music editor of the short-lived *Planet on Sunday* newspaper, a well meaning publication which sowed the seeds of its own destruction when it announced that it would not have any advertising. Things got worse when, after some sort of computer malfunction, its publication was put back a week despite the fact all the rather nasty looking but expensive TV adverts had been show the weekend before. I was surprised that it lasted the seven weeks that it did, although I was only paid for five of them due to the involvement of the DSS. But that, like the children's books of Sir John Verney, is another story.

And then I spent twelve years doing other things, burying both my parents, drinking too much, travelling around the world, and meeting and marrying my second wife, until meeting up once again with Rob Ayling, and throwing my horseshoes into the middle of his particular three ring circus.

So that brings us to the present day. This month, *Gonzo Weekly* which is basically the culmination of all the different things that I have tried to do in music magazine publishing over the years, but with better production values and less spelling mistakes, is now three years old. And, touching every bit of wood that I can find in a desperate attempt not to jinx this next statement, we seem to be doing alright, and I see no reason that she (I always think of my magazines as being female, for some reason, probably because like the unnamed woman in Sir Walter Scott's poem they are "uncertain, coy, and hard to please") will not carry on for the foreseeable future. I certainly hope so.

So, thank you for reading about my history as a music journalist. I realise that I have missed out the various things that I wrote for *Record Collector* and other magazines, but so what. The important reason behind this (and all my editorials) is not for me to rant on about all the different publications that I have written for in the past, but to get you in the mood for reading this week's one.

This I hope I have done. If not, pah!

DO WE OWE HIM A PORTRAIT?

The other day I was on Facebook. I dislike Facebook massively, but it is an undeniably useful tool for journalists. Once upon a time one had to spend long hours in a public library pouring through books like *Who's Who* and the *Writers and Artists Yearbook* to get contact details for people. Now it only takes 10 minutes and a few clicks of the mouse.

Facebook is also useful for alerting scribes like me to potentially interesting news items. As regular readers will know, anarchist punk band Crass were of pivotal importance in shaping the moral and political compass of the man I eventually turned out to be. They will also know that last week I interviewed one-time Crass lead singer Steve Ignorant for the front cover story in the magazine. He is a delightful fellow, and I always enjoy speaking to him.

I was posting up notifications of the existence of this magazine featuring Igs on Monday or Tuesday when I came across an extraordinarily lyrical painting of the man himself. It was by a bloke called Daniel Roberson, and it seemed that it was part of a series. So, I carried out the requisite couple of mouse clicks and dropped him a line.

He replied within a few minutes, and so I asked him why, when artists traditionally paint bowls of fruit, naked women, or glorious sunsets, he had chosen to paint my old mate Igs. Why?

He replied:

"I'm working towards my next exhibition at the moment...'Pivotal moments and Memories 1975-2015', Punk Rock has been a part of my life for a long time and I wanted to reference that in my work...

I remember one Saturday morning aged 13/14 or so, paying my weekly pilgrimage to the record stall on Chesham market. The bloke says "you like punk music don't you?", he hands me a copy of Feeding of the 5000 by CRASS. I get it home, carefully inspect every inch of the cover and artwork and stick it on the record player.

The first two minutes of intro worry me slightly but then Steve's voice kicks in and bang, my life takes a path that it might not have done if I hadn't stumbled upon Steve Ignorant.

I asked an old mate Gaz Suspect who I knew was mates with Steve if he'd ask him if he might be interested in having his portrait painted... he said he'd be honoured."

I was particularly impressed by the way that the style of the painting seemed to reflect various other aspects of Steve Ignorant's life away from that of being the Tourette's punk shouter, like his long time interest in the history of Punch and Judy shows, and his long time career as a Punch and Judy Professor.

Interesting that you made that link, originally the painting had a few references to his history in the background, including a punch and Judy theatre. It all got painted out eventually apart from the fragmented Crass symbol. I was reading Steve's book 'The rest is Propaganda' whilst working on the painting and I guess that had an effect on what happened on the canvas... it's quite a spontaneous process, so not intentional."

I asked what was going to happen to the painting now. He replied:

"*Now the painting goes into my exhibition at the Museum of Modern Art Wales. It starts on the 28th November. After that, I've entered it into a painting competition, if it gets accepted it'll be on show at the Mall Gallery in London next year. I'd also like to produce a limited edition print of it, which will be sold in aid of a charity of Steve's choosing (I'm guessing the lifeboat, but shouldn't presume).*"

If any of you are interested in checking out any more of his remarkable pictures please check out his Facebook page Daniel Roberson Art and his website www.danielroberson.co.uk

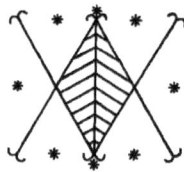

REVIEW

LEE BRILLEAUX: ROCK'N'ROLL GENTLEMAN
by Zoe Howe

I may have been born in 1959, but I am a child of the 1970s; those were the years when I first did most of the things that I have been doing ever since. And those things include rock and roll. I was sixteen when the first Dr Feelgood album came out, and I still remember, upstairs at a short lived record shop in Bideford's Mill Street, above what is now a small supermarket, looking at the record and being confused about the boast that it was recorded in mono. Surely that was so old fashioned as to make it completely out of synch with anything that was happening. But the music I was listening to had nothing to do with the raw estuarine blues of *Down by the Jetty*. A few years later I heard *Milk and*

Alcohol, and quite liked it, but I am afraid to say that at the time Dr Feelgood practically completely passed me by.

Like so many people I think that it was watching Julien Temple's *Oil City Confidential,* which is quite probably one of the greatest rockumentaries ever made, that turned me on to the band three decades too late. That and the incredibly brave, and gentlemanly way that Wilko Johnson faced the news of his own imminent demise with such dignity, that if he hadn't been before, he was immediately transported into national treasure territory without breaking sweat. I almost broke down at the pictures of Wilko standing bravely at Mick Farren's graveside with a copy of *Vamoires stole my Lunch Money,* and he won a place in my alcohol enlarged heart forever.

As we know, Wilko was granted a remarkable (some might say miraculous) reprieve, and is still with us today. But all this had one important effect on me - it made me a Dr Feelgood fan.

A year or so ago I interviewed Dylan (son of Steve) Howe, and I have been kicking myself ever since for not realising that he was a permanency at the drumstool behind Wilko, and that his wife Zoe had co-written Wilko's autobiography. If I had known either if these things at the time, I am sure that I would have asked him questions about them rather than about his forthcoming album, which would probably not have been a good thing, so things have worked out for the best in the end.

Now, Zoe has written a second Feelgood book; a biography of their star-crossed singer Lee Brilleaux, who died of cancer at the ridiculously young age of 41. And what a corker it is! I devoured it in three sittings whilst I was supposed to be doing something else - it is a measure of quite how good a writer she is, and quite what a good book this is, that I ignored a series of fascinating aberrations of British butterflies that have recently come to light, in order to read it.

Brilleaux comes across as a legendary character, the sort of socially motile (yes, I mean motile not mobile) character that could only come from England. A product of one of the strangest places in the country - Canvey Island in Essex - he carved a gloriously boozy swathe across the music industry, in a wonderfully louche Pilgrim's Process which would end up exactly where it began.

As part of my Feelgood odyssey I listened to all the albums on Spotify, and found - not altogether to my surprise - that the music rapidly declined away from my own particular tastes as soon as Wilko left the band. But, just as the book led me to believe, it got dramatically better again, as Brilleaux lived out his extraordinary life. Indeed, the live album recorded at his final ever shows, and released a few weeks after his death is as good as anything that the band ever recorded during their two decades in existence. I seem to be using the word 'poignant' rather a lot in this review, but I felt emotional reading the words of Mick Farren at various places in the narrative. He was someone of whom I was very fond, and listening to the Feelgood's rough tough but never nasty urban blues makes me realise why he appreciated the band so much. They were basically soulmates.

One could see the whole range of reasons why Brilleaux and Wilko parted company in 1977. Indeed one can also see the reason why the other two original members left a few years later. It is not easy being in a working partnership with someone who is driven by their own inner demons, as people who have worked with me over the years will bear testament. It is also not easy being in a working relationship with someone whose regime of substance abuse is different to yours.

It is actually the subject of alcohol that is one of the most singular things both about Brilleaux and about this book. We live in an age when anyone who drinks over the twenty one units that is deemed socially responsible by the nanny state is in danger of being labelled an alcoholic. But although Zoe Howe pulls no punches about Brilleaux and other band members' prodigious alcohol intake, she doesn't fall into the trap of criticising him for it. Indeed she even includes an amusing, if cautionary, anecdote in which Brilleaux sacks a drummer (later on in the band's career) for being drunk at ten in the morning rather than waiting for six in the evening like a gentleman. For the title of this book is a particularly apposite one. Lee Brilleaux was a cultured, intelligent gentleman, albeit a rock and roll gentleman, and the only regret that I have after finishing this extraordinarily poignant book is that I never had the chance to meet him. I feel sure that we would have got on rather well.

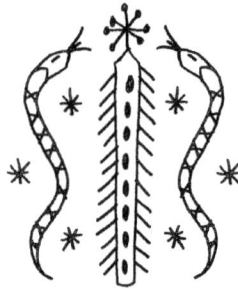

UNLUCKY FOR SOME

I am not particularly superstitious but I will admit to being paraskevidekatriaphobic, and today is Friday the Thirteenth and I will be the first to admit that I am on edge because things are - as they always do - going wrong.

According to Wikipedia Triskaidekaphobia (from Greek tris meaning "three", kai meaning "and", deka meaning "10" and phobos meaning "fear" or "morbid fear") is fear of the number 13 and avoidance to use it; it is a superstition and related to the specific fear of the 13th person at the Last Supper being Judas, who betrayed Jesus Christ and ultimately hanged himself. It is also a reason for the fear of Friday the 13th, called paraskevidekatriaphobia (from Παρασκευή Paraskevi, Greek for Friday) or friggatriskaidekaphobia (after Frigg, the Norse goddess after whom Friday is named in English).

My personal reasons for disliking the date reach back to my first days at Primary School back in Hong Kong when a teacher told us (one Friday 13th) that the belief in bad luck on this day was just a silly superstition. I had never actually heard of this before, but as an avid believer that all I was told by those in authority was wrong, I went on to have a particularly bad day (think hurting myself in an accident followed by a bout of physical chastisement from my paterfamilias) and I have disliked the day ever since.

There. I have shared one of my deepest, darkest and silliest secrets with you.

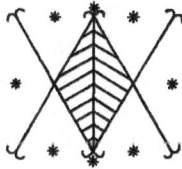

HISTORY BEING MADE

Last week I tried extremely hard to get the magazine finished in time for me to have a restful weekend. Things have been getting on top if me recently, and I really wanted some time off. I finished my bits quite early in the afternoon, but for all sorts of reasons (think Graham having to change the filament on Corinna's huge industrial size oven ... No that isn't a euphemism, and it involved far more faffing around, drilling holes in the wall, and the purchase of a new hammer action drill, whatever that is) it was mid evening before Corinna had finished doing her bits. Then, just before we went to press history was made.

OK, I want to qualify this. History is being made every day. One of the things that I love about history is that we live it and make it every day. I always remember when I was a stripling of eleven or so, my father explaining to me about the living veracity if historical process. At that time (1971) my paternal

Grandmother was an old lady in her eighties, and - so my Father told me - when she had been a little girl living in Clovelly (a village only a few miles away from where we live now) her family had a jobbing gardener, a very old man who had been a boy soldier at the Battle of Waterloo.

This got me thinking, and in one of the minor epiphanies that growing minds are wont to have, I realised that when the 21st Century dawned, there would be some people alive who were born in the 19th Century, and would then have experienced part of three whole centuries. In fact there are still two old ladies - one in Italy and one in The USA - for which this is true.

But I digress, and I have digressed even worse than I usually do, and that is saying something.

On Friday night, however, just as we were going to press, a historical event took place, and furthermore it was a historical event that shall, if I am not very mistaken, reverberate down through the years, if not decades, to come.

Back in 2001 I was working as the Deputy Editor of a tropical fish magazine, which was slowly and surely going down the drain because the owner/editor was a chronic alcoholic who was (quite literally) drinking himself to death. I remember in the days after 9-11 feeling punchdrunk, and worse, feeling that sitting at my computer in my little sitting room in Exeter, trying to write deathless prose about breeding angelfish was both irrelevant, and somehow inappropriate as - like most of the rest of the world - I was trying to come to terms with what had happened.

And I feel much the same now. Trying to get back into my daily routine when my mind is still full of the images of the carnage in France seems somehow disrespectful. But, of course, its not.

If we don't get on with our normal routines, which for me means sitting trying to write deathless prose about cryptozoology, aberrations of British butterflies, and rock music spattered with a teensy weensy bit of history and politics, then they have won! Whilst I was not a supporter of the Iraq War, believing it to be both illegal and unfounded, and - like many others - I warned against an inevitable backlash that would come as a result of it, I was shocked at the precise scale of the backlash, and am terrified at its implications.

Whatever happens next, and although I have my suspicions, I know no more than the rest of us, the world is never going to be the same again.

And am I going to continue writing amusing bollocks about mystery animals, butterflies and rock music. Of course I am. Terrorism is aimed at destabilising society and making it too afraid to function. Although I am sure that the Islamic State would find the Fortean stuff with which I deal blasphemous superstition, and much of the stuff that appears in this magazine to be decadent beyond extreme, it would be completely ludicrous for me to claim that the men from the deserts have any interest at all in stopping me personally. But they want to stop us ALL from functioning, and to continuing what we do normally is the best way to defy them.

I am sure that there will be some people who accuse me of not being sympathetic to the cause, because I have not draped this week's issue in the French tricolour. I am not draping it in the Lebanese flag or the Russian flag either, and both those countries suffered brutal terrorist attacks within a few weeks of those in Paris.

ISIL are a rogue organisation who, as far as I am aware, are not recognised as a legitimate government by any country on Earth. It his interesting, therefore to see another rogue, organisation, and furthermore one who have appeared in these pages before, facing up to them. In Monday's *Daily Mirror* a leader article states that "Hacker group Anonymous have declared war against ISIS after the attacks in Paris on Friday night. Posting a video on YouTube, the group said it would use its knowledge to "unite humanity" and warned the terrorists to "expect us".

Behind their signature mask, a spokesperson speaking in French said: "Anonymous from all over the world will hunt you down. You should know that we will find you and we will not let you go.

"We will launch the biggest operation ever against you."

As friends and relatives of mine covered their Facebook avatars in the bricoleur to show solidarity with the victims, another friend of mine wrote: "When literally hundreds of thousands of innocents are butchered in the DRC, Sudan or some other 'unfashionable' African country, why don't we see folks adorning their FB pages with THOSE flags or tearful declarations of "We are all Congolese" or "We are all Sudanese"? But suddenly "we're all Parisians" now?"

It is easy to see what he means, and I mostly agree with him. As Claire Bernish wrote: "Without question, I mourn for Paris' recent victims and their families — and I would never claim knowledgeable firsthand experience of the same.

But I refuse — despite my partial French heritage — to cloak myself in nationalism of any stripe or star, particularly not now. Because, besides victims in Paris, an incomprehensibly astronomic number of people have been grieving loss of the highest order for some time — in places whose names roll off our tongues as if it's accepted that violence simply happens there — and a majority likely couldn't guess the colours on these victims' flags."

Me? I am staying on the sidelines in my tumbledown potato shed, on the outskirts of a village nobody has heard of in rural North Devon. I am praying for Peace, but expecting War, and I really wish Mick Farren were still here....

Praise be to Nero's Neptune
The Titanic sails at dawn
Everybody's shouting
"Which side are you on?"
And Ezra Pound and T. S. Eliot
Fighting in the captain's tower
While calypso singers laugh at them
And fishermen hold flowers
Between the windows of the sea
Where lovely mermaids flow
And nobody has to think too much
About Desolation Row

For *Desolation Row* read Facebook.

STONES TOURING PARTY: A JOURNEY THROUGH AMERICA WITH THE ROLLING STONES
by Robert Greenfield

This is one of my favourite rock music biographies ever, and it tells the story of the events (both on and offstage) surrounding the 1972 North American tour by The Rolling Stones, promoting their then recent album Exile on Main Street. I first read it when I was sixteen and in many ways it was the book that shaped much of my life for the next few decades.

It was the book that first introduced me to the concept of the elegantly wasted debauchery of life on the road, and inspired me forthe next twenty years or so to try and emulate it. Eventually, of course, I grew up, and discovered that this sort of shocking behaviour comes at a price, even if you were part of the greatest rock and roll band of all time's entourage, and that life for most musicians on the road was nothing like that.

Re-reading it now, it is still a massively impressive book, but these days it is the social history and the shibboleths surrounding the events on stage which are more interesting to me than the accounts of cocaine sniffed and groupies fucked en masse. For example, I find it particularly interesting to see how the social establishment of the time tried to muscle in on the band to no avail, and how The Rolling Stones managed to avoid being lionized by the Truman Capotes and Princess Radziwells of their day who were trying to use them for their own nefarious ends.

Capote, for example was an even worse mess than Keith Richards at the time. His appetites for alcohol and drugs were prodigious, and he was desperately trying to use the band to help him relaunch a career that had never fulfilled its early promise. He had been commissioned to write an article about the tour, and he totally abused his position as celebrity journalist to swan around on the tour, take drugs and get in the way. He never actually wrote the article, and his most memorable contribution was to describe Mick Jagger as being "about as sexy as a pissing toad", an epithet which made me laugh when I first read it, and which still amuses me today.

Truman Capote was commissioned to cover the tour for Rolling Stone. Accompanied by prominent New York socialites Lee Radziwill and Peter Beard, Capote did not mesh well with the group; he and his entourage abandoned the tour in New Orleans, only to resurface for the final shows at Madison Square Garden. He did not complete his feature, tentatively entitled "It Will Soon Be Here". Rolling Stone ultimately recouped its stake by assigning Andy Warhol to interview Capote about the tour in 1973.

On the first show of the tour, 3 June in Vancouver, British Columbia, 31 policemen were treated for injuries when more than 2,000 fans attempted to crash the Pacific Coliseum. In San Diego on 13 June there were 60 arrests and 15 injured during disturbances. In Tucson, Arizona on 14 June, an attempt by 300 youths to storm the gates led to police using tear gas. Eighty-one people were arrested at the sellout Houston shows, mostly for marijuana possession and other drug offences.

There were 61 arrests in the large crowd at RFK Stadium in Washington, D.C. on the

Fourth of July. On 13 July police had to block 2,000 ticket-less fans from trying to gain access to the show in Detroit. On 17 July at the Montreal Forum a bomb blew up in the Stones' equipment van, and replacement gear had to be flown in; then it was discovered that 3,000 forged tickets had been sold, causing a fan riot and a late start to the concert. The next day, 18 July, the Stones' entourage got into a fight with photographer Andy Dickerman in Rhode Island, and Jagger and Richards landed in jail, imperilling that night's show at the Boston Garden. Boston Mayor Kevin White, fearful of a riot if the show were cancelled, intervened to bail them out; the show went on, albeit with another late start. Dickerman would later file a £22,230 lawsuit against the band.

Don Law: Kevin White, who still had serious national political aspirations, came out said, "My city is in turmoil tonight and I need to pull the police out of here. But I have bad news: The Rolling Stones were fogged out of Boston, had to land in Rhode Island, and were arrested." The whole place boos. Then Kevin White said, "But I called and we've gotten them out and they are on their way." There was so much cheering it was like the Bruins won the Stanley Cup. The tour ended with three consecutive nights at New York's Madison Square Garden, the first night of which saw 10 arrests and two policemen injured, and the last leading to confrontations between the crowd outside Madison Square Garden and the police.

While in Chicago, the group stayed in Hugh Hefner's Playboy Mansion. The last show on 26 July, Jagger's birthday, had balloons and confetti falling from Madison Square Garden's ceiling and Jagger blowing the candles off a huge cake. Pies were also wheeled in, leading to a pie fight between the Rolling Stones and the audience. Afterwards a party was held in Jagger's honor by Ahmet Ertegun, that included Bob Dylan, Woody Allen, Andy Warhol, the Capote entourage, and Zsa Zsa Gabor, with music from Count Basie. Dylan referred to the event as "the beginning of an all-encompassing consciousness".

One vague mystery which I have never been able to solve involves a nameless character who turns up, having a hatred of Keith Richards. He is described as being a legendary figure whose beat years are long behind him, who used to play with a great rock band and now plays with a succession of ever more unimpressive pop groups. I have never been able to work out who this character is, and would be fascinated if someone out there in Gonzo readerland could enlighten me.

The real star of this book is Edward Herbert Beresford "Chip" Monck (born March 5, 1939 in Wellesley, Massachusetts), an American Tony Award nominated lighting designer, most famously serving as the master of ceremonies at the 1969 Woodstock Festival. After the Boston show was delayed Monck is on stage reading Jonathan Livingston Seagull to the crowd. He comes over as a perfect rock and roll gentleman; resourceful, intelligent and kind, and above all damn good at his job. Another inspiration to me over the years.

This is still an awesome book, and if you have 't read it, and enjoy this magazine, I heartily recommend that you go out and buy it. You have my personal guarantee that you will enjoy it.

And so another week judders towards a close like a wheezy and arthritic juggernaut. I am not going to pretend that it has been the most fun week that we have ever had here in the potato shed, but it has been a pretty productive one, and – so far, touch wood – nothing spectacular has gone wrong.

I don't know how many of you read my ramblings last Friday about my (mostly) irrational dislike (I wont go as far as to call it fear) of Friday the 13th. But it was only last night that I realised that this was the precise date on which the appalling events in Paris took place. I am sure it is a coincidence, but it is not going to do anything to make me like the date anymore. However, Jessica has just pointed out that she had a very good Friday the 13th even though she doesn't like the date either, so that argument pretty well goes out of the window.

The events of last Friday have taken over so many aspects our collective consciousness that no matter how hard one tries, one cannot ignore them. This week's magazine is testament to that, as the vast majority of articles in it reference the tragedy in some way or other I have a feeling that it will be a long time before our collective psyche is free of the horrors of that night. However, as I have been saying in these pages for the last three years we are living is strange and disturbing times, and I think that it would be unwise in the extreme to treat these events as if they were a one off. the ostrich is popularly believed to have a habit of putting in head in a hole in the sand whenever it is in danger, believing that if it cannot see the danger then it doesn't exist, this is, believe it or not, a complete fallacy. The human race however, has a long and ignoble habit of doing much the same thing. Out reaction to the global climate change crisis, is a good example of this. And the events in the Middle East, and indeed those in Paris will not go away. If we do not do something about this, then as a species we are in even deeper shit then we are at the moment.

And it is at times like these when, I believe, the little community for which this magazine is a hub, becomes evermore important. in a world full of hatred and bad vibes, the good vibes spread by music, friendship, and yes… love, become of paramount importance. I am still naive enough to believe that although love is not all that one needs, it is a damn good start, and that if we are ever going to progress as individuals and as a species that we should damn well start embracing the light instead of the dark. Ok that's it for today. I'm getting off my soap box now, and I hope all of you have a peaceful and pleasant week until we meet again.

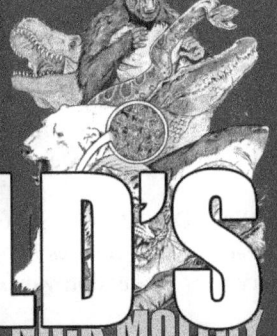

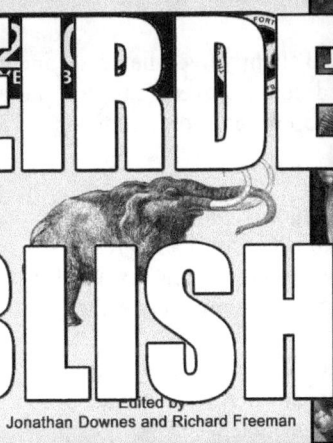

THE WORLD'S WEIRDEST PUBLISHING COMPANY

HOW TO START A PUBLISHING EMPIRE

Unlike most mainstream publishers, we have a non-commercial remit, and our mission statement claims that "we publish books because they deserve to be published, not because we think that we can make money out of them". Our motto is the Latin Tag *Pro bona causa facimus* (we do it for good reason), a slogan taken from a children's book *The Case of the Silver Egg* by the late Desmond Skirrow.

WIKIPEDIA: "The first book published was in 1988. *Take this Brother may it Serve you Well* was a guide to Beatles bootlegs by Jonathan Downes. It sold quite well, but was hampered by very poor production values, being photocopied, and held together by a plastic clip binder.

In 1988 A5 clip binders were hard to get hold of, so the publishers took A4 binders and cut them in half with a hacksaw. It now reaches surprisingly high prices second hand.

The production quality improved slightly over the years, and after 1999 all the books produced were ringbound with laminated colour covers. In 2004, however, they signed an agreement with Lightning Source, and all books are now produced perfect bound, with full colour covers."

Until 2010 all our books, the majority of which are/were on the subject of mystery animals and allied disciplines, were published by `CFZ Press`, the publishing arm of the Centre for Fortean Zoology (CFZ), and we urged our readers and followers to draw a discreet veil over the books that we published that were completely off topic to the CFZ.

However, in 2010 we decided that enough was enough and launched a second imprint, `Fortean Words` which aims to cover a wide range of non animal-related esoteric subjects. Other imprints will be launched as and when we feel like it, however the basic ethos of the company remains the same: Our job is to publish books and magazines that we feel are worth publishing, whether or not they are going to sell. Money is, after all - as my dear old Mama once told me - a rather vulgar subject, and she would be rolling in her grave if she thought that her eldest son was somehow in `trade`.

Luckily, so far our tastes have turned out not to be that rarified after all, and we have sold far more books than anyone ever thought that we would, so there is a moral in there somewhere…

Jon Downes,
Woolsery, North Devon
July 2010

CFZ PRESS

CFZ Press is our flagship imprint, featuring a wide range of intelligently written and lavishly illustrated books on cryptozoology and the quirkier aspects of Natural History.

TRADE   BEWARE OF IMITATIONS   MARK

CFZ CLASSICS

CFZ Classics is a new venture for us. There are many seminal works that are either unavailable today, or not available with the production values which we would like to see. So, following the old adage that if you want to get something done do it yourself, this is exactly what we have done.

Desiderius Erasmus Roterodamus (b. October 18th 1466, d. July 2nd 1536) said: "When I have a little money, I buy books; and if I have any left, I buy food and clothes," and we are much the same. Only, we are in the lucky position of being able to share our books with the wider world. CFZ Classics is a conduit through which we cannot just re-issue titles which we feel still have much to offer the cryptozoological and Fortean research communities of the 21st Century, but we are adding footnotes, supplementary essays, and other material where we deem it appropriate.

http://www.cfzpublishing.co.uk/

Fortean Words is a new venture for us. The F in CFZ stands for "Fortean", after the pioneering researcher into anomalous phenomena, Charles Fort. Our Fortean Words imprint covers a whole spectrum of arcane subjects from UFOs and the paranormal to folklore and urban legends. Our authors include such Fortean luminaries as Nick Redfern, Andy Roberts, and Paul Screeton. . New authors tackling new subjects will always be encouraged, and we hope that our books will continue to be as ground-breaking and popular as ever.

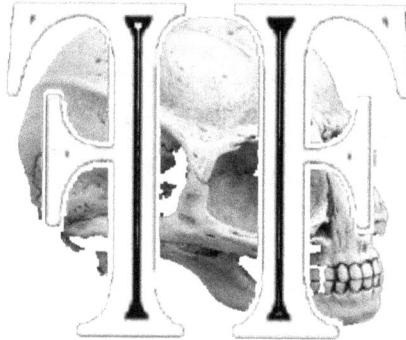

Just before Christmas 2011, we launched our third imprint, this time dedicated to - let's see if you guessed it from the title - fictional books with a Fortean or cryptozoological theme. We have published a few fictional books in the past, but now think that because of our rising reputation as publishers of quality Forteana, that a dedicated fiction imprint was the order of the day.

http://www.cfzpublishing.co.uk/

www.ingramcontent.com/pod-product-compliance
Lightning Source LLC
LaVergne TN
LVHW022340080426
835508LV00012BA/1289